KT-177-149

Footprint Handbook

C016088896

This is
Guatemala

Guatemala has a monopoly on colour: from the red lava tongues of the volcanoes in the western highlands to the creamy shades of the southern Petén caves, and from the white sand of the Caribbean coast to the black sand and fabulous orange sunsets over the Pacific. And that's just nature's palette. Completing this work of art are traditional Maya fiestas, arcane religious rituals where idol worship and Roman Catholicism merge, and jungle temples where ancient ruins tell of long-lost civilizations.

Deep in Guatemala's northern jungle, the majestic cities of the Maya are buried. Temples, stelae and plazas have been discovered here, along with evidence of human sacrifice and astronomical genius.

Antigua is the colonial centre of the New World. Gracefully ruined after an 18th-century earthquake, its cobbled streets are lined with columned courtyards, toppled church arches, preserved pastel-coloured houses, flowers and fountains galore.

Lake Atitlán and its three volcanoes are truly breathtaking. Further west, the bustling city of Quetzaltenango makes an excellent base from which to explore the volcanoes, markets and villages of the western highlands, such as the mountain community of Todos Santos, where the colourful clothes of the Maya and the All Saints' Day horse race are major attractions.

In the Verapaces, rivers run through caves stuffed with stalagmites and stalactites. On the humid lower slopes of the Pacific, Olmec-influenced ruins are buried among coffee bushes and turtles nest on the shore, while on the Caribbean coast, the Garífuna rock to the sound of the punta and dolphins frolic in the sea.

Richard Arghiris

Best of
Guatemala

❶ Antigua

Backed by a simmering panorama of jagged volcanic peaks, the outstandingly baroque, partially ruined and unrepentantly hedonistic city of Antigua was the de facto capital of Central America for two centuries, resulting in an unrivalled architectural legacy that has earned it UNESCO World Heritage Site status. Page 39.

❷ Lake Atitlán

Described by Alexander Von Humboldt as 'the most beautiful lake in the world' and by Aldous Huxley as 'too much of a good thing', Lake Atitlán is an entrancing body of water fringed by Mayan villages and hazy blue volcanoes. Laze in a hammock or explore local communities; it's up to you. Page 59.

❸ Chichicastenango

An hour north of Lake Atitlán is the famous market of Chichicastenango, a town where Maya and visitors converge in a twice weekly frenzy of buying general goods and produce, alongside textiles and tapestry. The market is alive with colour and is a must for any visitor. Also here is an atmospheric Mayan shrine. Page 84.

❹ Todos Santos Cuchumatán

This mountain community is famous for the distinctive colourful clothes of its indigenous Mam inhabitants and its All Saints' Day horse race, one of the most celebrated and spectacular in Central America. Page 102

❺ Around Quetzaltenango

Maya villages and market towns, hot springs and volcanoes dot the mountains within easy reach on foot or by bus from the busy highland settlement of Quezaltenango. Highlights include the village of San Andrés Xecul, famous for its mustard-coloured domed church, and Zunil, with relaxing thermal baths. Page 106.

❻ Monterrico

Along the Pacific coast, the turtle-nesting sites of Monterrico are attracting visitors to this little-explored district of Guatemala. The journey to the long black sand beach takes you by boat through tangled mangrove swamps, teeming with birdlife. Page 124.

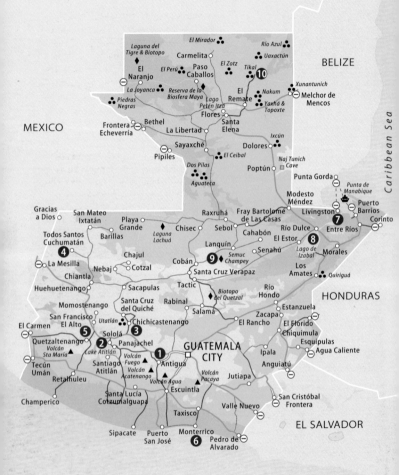

El Mirador
Río Azul
Carmelita
El Zotz
Uaxactún
Tikal **10**
El Perú
Paso Caballos
Xunantunich
Nakum
El Remate
Yaxhá & Topoxte
Melchor de Mencos

BELIZE

Laguna del Tigre & Biotopo
El Naranjo
La Joyanca
Reserva de la Biosfera Maya
Lago Petén Itzá

Piedras Negras
Flores
Santa Elena

MEXICO

Frontera Echeverría
Bethel
La Libertad
Ixcún
Sayaxché
Dolores

Pipiles
Dos Pilas
El Ceibal
Naj Tunich Cave
Aguateca
Poptún

Punta Gorda

Punta de Manabique

Modesto Méndez
Livingston
Puerto Barrios

Caribbean Sea

Gracias a Dios
San Mateo Ixtatán
Playa Grande
Chisec
Raxruhá
Fray Bartolomé de Las Casas
Sebol
Río Dulce
Corinto

Todos Santos Cuchumatán **4**
Barillas
Laguna Lachuá
Cahabón
El Estor **8**
Entre Ríos **7**

La Mesilla
Chajul
Lanquín
Senahú
Lago de Izabal
Morales

Chiantla
Nebaj
Cotzal
Cobán
9 Semuc Champey
Santa Cruz Verapaz
Los Amates
Quiriguá

Huehuetenango
Sacapulas
Tactic
Río Hondo

HONDURAS

Momostenango
Santa Cruz del Quiché
Biotopo del Quetzal
Rabinal
Salamá
Estanzuela

El Carmen
El Alto
Utatlán **5**
Chichicastenango
Zacapa
El Florido

Quetzaltenango
Solólá
Panajachel
El Rancho
Chiquimula
Esquipulas

Volcán Sta María
3
GUATEMALA CITY
Agua Caliente

Tecún Umán
Santiago Atitlán
Lake Atitlán
Volcán Fuego
1
Antigua
Volcán Pacaya
Ipala
Anguiatú

Retalhuleu
Volcán Acatenango
Volcán Agua
Jutiapa

Champerico
Santa Lucía Cotzumalguapa
Escuintla
San Cristóbal Frontera

Taxisco
Valle Nuevo
EL SALVADOR

Sipacate
Puerto San José
Monterrico
6
Pedro de Alvarado

Pacific Ocean

N

50 km
50 miles

❾ Semuc Champey

The numinous spectacle of Semuc Champey consists of multiple turquoise pools fed by low waterfalls. Set in the remote karst landscape of Guatemala's Alta Verapaz, you'll have to travel off the beaten track to reach this natural wonder, one of the most enchanting in Central America. Page 160.

❼ Lívingston

The relaxed Caribbean village of Lívingston, accessible only by boat, is home to the Guatemalan Garífuna, and the starting point for trips north to Punta Gorda in Belize or, via Puerto Barrios, Placencia in Belize, or south overland to Honduras. Page 141.

❿ Tikal

The ruined city of Tikal earned its place in sci-fi history as the location for a rebel moon in George Lucas's Star Wars. Once one of the most powerful polities in the Mayan world, it has astoundingly tall pyramids that reach high above the rainforest canopy. Page 176.

❽ Lago de Izabal and Río Dulce

The expansive Lago de Izabal narrows to form the fabulous Río Dulce gorge. Skirting the northern shores of the lake is the Bocas del Polochic Wildlife Reserve, which is full of monkeys, birds and other wildlife, or you can spot manatees at the lakeside village of El Estor. Page 146.

Quetzal feathers

Route planner

Many visitors will start their trip in Guatemala City, if they're flying into the country. But if you're travelling through the region, the most natural route in Guatemala is to enter the country from the north from Mexico or Belize, visit Tikal and then head south.

One week to ten days
colonial town, volcanic landscapes and Maya market

Guatemala City is a modern, polluted capital. It is the main entry point for travellers by air and long-distance bus. While there are some sites of interest, a couple of excellent museums in the city centre and some great nightlife, most head west to the clean air of **Antigua**. A dramatic location at the foot of three volcanoes, handsome colonial architecture and a relaxed atmosphere make Antigua a good base acclimatize for a day or two.

After Antigua, head further into the western highlands to **Lago Atitlán**, a spectacular and sacred lake protected on all sides by silent volcanic peaks. Take your pick from several villages dotted around the lake shores, linked by ferries and hiking trails. Spend a few days in **San Pedro La Laguna**, the chief chill-out spot, or **San Marcos**, the favourite place for true relaxation, or visit any of the other less touristy and more interesting options.

Not to be missed an hour north of Lake Atitlán is the famous, colourful market of **Chichicastenango**, a town where Maya and visitors converge in a twice-weekly frenzy of buying general goods and produce, alongside textiles and tapestry. If heading north to Mexico from here, there are more good opportunities for discovering the charms of western Guatemala, including the volcanoes and Maya communities around **Quetzaltenango**, **Retalhuleu** and **Huehuetenango**.

Three weeks or more

Three to four weeks is a good amount of time to visit Guatemala; any less and you'll have to rush around. With some extra time, it's also worth considering taking a short Spanish course in either Antigua or Quezaltenango, the main centres for language study. In the western highlands, once you've explored Antigua and Lago Atitlán, head north into the heart of the Cuchumatanes mountains and to **Todos Santos Cuchumatán**, a town with restricted Western influences and which is increasingly popular as a place to learn about the Mam way of life, including language and weaving classes.

It's worth taking a detour south of the highlands, along the Pacific coastline, to the turtle-nesting sites of **Monterrico**, which are attracting visitors to this little-explored district of Guatemala.

Heading northeast from Guatemala City are the highlands of the Verapaz region, which are well worth exploring for a few days. **Cobán** is the main focus, with access to the caves at **Lanquín**, the natural bridge of **Semuc Champey** and, at Purulhá, the **Mario Dary Rivera Reserve** which protects the habitat of the quetzal, Guatemala's national bird.

East of the Verapaz region is **Lago de Izabal**, with the **Bocas del Polochic Wildlife Reserve** on its northern shores. The reserve is full of monkeys, avifauna and other wildlife. South of the lake, the highway runs close to **Quiriguá**, which once competed with Tikal and nearby Copán, in Honduras, for dominance of the Maya heartlands.

It's worth spending a few days on and around Guatemala's short Caribbean shore. **Lívingston** is popular with young travellers and nearby is **El Golfete Biotopo Chocón Machacas**, a manatee and wildlife reserve, and the fabulous **Río Dulce** gorge. From Lívingston boats go inland to Río Dulce, north to Punta Gorda in Belize, or head for Puerto Barrios for Placencia in Belize, or south overland to Honduras.

Don't miss a trip further north to the forested northern lowlands of **El Petén**, which hide most of Guatemala's archaeological sites. The majestic **Tikal** is the most developed for tourism, but with some extra time, many others can be reached including **Uaxactún**, **Yaxhá** and **El Ceibal**. **Flores**, sitting on an island in Lago Petén Itzá, is the centre for exploring El Petén with routes from here to Belize and Mexico.

If you then go south again, there are many options for crossing the border to Honduras. Head for El Florido, for best access to Copán, or out to the Caribbean and the crossing at Entre Ríos Corinto near Puerto Barrios for the Bay Islands.

When to go

...and when not to

Climate

The best time to go is between November and April, when there is virtually no rain, although there are slight regional variations and a handful of microclimates that do not obey the rule. Local weather is dependent upon altitude and varies greatly. Most of the population lives at between 900 m and 2500 m, where the climate features warm days and cool nights, so you'll need warm clothes at night. The majority of visitors spend most of their time in the highlands, where the dry season lasts from November to April. However, don't be put off by the term 'rainy season'; most years, the rains only affect travellers for an hour or two a day, depending on where you are.

The central region around Cobán has an occasional drizzle-like rain called *chipi chipi* in February and March. Some places enjoy a respite from the rains (the *canícula*) in July and August. On the Pacific and Caribbean coasts you can expect rain all year round, heaviest on the Pacific in June and September with a dry spell in between, but with no dry season on the Caribbean. In the lowlands of El Petén, the wet season is roughly May to October, when the mosquitoes are most active. December to February are cooler months, while March and April are hot and dry. In terms of festivals, the key events are Semana Santa at Easter in Antigua, see page 49, and All Saints' Day in Todos Santos, see page 103.

Weather Guatemala City

January	February	March	April	May	June
12°C 22°C 0mm	13°C 23°C 0mm	14°C 25°C 6mm	15°C 25°C 12mm	16°C 25°C 152mm	16°C 23°C 274mm

July	August	September	October	November	December
16°C 23°C 203mm	16°C 23°C 198mm	16°C 22°C 231mm	16°C 22°C 173mm	14°C 22°C 9mm	13°C 22°C 3mm

If the time and mood is right, there is little to beat a Latin American festival. Fine costumes, loud music, the sounds of firecrackers tipped off with the gentle wafting of specially prepared foods all (normally) with a drink or two. Whether you're seeking the carnival or happen to stumble across a celebration, the events – big or small – are memorable. If you want to hit the carnivals there are a few broad dates generally significant throughout the region. Carnival is normally the week before the start of Lent, while Semana Santa (Easter Week) is an understandably more spiritual affair. It's particularly colourful in Antigua with floats carrying Christ over wonderfully coloured and carefully placed carpets of flowers, but is also spectacular in **Santiago Atitlán**. On 2 November is Día de los Muertos (Day of the Dead), when families visit cemeteries to honour the dead. In the small mountain town of **Todos Santos Cuchumatán**, All Saints' Day is famously celebrated with a colourful and drunken horse race accompanied by lots of dancing and antics; see box, page 103. Christmas and New Year result in celebrations of some kind, but these are not always public.

Guatemala celebrates wildly on Independence Day on 15 September. Other important local fiestas are also busy times; book ahead. August is holiday time so accommodation can be scarce, especially in the smaller resorts.

Public holidays lead to a complete shut-down in services. There are no banks, government offices and usually no shops open, and often far fewer restaurants and bars. It is worth keeping an eye on the calendar to avoid changing money or trying to make travel arrangements on public holidays.

Festivals and public holidays

Although specific dates are given for fiestas, there's often a week of jollification beforehand.

1 January New Year.

March/April Holy Week (four days). Easter celebrations are exceptional in Antigua and Santiago Atitlán. Bus fares may be doubled.

1 May Labour Day.

15 August Public holiday in Guatemala City only.

15 September Independence Day.

12 October Discovery of America. Not a business holiday.

20 October Revolution Day.

1 November All Souls' Day. Celebrated with abandonment and drunkeness in Todos Santos. In Santiago Sacatepéquez, the Día de los Muertosis characterized by colourful kite-flying (barriletes).

24 December Christmas Eve. From noon, although not a business holiday.

25 December Christmas Day.

31 December Public holiday from noon.

What to do

from caving to diving to whitewater rafting

Archaeology

Archaeological sites run the gamut from a handful of unexcavated mounds to heavily restored citadels with vast pyramids and palatial complexes. Along with a quiet, contemplative attitude, solitude is key to experiencing the ruins and their subtle atmosphere. Set out as early as possible in the day, to avoid hordes of tourists at sites such as Tikal; opening time is best. If the site is shrouded in forests, you have a better chance of seeing wildlife in the early morning too, and there may be photogenic mists. To comprehend the richness and complexity of Mayan civilization, it is worth reading in-depth before setting out. We recommend anything and everything by Linda Schele.

Birdwatching and wildlife observation

In typical tropical exuberance, Guatemala is brimming with wildlife and you won't have to venture far out of urban settings to encounter it. Casual strolling at any of the larger archaeological sites is often rewarded with the sight of iguanas sunning themselves on rocks, scampering agoutis, coatis and other rodents, mot-mots, hawks and occasional monkeys in the trees. The Maya Biosphere Reserve is the big natural attraction, encompassing more than 57,000 ha of teeming rainforest and dry forest, and numerous archaeological sites, including Tikal; the wildlife observation is superb. The majority of tour operators listed in this guide will offer nature-oriented tours. There are several national parks, biotopes and protected areas in Guatemala, each with their highlights.

Climbing and hiking

Guatemala represents a wealth of opportunity for climbers, with more than 30 volcanoes on offer. There are also the heights of the Cuchumatanes Mountains in the highlands, which claims the highest non-volcanic peak in the country at 3837 m, and those of the relatively unexplored Sierra de Las Minas in eastern Guatemala close to the Río Motagua Valley. **Fundación Defensores de la Naturaleza** ① *4a Avenida 23-01 Zona 14, Guatemala City, T2310-2929, www.defensores.org.gt*, are the people to contact for *a permiso* to climb in the Sierra de las Minas Biosphere Reserve. **Turismo Ek Chuah** ⓘ *3 Calle 6-24, Zona 2, T2232-0745, www.ekchuah.com*, offer volcano-specific tours, see page 34. For other operators offering volcano climbing around Guatemala City and Antigua, see page 51.

A network of paths and tracks covers much of Guatemala, with the Petén being the most popular hiking destination with a variety of routes connecting jungle-shrouded ruins, some of them very remote. You will need to be physically fit to complete the 5- to 7-day odyssey to El Mirador, but lighter day treks to other interesting sites are possible too; Flores is the usual jumping-off point. The countryside around Quetzaltenango, Antigua and Lake Atitlán offers many opportunities for casual walking and volcano climbing. Always check on the security situation before setting out.

Even if you only plan to be out a couple of hours you should have comfortable, safe waterproof footwear and a daypack to carry your sweater and waterproof. At high altitudes the difference in temperature between sun and shade is remarkable. The longer trips mentioned in this book require basic backpacking equipment. Essential items are: a good backpack, sleeping bag, foam mat, stove, tent or tarpaulin, dried food (not tins), water bottle, compass and trowel for burying human waste. Hikers have little to fear from the animal kingdom

apart from insects; robbery and assault are rare. You are much more of a threat to the environment than vice versa. Leave no evidence of your passing; don't litter and don't give gratuitous presents of sweets or money to rural villagers. Respect their system of reciprocity; if they give you hospitality or food, then is the time to reciprocate with presents.

Guatemala has an Instituto Geográfico, which sells topographical maps of a scale 1:100,000 or 1:50,000. The physical features shown on these are usually accurate; the trails and place names less so. National park offices also sell maps.

Mountain biking

Mountain biking is an increasingly popular activity in Guatemala. There are numerous tracks and paths that weave their way across the country, passing hamlets as you go. **Old Town Outfitters** ⓘ *5 Av Sur 12 "C", Antigua, T7832-4171, www.adventureguatemala.com*, is a recommended operator, offering mountain bike tours starting at US$52 for a half day. They also deal in the gear.

Spiritual interest

There is a spiritual centre on the shores of Lake Atitlán that offers courses in accordance with the cycle of the moon: **Las Pirámides del Ka**, in San Marcos La Laguna, offers yoga and meditation as well as spiritual instruction year round (see page 83). At the **Takilibén Maya Misión** in Momostenango, day keeper Rigoberto

Itzep (leave a message for him on T7736-5537), 3 Av "A", 6-85, Zona 3, offers courses in Maya culture.

Textiles and weaving

It is possible to get weaving lessons in many places across the highlands. Weaving lessons can also be organized through Spanish schools.

Whitewater rafting

Rafting is possible on a number of rivers in Guatemala across a range of grades. However, trips have to be arranged in advance. In general, the larger the group, the cheaper the cost. **Maya Expeditions** ⓘ *www.mayaexpeditions.com*, is the country's best outfitter. It rafts the Río Cahabón in Alta Verapaz (Grade III-V), the Río Naranjo close to Coatepeque (Grade III), the Río Motagua close to Guatemala City (Grade III-IV), the Río Esclavos, near Barbarena (Grade III-IV), the Río Coyolate close to Santa Lucía Cotzumalguapa (Grade II-III) and the Río Chiquibul in the Petén (Grade II-III). It also runs a rafting and caving tour in the Petén and a combined archaeology and rafting tour where you would raft through a canyon on the Río Usumacinta (Grade II). For a little extra excitement, Maya Expeditions also arrange bungee jumping in Guatemala City.

Where to stay

from homestays to hammocks

Hotels and guesthouses

Hotels are widespread in all major towns and cities, but less prevalent in villages and small communities. Most rooms come with their own bathroom, running hot and/or cold water, cable TV, a fan, writing desk and Wi-Fi. Air conditioning will ratchet up the price, sometimes by an extra US$10-20. The very cheapest rooms have a shared bathroom (note that in the text the term 'with bath' usually means 'with shower and toilet', not 'with bathtub'). Couples should ask for a room with a *cama matrimonial* (double bed), which is cheaper than a room with two beds.

Rates vary seasonally, especially on the coast. You may also be charged 'gringo rates' based on your appearance and command of Spanish. Many hotels have a few cheap and very basic rooms set aside from their standards; politely ask if they have something *más económico*. A cheap but decent hotel might be around US$15 a night. In many popular destinations there is often an established preferred choice budget option.

Making reservations is a good idea, particularly at times you know are going to be busy or if you are travelling a long distance and won't have the energy to look around for a room. At the lower end of the market, having reservations honoured can be difficult. Ask the hotel if there is anything you can do to secure the room. If arriving late, make sure the hotel knows what

Price codes

Where to stay	
$$$$	over US$150
$$$	US$66-150
$$	US$30-65
$	under US$30

Price of a double room in high season, including taxes.

Restaurants	
$$$	over US$12
$$	US$7-12
$	US$6 and under

Prices for a two-course meal for one person, excluding drinks or service charge.

time you plan to arrive. Beware 'helpers' who try to find you a hotel, as rates increase to pay their commission. Try www.airbnb.co.uk for stays with local hosts in apartments or houses. Although owners are not always necessarily present in the property while you're there, they will answer any questions before you get there and welcome you on arrival.

For those on a really tight budget, look for a boarding house, called a *casa de huéspedes, hospedaje, pensión, casa familial* or *residencial*; they are normally found in abundance near bus stations and markets. They are usually quite basic and family-run and may or may not have television, running hot water, windows or sunlight. 'Love motels' can be found on highways, designed with discretion in mind. Although comfortable if occasionally seedy, their rates tend to be hourly.

B&Bs

Throughout the region, the extent and popularity of B&Bs has taken off in recent years and most of them imply a level of quality, comfort and personal service above and beyond your bog-standard hotel. Some of the converted townhouses in the big colonial cities are especially beautiful. On the beach, luxury 'rustic chic' *cabañas* have become de rigueur. Most B&Bs cost upwards of US$50 per night and it's worth shopping around as style, comfort, intimacy and overall value vary greatly between establishments. Also check what kind of breakfast is included, as some do not extend to a full cooked spread. It's worth checking out www.airbnb.co.uk too, which has plenty of great value places listed to stay in the region.

> **Tip...**
> Used toilet paper should be placed in the receptacle provided and not flushed down the pan, even in quite expensive hotels. Failing to do this blocks the pan or drain.

The web has spawned some great communities and independent travellers should take a look at www.couchsurfing.com. It's a way of making friends by kipping on their sofa. It's grown rapidly in the last few years and appears to be a great concept that works.

Nature lodges

Nature lodges are famed for their romantic settings and access to areas of outstanding natural beauty, including rainforests, cloudforests, mountains and beaches. They are among the world's best places for wildlife observation, especially for birds. Although nature lodges are comparatively expensive – most fall in our $$$ and $$$$ range – they promise a unique and intimate experience of the wilderness that is sure to leave lasting impressions. Everyone should consider splashing out at least once.

Homestays
Homestays are a great way to learn about local culture and are best arranged through Spanish schools or community tourism projects. Reasonably comfortable options are available in big towns and cities, but in more remote places, expect rustic conditions, including an outdoor toilet, little or no electricity, and cold running water (or just a bucket and wash bowl). Simple meals are usually included in rates.

Camping
There are few official campsites in Guatemala but camping is generally tolerated. Obey the following rules for wild camping: arrive in daylight and pitch your tent as it gets dark; ask permission to camp from a person in authority; never ask a group of people – especially young people; avoid camping on a beach (because of sandflies and thieves). If you can't get information, camp in a spot where you can't be seen from the nearest inhabited place and make sure no one saw you go there. Camping supplies are usually only available in the larger cities, so stock up on them when possible. In some national parks, simple rangers' station offer rustic lodging in cots. Bring your own food and water and some warm bedding; the rainforest can get quite chilly in the early hours.

Hammocks

A hammock can be an invaluable piece of equipment, especially if travelling on the cheap. It will be of more use than a tent because many places have hammock hooks, or you can sling a hammock between trees or posts. A good tip is to carry a length of rope and some plastic sheeting. The rope gives a good choice of tree distances and the excess provides a hanging frame for the plastic sheeting to keep the rain off. Metal S-hooks or a couple of climbing karabiners can also be very useful, as can strong cord for tying out the sheeting. Don't forget a mosquito net if travelling in insect-infested areas.

Food
& drink

Food

Most restaurants serve a daily special meal, usually at lunchtime called a *comida corrida* or *comida corriente*, which works out much cheaper and is usually filling and nutritious. Vegetarians should list all the foods they cannot eat; saying '*Soy vegetariano/a*' (I'm a vegetarian) or '*No como carne*' (I don't eat meat) is often not enough. Universally the cheapest place to eat is the local market.

Traditional Central American/Mexican food such as tortillas, *tamales*, *tostadas*, etc, are found everywhere. Tacos are less spicy than in Mexico. *Chiles rellenos* (chillies stuffed with meat and vegetables) are a speciality in Guatemala and may be *picante* (spicy) or *no picante*. *Churrasco*, charcoal-grilled steak, is often accompanied by *chirmol*, a sauce of tomato, onion and mint. Guacamole is also excellent. Local dishes include *pepián* (thick meat stew with vegetables) in Antigua, *patín* (small fish from Lake Atitlán wrapped in leaves and served in a tomato-based sauce) from Lake Atitlán, *cecina* (beef marinated in lemon and bitter orange) from the same region. *Fiambre* is widely prepared for families and friends who gather on All Souls' Day (1 November). It consists of all kinds of meat, fish, chicken, vegetables, eggs or cheese served as a salad with rice, beans and other side dishes. Desserts include *mole* (plantain and chocolate), *torrejas* (sweet bread soaked in egg and *panela* or honey) and *buñuelos* (similar to profiteroles) served with hot cinnamon syrup. For breakfast try *mosh* (oats cooked with milk and cinnamon), fried plantain with cream and black beans in various forms. *Pan dulce* (sweet bread), in fact bread in general, and local cheese are recommended. Try *borracho* (cake soaked in rum).

Drink

Local beers are good (Monte Carlo, Cabra, Gallo and Moza, a dark beer); bottled, carbonated soft drinks (*gaseosas*) are safest. Milk should be pasteurized. Freshly made *refrescos* and ice creams are delicious and made of local fruits; *licuados* are fruit juices with milk or water, but hygiene varies, so take care. Water should be filtered or bottled. By law alcohol cannot be consumed after 2000 on Sundays.

Essential Guatemala City

Finding your feet

Any address not in Zona 1 – and it is absolutely essential to quote zone numbers in addresses – is probably some way from the centre. Addresses themselves, being purely numerical, are usually easy to find. For example, 19 Calle, 4-83 is on 19 Calle between 4 Avenida and 5 Avenida at No 83.

If driving, Avenidas have priority over calles (except in Zona 10, where this rule varies).

Best places to stay
Posada Belén, page 28
La Inmaculada, page 29
Quetzalroo, page 30

Getting around

You can walk between the main sights in central Zona 1 but will need to take a bus or taxi to Zonas 9, 10 and 14. Cheap city buses run all day until 2000. Otherwise, take a taxi but for safety reasons make sure it's an official one; see page 37 for more information.

Safety

As with any big city, take precautions, especially on public transport or in

Best restaurants
Gracia Cocina de Autor, page 31
Hotel Pan American restaurant, page 30
Restaurante Vegetariano Rey Sol, page 31

crowded areas such as markets or bus stations. Be vigilant in all zones of the city, even in upmarket areas, and after dark, when it's advisable to take a radio taxi (see also Getting around above) rather than walk. Avoid withdrawing large sums of money from the bank. Don't wear jewellery or display valuable items such as cameras or phones. It may be best to avoid the Carretera Salvador from the city to the El Salvador border as car-jackings and holdups are becoming increasingly common on that route. To report an incident, contact INGUAT's tourist assistance on T1500, or the police on T110 or T120.

When to go

Temperatures normally average around the mid-20°Cs, but it can be chilly due to the high altitudes. Wet season is May to October. See also weather chart, page 11.

Time required

Two days.

Guatemala City

Smog-bound and crowded, Guatemala City, known simply as 'Guate', is the commercial and administrative centre of the country. Sketchy in parts and rarely rated by visitors, this is the beating heart of Guatemala and is worth a couple of days if you have time and can bear the noise and pollution in Zona 1. Guatemala City is surrounded by active and dormant volcanoes easily visited on day trips.

Sights

industrial sprawl sprinkled with architectural treasures and urban sculpture

The old centre of Guatemala City (population 1.2 million, altitude 1500 m) is Zona 1. It is still a busy shopping and commercial area, with some good hotels and restaurants, and many of the cheaper places to stay. However, the main activity of the city has been moving south, first to Zona 4, now to Zonas 9, 10 and 14. With the move have gone commerce, banks, embassies, museums and the best hotels and restaurants. The best residential areas are in the hills to the east, southeast and west.

Around Zona 1

At the city's heart lies the **Parque Central**. It is intersected by the north–south-running 6 Avenida, the main shopping street. The eastern half has a floodlit fountain; on the west side is **Parque Centenario**, with an acoustic shell in cement used for open-air concerts and public meetings. The Parque Central is popular on Sunday with many *indígenas* selling textiles.

To the east of the plaza is the **cathedral**. It was begun in 1782 and finished in 1815 in classical style with notable blue cupolas and dome. Inside are paintings and statues from ruined Antigua. Solid silver and sacramental reliquary are in the east side chapel of the Sagrario. Next to the cathedral is the colonial mansion of the Archbishop. Aside from the cathedral, the most notable public buildings constructed between 1920 and 1944, after the 1917 earthquake, are the **Palacio Nacional** ① *Mon-Sat 0900-1200 and 1400-1700, entrance and guided tour US$4*, built of light green stone and concealing a lavish interior filled with murals and chandeliers, the police headquarters, the Chamber of Deputies and the post office, which is now home to a small cultural centre. To the west of the cathedral are the Biblioteca Nacional and the Banco del Ejército. Behind the Palacio Nacional is the Presidential Mansion.

Zona 1

➡ **Guatemala City maps**
1 Guatemala City: Zona 1, page 24
2 Guatemala City: Zona 9, 10, 13, page 27

N

300 metres
300 yards

Where to stay 🛏
Ajau 2 *D2*
Pan American 7 *A2*
Pensión Meza 8 *B3*
Posada Belén 1 *C3*
Theatre International 3 *C2*

Restaurants 🍴
Altuna 1 *C2*
Café de Imeri 3 *A1*
Helados Marylena 5 *A1*
Rey Sol 7 *A2*

Bars & clubs 🍸
El Portal 12 *A2*
Europa 4 *B2*
La Bodeguita del Centro 10 *B1*
Las Cien Puertas 14 *A2*

Transport 🚌
ADN to Santa Elena 5 *C2*
Escobar y Monja Blanca to Cobán 1 *C2*
Fuente del Norte to Río Dulce & Santa Elena/Flores 2 *D2*
Línea Dorada to Río Dulce & Flores 3 *D3*
Marquensita to Quetzaltenango 6 *E1*

Rutas Orientales to Chiquimula & Esquipulas 7 *D3*
Transportes Galgos to Mexico 12 *D2*
Transportes Litegua to Puerto Barrios & Río Dulce 13 *C3*

Museums in Zona 1 include the **Museo Nacional de Historia** ⓘ *9 Calle, 9-70, T2253-6149, www.mcd.gob.gt, Mon-Fri 0900-1700, US$1.50,* which has historical documents and objects from Independence onward. The **Museo de la Universidad de San Carlos de Guatemala (MUSAC)** ⓘ *9 Av, 9-79, T2232-0721, www.musacenlinea.org, Mon, Wed-Fri 0930-1730, Sat 0930-1700, US$1; guided tours at 1000 and 1400,* charts the history of the university. The Salón Mayor is where Guatemala signed its Independence from Mexico in 1823, and in 1826 the Central American Federation, with Guatemala as the seat of power, abolished slavery in the union. Also, Doctor Mariano Gálvez, the country's president from 1831-1838, is buried behind part of the salon wall and a marble bust of him sits outside the door. The Universidad de San Carlos was the first university in Guatemala City. **Casa MIMA** ⓘ *8 Av, 14-12, T2253-6657, casamima@hotmail.com, Mon-Sat 0900-1230, 1400-1500, US$1, no photography,* is the only authentic turn-of-the-19th-century family home open to the public, once owned by the family Ricardo Escobar Vega and Mercedes Fernández Padilla y Abella. It is furnished in European-influenced style with 15th- to mid-20th-century furniture and ornaments.

Churches Most of the churches worth visiting are in Zona 1. **Cerro del Carmen** ⓘ *11 Av y 1 Calle A,* was built as a copy of a hermitage destroyed in 1917-1918, containing a famous image of the Virgen del Carmen. Situated on a hill with good views of the city, it was severely damaged in the earthquake of 1976 and remains in poor shape. **La Merced** ⓘ *11 Av y 5 Calle,* dedicated in 1813, has beautiful altars, organ and pulpit from Antigua as well as jewellery, art treasures and fine statues. **Santo Domingo** ⓘ *12 Av y 10 Calle,* built between 1782 and 1807, is a striking yellow colour, reconstructed after 1917, with an image of Nuestra Señora del Rosario and sculptures. **Sagrado Corazón de Jesús**, or **Santuario Expiatorio** ⓘ *26 Calle y 2 Av,* holds 3000 people; the colourful, exciting modern architecture was by a young Salvadorean architect who had not qualified when he built it. Part of the complex, built in 1963 (church, school and auditorium) is in the shape of a fish. The entrance is a giant arch of multicoloured stained glass, wonderfully illuminated at night. The walls are lined with glass confessionals. **Las Capuchinas** ⓘ *10 Av y 10 Calle,* has a very fine St Anthony altarpiece, and other pieces from Antigua. **Santa Rosa** ⓘ *10 Av y 8 Calle,* was used for 26 years as the cathedral until the present building was ready. The altarpieces are from Antigua (except above the main altar). **San Francisco** ⓘ *6 Av y 13 Calle,* a large yellow and white church that shows earthquake damage outside (1976), has a sculpture of the Sacred Head, originally from Extremadura in Spain. **Carmen El Bajo** ⓘ *8 Av y 10 Calle,* was built in the late 18th century; again the façade was severely damaged in 1976.

North of the centre
Parque Minerva ⓘ *Av Simeón Cañas, Zona 2, www.mapaenrelieve.org, 0900-1700, US$4,* has a huge relief map of the country made in 1905 to a horizontal scale of 1:10,000 and a vertical scale of 1:2,000. The park has basketball and baseball courts, bar and restaurant and a children's playground (unsafe at night). To get there, take

BACKGROUND

Guatemala City

Guatemala City was founded by decree of Carlos III of Spain in 1776 to serve as capital after earthquake damage to the earlier capital, Antigua, in 1773. Almost completely destroyed by earthquakes in 1917-1918, it was rebuilt in modern fashion, or in copied colonial, only to be further damaged by earthquake in 1976. Most of the affected buildings have been restored.

bus V21 from 7 Avenida, Zona 4. Just beyond is a popular park, the **Hipódromo**, which is packed on Sundays with bumper cars and mechanical games, and a great little train for kids.

South of the centre: Avenida La Reforma

The modern **Centro Cívico**, which links Zona 1 with Zona 4, includes the Municipalidad, Palacio de Justicia, Ministerio de Finanzas Públicas, Banco de Guatemala, the mortgage bank, the social-security commission and the tourist board. The curious **Teatro Nacional** ⓘ *Mon-Fri 0800-1630 for tours, US$4*, with its blue and white mosaic, dominates the hilltop of the west side of the Centro Cívico. There is an excellent view of the city and surrounding mountains from the roof. An old Spanish fortress provides a backdrop to the open-air theatre adjoining the Teatro Nacional.

Cuatro Grados Norte, located on Vía 5 between Ruta 1 and Ruta 2, is a pedestrianized area that has grown up around the IGA theatre and bookshop (a cultural centre, which sometimes has interesting concerts and exhibitions). Cafés and bars have tables on the street and it's safe and fun to wander around at night. The **Centro Cultural de España** is located here with live music, films, exhibitions and conferences, and there is also a branch of **Sophos**, an excellent bookshop. On Saturdays there is a street market with craft and jewellery stalls, often cultural events in the street. On Sundays there are clowns and events for children. It's a strange mix of wealthy Guatemalans strolling with their poodles and alternative street-market types; sit back and enjoy watching the people.

To see the finest residential district go south down 7 Avenida to Ruta 6, which runs diagonally in front of Edificio El Triángulo, past the orange **Capilla de Yurrita** (Ruta 6 y Vía 8). Built as a private chapel in 1928 on the lines of a Russian Orthodox church, it has been described as an example of "opulent 19th-century bizarreness and over-ripe extravagance". There are many woodcarvings, slender white pillars, brown/gold ornamentation and an unusual blue sky window over the altar. Ruta 6 runs into the wide tree-lined Avenida La Reforma.

To the east, in Zona 10, are some excellent museums. **Museo Ixchel del Traje Indígena** ⓘ *Campus of Universidad Francisco Marroquín, 6 Calle Final, T2331-3623, www.museoixchel.org, Mon-Fri 0900-1700, Sat 0900-1300, US$4.60*, has a collection of indigenous dress. In addition to the clothes there are photos from the early 20th century, paintings and very interesting videos. A shop sells beautiful textiles that aren't available on the tourist market, prices are fixed, and quality costs. **Museo Popol Vuh de Arqueología** ⓘ *6 Calle Final, T2338-7896, www.popolvuh.ufm.edu. gt, Mon-Fri 0900-1700, Sat 0900-1300, US$4.60, US$3 for photos*, has an extensive collection of pre-Columbian and colonial artefacts, as well as a replica of the Dresden Codex, one of the only Maya parchment manuscripts in existence. **Museo de Historia Natural de la USAC y Jardín Botánico** ⓘ *Calle Mcal Cruz 1-56, T2334-6065, Mon-Fri 0800-1600, Sat 0830-1230, US$1.30*, has gardens, stuffed animals and live snakes.

In **Parque Aurora**, Zona 13, in the southern part of the city, are La Aurora International Airport, the Observatory, racetrack and **Parque Zoológico La Aurora** ⓘ *T2472-0507, www.aurorazoo.org.gt, Tue-Sun 0900-1700, US$3.30*. The newer areas show greater concern for the animals' wellbeing. There are also several

Zona 9, 10 & 13

Where to stay 🛏
Comfort Hostel **1**
Dos Lunas Guest House **2**
Hostal Guatefriends **3**
La Inmaculada **4**
Mariana's Petit Hotel **5**
Quetzalroo **6**
Residencial Reforma
  La Casa Grande **7**
San Carlos **8**
Villa Toscana **9**

Restaurants 🍴
Gracia Cocina de Autor **3**
Hacienda de los Sánchez **1**
Hacienda Real **2**
Kacao **5**
Khawp Khun Kha **4**
Los Alpes **6**
Panadería San Martín **7**
Splendido **8**
Tamarindos **12**

Bars & clubs 🍸
Cheers **9**
Shakespeare's Pub **11**

➜ **Guatemala City maps**
1 Guatemala City: Zona 1, page 24
2 Guatemala City: Zona 9, 10, 13, page 27

600 metres
600 yards

museums: the **Museo Nacional de Antropología y Etnología** ⓘ *Salón 5, Parque Aurora, Zona 13, T2475-4406, www.munae.gob.gt, Tue-Fri 0900-1600, Sat-Sun 0900-1200, 1330-1600, US$7.90, no photos,* has outstanding Maya pieces including stelae from Piedras Negras and typical Guatemalan dress, as well as good models of Tikal, Quiriguá and Zaculeu. There are sculptures, murals, ceramics, textiles, a collection of masks and an excellent jade collection. Around the corner is the **Museo Nacional de Historia Natural** ⓘ *6 Calle, 7-30, Zona 13, T2472-0468, Mon-Fri 0900-1600, Sat-Sun 0900-1200, 1400-1600, US$6.50,* which houses a collection of national fauna, including stuffed birds, animals, butterflies, geological specimens, etc. Opposite the archaeology museum, the **Museo de Arte Moderno** ⓘ *Salón 6, Parque Aurora, Zona 13, T2472-0467, US$4, Tue-Fri 0900-1600,* has a modest but enjoyable collection. Next door is the **Museo de los Niños** ⓘ *T2475-5076, Tue-Fri 0830-1200, 1300-1630, US$4,* an interactive museum with a gallery of Maya history and the Gallery of Peace which houses the world's largest single standing artificial tree – a *ceiba.*

Listings Guatemala City *maps p24 and p27*

Tourist information

INGUAT
7 Av, 1-17, Zona 4 (Centro Cívico), 24 hrs T1801-464-8281, T2421-2800, www. visitguatemala.com. Mon-Fri 0800-1600.
They are very friendly and English is sometimes spoken. They provide a hotel list, a map of the city, and general information on buses, market days, museums, etc. There is also an office in the airport arrivals hall (T2331-4256, open 0600-2100) where staff are exceptionally helpful and on the ball.

Where to stay

You can get better prices in the more expensive hotels by booking corporate rates through a travel agent or simply asking at the desk if any lower prices are available. Hotels are often full at Easter and Christmas. At the cheaper hotels, single rooms are not always available. There are many cheap *pensiones* near bus and railway stations

and markets; those between Calle 14 and Calle 18 are not very salubrious.

Hoteles Villas de Guatemala, reservations 8 Calle 1-75 Zona 10, T2223-5000, www.villasdeguatemala.com, rents luxury villas throughout Guatemala.

Zona 1

$$ Pan American
9 Calle, 5-63, T2232-6807, www.hotelpanamerican.com.gt.
This one time art deco jewel of the Centro Histórico is well past its heyday, but worth a look nonetheless. They offer quiet, comfortable, reasonable rooms with TV, but try to avoid those on the main-road side. Award-winning restaurant with good food (see Restaurants, below). Parking, and breakfast included.

$$ Posada Belén
13 Calle "A", 10-30, T2232-9226, www.posadabelen.com.
A colonial-style house run by the friendly Francesca and René Sanchinelli,

who speak English. Quiet, comfy rooms with good hot showers. Laundry, email service, luggage store and good meals. Parking. Tours available. A lovely place to stay. Highly recommended.

$ Ajau
8 Av, 15-62, T5205-5137,
www.hotelajau.com.
This converted early 20th-century house has 45 simple, adequate, economical rooms set around a central courtyard, with or without private bath. Services include Wi-Fi, internet terminal, airport transfer, laundry and meals. A typical old school cheapie, helpful, secure and no frills.

$ Pensión Meza
10 Calle, 10-17, T2232-3177.
A large ramshackle place with beds in dorms. It's popular with helpful staff and English is spoken. It's sometimes noisy and some rooms are damp. Other rooms are darker than a prison cell, but cheered by graffiti, poetry and paintings. There is table tennis, book exchange, internet at US$8 per hr and or free Wi-Fi.

$ Theatre International
8 Av, 14-17, T4202-5112,
www.theatreihostel.com.
Located to the side of the Teatro Abril, this 70-bed party hostel features 2 patios, kitchen, Wi-Fi and complimentary pancake breakfasts. There is a range of accommodation to suit all budgets, include thrifty 8- and 14-bed dorms, and private rooms with or without private bath. One for the whippersnappers and sadly a bit stuck up ("entrance is not allowed for people older than 45").

South of the centre:
Avenida La Reforma

$$$ Comfort Hostel
17 Calle, 14-35, Zona 10, T2367-0754,
www.comforthostel.com.
This small, secluded and professionally managed B&B features a very reasonable restaurant and a small patio where you can relax or work. Rooms are spacious, tranquil, tasteful and well-equipped with cable TV, clock radio, Wi-Fi, safety boxes and sparkling bathrooms with hot water. Simple but personal.

$$$ La Inmaculada
14 calle 7-88, Zona 10, T2314-5100,
www.inmaculadahotel.com.
With Egyptian cotton linens, complimentary L'Occitane toiletries and slick contemporary design, La Inmaculada is indeed immaculately stylish, a great option for couples or hip young things. Services include spa treatments and business centre. Very tasteful and highly recommended.

$$$ Residencial Reforma La Casa Grande
Av La Reforma, 7-67, Zona 10, T2332-0914, www.casagrande-gua.com.
Near the US embassy, a very attractive colonial-style house dating to the early 20th century, complete with whitewashed courtyard and lavish statues. Rooms and suites are comfortable but also rather simple and pricey for what you get. Good, small restaurant, open 0630-2100, also a bar and internet service.

$$$ San Carlos
Av La Reforma, 7-89, Zona 10, T2362-9076, www.hsancarlos.com.
A small, charming hotel set in a sumptuous historical property with a small pool and leafy garden. Rooms are

modern, middle-of-the-road and fully equipped with Wi-Fi and cable TV; suites and apartments are more luxurious. Rates includes breakfast and airport transfer.

$$ Villa Toscana
16 Calle 8-20, Zona 13, Aurora I, T2261-2854, www.hostalvillatoscana.com.
Stylish B&B adorned in tones of gold and cream. Rooms come with cable TV, Wi-Fi, handmade hardwood furniture and floral wall sculptures. The garden, where breakfast is served under a canopy, features a trim green lawn and well-tended flowers. Lovely and relaxing. Airport shuttle included.

$$-$ Hostal Guatefriends
16 Calle, 7-40, Zona 13, Aurora I, T5308-3275, www.hostalguatefriends.com.
Brightly painted hostel accommodation by the night or the month, including 4-person dorms ($, but still a bit pricey for Guatemala) and private rooms ($$) with cable TV and Wi-Fi. Rates include breakfast and airport shuttle. Friendly, safe and helpful.

$$-$ Mariana's Petit Hotel
20 Calle, 10-17, Zona 13, Aurora II, www.marianaspetithotel.com.
Located close to the airport with free pickup and drop-off, this simple and homely B&B has a range of comfortable, quiet and unpretentious rooms, all with cable TV and Wi-Fi. Upstairs there's a lovely roof terrace where you can soak up the sun. Great breakfasts. Helpful and hospitable.

$$-$ Quetzalroo
6 Av, 7-84, Zona 10, T5746-0830, www.quetzalroo.com.
This successful Australian/Guatemalteco-owned youth hostel is recommended as the best of its kind in the city. The staff

are super-friendly and helpful; rooms are simple, comfortable and cosy ($$); dorms are low-key ($). They do a city tours by bike and a basic breakfast is included. Sociable, quiet and relaxed.

$ Dos Lunas Guest House
21 Calle, 10-92, Zona 13, T2261-4248, www.hoteldoslunas.com.
Private rooms and dorms in a comfy B&B. Very close to the airport with free transport to or from the airport. Storage service, free breakfast and water and tourist information. Lorena, the landlady, also organizes shuttles and taxis and tours. English spoken. Reservations advisable as often full.

Restaurants

Zona 1
There are all kinds of food available in the capital, from the simple national cuisine to French, Chinese and Italian food. There is a plethora of fast-food restaurants and traditional *comedores* where you will get good value for money; a reasonable set meal will cost no more than US$3. The cheapest places to eat are at street stalls and the various markets – take the normal precautions.

$$$ Altuna
5 Av, 12-31, www.restaurantealtuna.com.
This establishment has a beautiful traditional Spanish bar interior and serves tasty Spanish food in huge portions, including paella and seafood. Lobster is available but expensive. Delicious coffee. There is a branch in Zona 10 at 10 Calle, 0-45.

$$$-$$ Hotel Pan American
See Where to stay, above.
Regional and international cuisine served in the central courtyard of this hotel, a faded but distinctive art deco

beauty that was once the haunt of the rich and famous. An award-winning establishment with lots of ambience and an affordable lunchtime menu.

$$-$ Café de Imeri
6 Calle, 3-34. Closed Sun.
Sandwiches, salads, soups and pastries in a patio garden. Set lunch and excellent cakes. It's popular with young professional Guatemalans. Try the *pay de queso de elote* (maize cheesecake). Its bakery next door has a rare selection of granary breads, birthday cakes, etc.

$ Restaurante Vegetariano Rey Sol
8 Calle, 5-36. Closed Sun.
A prize vegetarian find – wholesome food and ambience oasis amid the fumes of Zona 1, and popular with the locals. Delicious veggie concoctions at excellent prices served canteen-style by friendly staff. Breakfasts and *licuados* also available. Newer, larger and brighter branch at 11 Calle, 5-51.

Ice cream parlours

Helados Marylena
6 Calle, 2-49. Daily 1000-2200.
Not quite a meal but almost. This establishment has been serving up the weirdest concoctions for 90 years. From the probably vile – fish, chilli, yucca and cauliflower ice cream – to the heavenly – beer and sputnik (coconut, raisins and pineapple). The *elote* (maize) is good too. This city institution is credited with making children eat their vegetables! Anyone travelling with fussy eaters should stop by here.

South of the centre: Avenida La Reforma
Most of the best restaurants are in the **Zona Viva**, within 10 blocks of

the Av La Reforma on the east side, between 6 Calle and 16 Calle in Zona 10. **Zona 9** is just across the other side of Av La Reforma.

There are several options in the area around **Cuatro Grados Norte** providing tapas, sushi, *churros* and chocolate. Lively, especially on Fri and Sat nights.

$$$ Gracia Cocina de Autor
14 Calle y 4 Av, Zona 10, T2366 8699.
Modern and minimalist, Gracia Cocina de Autor serves an eclectic menu of flavourful gourmet dishes by chef Pablo Novales in a stylish setting. Recipes are international fusion with smoked salmon bagels and eggs benedict among the offerings for brunch, lamb chops and roast pork for lunch or dinner. Recommended.

$$$ Hacienda de los Sánchez
12 Calle, 2-25, Zona 10.
Good steaks and local dishes, but seriously crowded at weekends, and so not the most pleasant of settings compared with other steakhouses in the vicinity. Well-established and something of a classic on the scene.

$$$ Hacienda Real
5 Av 14-67, Zona 10, www.hacienda-real.com.
An excellent selection of grilled meats with a hint of smokiness. Great ambience, often buzzing, and the candles and palms create a garden-like setting. There's also a nice little bar with Mexican leather chairs on one side.

$$$ Kacao
1 Av, 13-51, Zona 10, www.kacao.com.gt.
A large variety of delicious local and national dishes, which are attractively prepared and served in ample portions. The setting is fantastic: a giant thatched room, *huipiles* for tablecloths and

beautiful candle decorations. Some options are expensive.

$$$ Khawp Khun Kha
13 Calle A, 7-19, Zona 10, Plaza Tiffany.
If the flavours of Central America have grown tired and old, try this hip Thai restaurant, serving spicy *panang* and green curries, pad Thai and other specialities sure to liven up your taste buds. Good and tasty, but definitely fusion cuisine and not quite authentically Thai (close enough though).

$$$ L'Osteria
Cuatro Grados Norte, Vía 5 between Ruta 1 and Ruta 2.
Popular Mediterranean restaurant on the corner, complete with a pleasant outdoor terrace. They serve tasty Greek fare, hummous and pitta bread, along with solid Italian favourites such as pizza and lasagne.

$$$ Splendido
12 Calle, 4-15, Zona 14, www.restaurantesplendido.com.
A very presentable bistro-style restaurant with impeccable service and delicious and predominantly French-flavoured fusion cooking. Main courses include scallops, shrimps, steaks and a selection of pasta. Specialities include sweet chilli tuna, chicken curry, peppered steak and key lime cheesecake.

$$$ Tamarindos
11 Calle, 2-19A, Zona 10, T2360-2815.
Mixed Asian, sushi, Vietnamese rolls, mushrooms stuffed with almonds and crab are some of the tantalizing options at this very smart Asian restaurant with spiral shades and soothing bamboo greens.

$$ Los Alpes
10 Calle, 1-09, Zona 10. Closed Mon.
A Swiss-Austrian place with light meals and a smorgasbord of excellent cakes and chocolates. Popular with Guatemalan families.

$$-$ Panadería San Martin
2 Av, Zona 10, www.sanmartinbakery.com.
San Martín is a very popular bakery with branches across Guatemala and El Salvador. In addition to baked goods, they offer cooked breakfasts and reliable international fare such as pizzas, salads, soups and sandwiches. Not outstanding, but easy and tasty enough.

Bars and clubs

Cheers
13 Calle, 0-40, Zona 10. Mon-Sat 0900-0100, Sun 1300-2400ish.
A basement sports bar with pool tables, darts and large cable TV. Happy hour until 1800. The awning outside features the logo from the hit TV show.

El Portal
Portal del Comercio, 8 Calle, 6-30, Zona 1. Mon-Sat 1000-2200.
This was a favourite spot of Che Guevara and you can imagine him sitting here holding court at the long wooden bar. A stuffed bull's head now keeps watch over drinkers. To get there, enter the labyrinths of passageways facing the main plaza at No 6-30 where there is a Coke stand. At the first junction bear round to the left and up on the left you will see its sign. *Comida típica* and marimba music, beer from the barrel.

Europa
11 Calle, 5-16, Zona 1. Mon-Sat 0800-0100.

Popular peace-corps/travellers' hangout. A sports bar, showing videos, with books for sale. They also serve grub.

La Bodeguita del Centro
12 Calle, 3-55, Zona 1, T2239-2976.
The walls of this hip place in an old stockhouse are adorned with posters of Che Guevara, Bob Marley and murdered Salvadorean Archbishop Romero. There's live music Thu-Sat at 2100, talks, plays, films, and exhibitions upstairs. Wooden tables are spread over 2 floors; seriously cheap nachos and soup are on the menu. It's an atmospheric place to spend an evening. Call in to get their *Calendario Cultural* leaflet.

Las Cien Puertas
Pasaje Aycinea, 7 Av, 8-44, just south of Plaza Mayor, Zona 1. Daily 1600-2400.
Has a wonderful atmosphere with political, satirical and love missives covering its walls. There's excellent food and outdoor seating and it's friendly.

Shakespeare's Pub
13 Calle, 1-51, Zona 10. Mon-Fri 1100-0100, Sat and Sun 1400-0100.
English-style basement bar with a good atmosphere, American owner, a favourite with expats and locals, safe for women to drink.

Entertainment

Cinema and theatre
There are numerous cinemas and they often show films in English with Spanish subtitles.
Teatro Nacional, *Centro Cívico, see page 26.* Most programmes are Thu-Sun.

Shopping

Bookshops
Museo Ixchel, *see page 26.* This museum has a bookshop.
Museo Popol Vuh bookshop, *see page 27.* Has a good selection of books on pre-Columbian art, crafts and natural history.

Maps
Maps can be bought from the **Instituto Geográfico Nacional (IGN)**, Av Las Américas, 5-76, Zona 13, T2332-2611. Mon-Fri 0900-1730. The whole country is covered by about 200 1:50,000 maps available in colour or photocopies of out-of-print sections. None is very up to date. There is, however, an excellent 1996, 1:15,000 map of Guatemala City in 4 sheets. A general *Mapa Turístico* of the country is available here, also at INGUAT, see Tourist information above.

Markets
The **Central Market** operates underground behind the cathedral, from 7 to 9 Av, 8 Calle, Zona 1. One floor is dedicated to textiles and crafts, and there is a large, cheap basketware section on the lower floor. Silverware is cheaper at the market than elsewhere in Guatemala City. Other markets include the **Mercado Terminal** in Zona 4, and the **Mercado de Artesanía** in the Parque Aurora, near the airport, which is for tourists. Large shopping centres are good for a wide selection of local crafts, artworks, funky shoes, and clothes. Don't miss the *dulces*, candied fruits and confectionery.

Shopping centres and supermarkets
The best shopping centres are **Centro Comercial Los Próceres**, 18 Calle and

3 Av, Zona 10, the **Centro Comercial La Pradera**, Carretera Roosevelt and Av 26, Zona 10. There is a large **Paiz** supermarket on 18 Calle and 8 Av and a vast shopping mall **Tikal Futura** at Calzada Roosevelt and 22 Av, Zona 11. *Artesanías* for those who shop with a conscience at the fair-trade outlet **UPAVIM**, Calle Principal, Col La Esperanza, Mesquital Zona 12, T2479-9061, www.upavim.org, Mon-Fri 0800-1800, Sat 0800-1200.

What to do

Clark Tours, *Plaza Clark, 7 Av 14-76, Zona 9, T2412-4700, www.clarktours.com. gt, and several other locations.* Long-established, very helpful, tours to Copán, Quiriguá, etc.
Four Directions, *1 Calle, 30-65, Zona 7, T2439-7715, www.fourdirections.travel.* Recommended for Maya archaeology tours. English spoken.
Maya Expeditions, *13 Av, 14-70, Zona 10, T2366-9950, www.mayaexpeditions. com.* Very experienced and helpful, with varied selection of short and longer river/hiking tours, whitewater rafting, bungee jumping, cultural tours, tours to Piedras Negras.
Trolley Tour, *T5907-0913, Tue-Sat 1000-1300, Sun 1000.* Pick-ups from Zona 10 hotels for 3-hr city tours, US$20, children US$10.
Turismo Ek Chuah, *3 Calle 6-24, Zona 2, T2220-1491, www.ekchuah.com.* Nationwide tours as well as some specialist and tailor-made tours on bicycle and horseback.

Transport

Air
The airport is in the south part of the city at La Aurora, 4 km from the Plaza Central, T2331-8392. It has banks, ATMs, internet,

bars and restaurants. A taxi to Zona 10 is US$8, Zona 1, US$10, and from Antigua, US$25-30. Shuttles from outside airport to Antigua meet all arriving flights, US$10.

Flights to **Flores** with **Grupo Taca** 0820, 1605 and 1850, and **TAG** at 1630 daily. For the following domestic airlines, phone for schedules: **Aerocharter**, T5401-5893, to **Puerto Barrios**. **Aeródromo**, T5539-9364, to **Huehuetenango**. **Aerolucía**, T5959-7008 to **Quetzaltenango**.

Bus
Local
Buses operate between 0600-2000, after which you'll have to rely on taxis.

In town, US$0.13 per journey on regular buses and on the larger red buses known as *gusanos* (worms) except on Sun and public holidays when they charge US$0.16. One of the most useful bus services is the **101**, which travels down 10 Av, Zona 1, and then cuts across to the 6 Av, Zona 4, and then across Vía 8 and all the way down the Av La Reforma, Zona 10. The **82** also travels from Zona 1 to 10 and can be picked up on the 10 Av, Zona 1 and the 6 Av, Zona 4. Bus **85**, with the same pickup points, goes to the cluster of museums in Zona 13. Buses **37**, **35**, **32** all head for the INGUAT building, which is the large blue and white building in the Centro Cívico complex. **R40** goes from the 6 Av, Zona 4, to the Tikal Futura shopping complex; a good spot to catch the Antigua bus, which pulls up by the bridge to the complex. Buses leaving the 7 Av, Zona 4, just 4 blocks from the Zona 4 bus terminal, for the Plaza Mayor, Zona 1, are *gusano* **V21**, **35**, **36**, **82**, and **101**.

Long distance

The Zona 4 chicken bus terminal between 1-4 Av and 7-9 C serves the Occidente (west), the Costa Sur (Pacific coastal plain) and El Salvador. The area of southern Zona 1 contains many bus offices and is the departure point for the Oriente (east), the Caribbean zone, Pacific coast area towards the Mexican border and the north, to Flores and Tikal. 1st-class buses often depart from company offices in Zona 1 (see map, page 24).

There are numerous bus terminals in Guatemala City. The majority of 1st-class buses have their own offices and departure points around Zona 1. Hundreds of chicken buses for the south and west of Guatemala leave from the Zona 4 terminal, as well as local city buses. Note that some companies have been moved from Zona 1 and Zona 4 out to Zona 7 and 12. There was a plan, at the time of writing, to redirect all buses for the southern region to leave from Central Sur, Col Villalobos.

Tip...
Watch your bags everywhere, but like a hawk in the Zona 4 terminal.

International buses (see below) have their offices scattered about the city. (The cheaper Salvador buses leave from near the Zona 4 terminal.) The Zona 4 bus terminal has to be the dirtiest and grimmest public area in the whole of the city.

The main destinations with companies operating from Guatemala City are:

Antigua, every 15 mins, 1 hr, US$1, until 2000 from Av 23 and 3 Calle, Zona 3. To **Chimaltenango** and **Los Encuentros**, from 1 Av between 3 y 4. Calle, Zona 7. **Chichicastenango** hourly from 0500-1800, 3 hrs, US$2.20 with Veloz Quichelense. **Huehuetenango**, with **Los Halcones**, Calzada Roosevelt, 37-47, Zona 11, T2439-2780, 0700, 1400, 1700, US$7, 5 hrs, and **Transportes Velásquez**, Calzada Roosevelt 9-56, Zona 7, T2440-3316, 0800-1630, every 30 mins, 5 hrs, US$7.

Panajachel, with **Transportes Rebulí**, 41 Calle, between 6 y 7 Av, Zona 8, T2230-2748, hourly from 0530-1530, 3 hrs, US$2.20; also to **San Lucas Tolimán** 0530-1530, 3 hrs US$2.10 **San Pedro La Laguna** with **Transportes Méndez**, 41 C, between 6 y and Av, Zona 8, 1300, 4 hrs. **Santiago Atitlán**, with various companies, from 4 C, between 3 y 4 Av, Zona 12, 0400-1700, every 30 mins, 4 hrs, US$4.

Quetzaltenango (Xela) and **San Marcos**. 1st-class bus to Xela with **Transportes Alamo**, 12 Av "A", 0-65, Zona 7, T2471-8626, from 0800-1730, 6 daily 4 hrs, US$7. **Líneas Américas**, 2 Av, 18-47, Zona 1, T2232-1432, 0500-1930, 7 daily, US$7. **Galgos**, 7 Av, 19-44, Zona 1, T2232-3661, between 0530-1700, 5 daily, 4 hrs, US$7 to **Tapachula** in Mexico through the El Carmen border; see also box, page 210. **Marquensita**, 1 Av, 21-31, Zona 1, T2230-0067. From 0600-1700, 8 a day, US$6.10, to Xela and on to San Marcos. To **Tecpán**, with **Transportes Poaquileña**, 1 Av corner of 3 and 4 Calle, Zona 7, 0530-1900, every 15 mins, 2 hrs, US$1.20.

To **Santa Cruz del Quiché**, Sololá and Totonicapán, buses depart from 41 Calle between 6 and 7 Av, Zona 8.

To **Biotopo del Quetzal** and **Cobán**, 3½ hrs and 4½ hrs respectively, hourly from 0400-1700, US$6 and US$7.50, with **Escobar y Monja Blanca**, 8 Av, 15-16, Zona 1, T2238-1409. **Zacapa**, **Chiquimula** (for **El Florido**, on the Honduran border) and **Esquipulas** with

Rutas Orientales, 19 Calle, 8-18, Zona 1, T2253-7282, every 30 mins 0430-1800. To Zacapa, 3¼ hrs, to Chiquimula, 3½ hrs, to Esquipulas, 4½ hrs, US$6.

Puerto Barrios, with Transportes Litegua, 15 Calle, 10-40, Zona 1, T2220-8840, www.litegua.com, 0430-1900, 31 a day, 5 hrs, US$6.80, 1st class US$12 and Río Dulce, 0600, 0900, 1130, 5 hrs, US$6.20.

El Petén with Fuente del Norte (same company as Líneas Máxima de Petén), 17 Calle, 8-46, Zona 1, T2251-3817, going to Río Dulce and Santa Elena/Flores. There are numerous departures 24 hrs; 5 hrs to Río Dulce, US$6.50; to Santa Elena, 9-10 hrs, US$12; buses vary in quality and price, breakdowns not unknown. The 1000 and 2130 departures are a luxury bus Maya del Oro with snacks, US$18, the advantage being it doesn't stop at every tree to pick up passengers. Línea Dorada, 16 Calle, 10-03, Zona 1, T2220-7990, www.tikalmayanworld.com, at 1000, US$16 to Flores, 8 hrs and on to Melchor de Mencos, 10 hrs. To Santa Elena ADN, 8 Av, 16-41, Zona 1, T2251-0050, www.adnautobuses delnorte.com, luxury service, 2100 and 2200, returns at 2100 and 2300, US$19, toilets, TV and snacks.

To Jalapa with Unidos Jalapanecos, 22 Calle 1-20, Zona 1, T2251-4760, 0430-1830, every 30 mins, 3 hrs, US$2.50 and with Transportes Melva Nacional, T2332-6081, 0415-1715, every 30 mins, 3 hrs 30 mins, US$2.50. Buses also from the Zona 4 terminal. To San Pedro Pinula between 0500-1800.

To Chatia Gomerana, 4 Calle y 8 Av, Zona 12, to La Democracia, every 30 mins from 0600-1630 via Escuintla and Siquinala, 2 hrs. Transportes Cubanita to Reserva Natural de Monterrico (La Avellana), 4 Calle y 8 Av, Zona 12,

at 1030, 1230, 1420, 3 hrs, US$2.50. To Puerto San José and Iztapa, from the same address, 0430-1645 every 15 mins, 1 hr. To Retalhuleu (Reu on bus signs) with Transportes Fortaleza del Sur, Calzada Aguilar Batres, 4-15, Zona 12, T2230-3390, between 0010-1910 every 30 mins via Escuintla, Cocales and Mazatenango, 3 hrs, US$6.80. Numerous buses to Santa Lucía Cotzumalguapa go from the Zona 4 bus terminal.

International buses

Reserve the day before if you can. Taking a bus from Guatemala City as far as, say, San José, is tiring and tiresome (the bus company's bureaucracy and the hassle from border officials all take their toll). For crossings to Honduras and El Salvador, see also boxes, pages 213 and 214. For Belize border information, see box, page 212, and for Mexico, see box, page 210.

To Honduras avoiding El Salvador, take a bus to Esquipulas, then a minibus to the border. Hedman Alas, 2 Av, 8-73, Zona 10, T2362-5072, www.hedmanalas. com, to Copán via El Florido, at 0500 and 0900, 5 hrs, US$30. Also goes on to San Pedro Sulas, US$45, and La Ceiba, US$52. Pullmantur to Tegucigalpa daily at 0700 via San Salvador, US$66 and US$94. Ticabus to San Pedro Sula, US$34 and Tegucigalpa, US$34 via San Salvador. Rutas Orientales, 19 C, 8-18, T2253-7282 goes to Honduras at 0530 via Agua Caliente, 8 hrs, US$28; see also box, page 213, for more on crossing into Honduras.

To Mexico with Trans Galgos Inter, 7 Av, 19-44, Zona 1, T2223-3661, www. transgalgosinter.com.gt, to Tapachula via El Carmen, 0730, 1330, and 1500, 7 hrs; see also box, page 210. Línea Dorada, address above, to Tapachula at 0800, US$24. **Transportes Velásquez**, 20 Calle, 1-37, Zona 1, T2221-1084, 0800-1100, hourly to **La Mesilla**, 7 hrs, US$5. **Transportes Fortaleza del Sur**, Calzada Aguilar Batres, 4-15, Zona 12, T2230-3390 to **Ciudad Tecún Umán**, 0130, 0300, 0330, 0530 via **Retalhuleu**, 5 hrs.

To **Chetumal** via **Belize City**, with **Línea Dorada** change to a minibus in Flores. Leaves 1000, 2100, 2200 and 2230, 2 days, US$42. Journey often takes longer than advertised due to Guatemala–Belize and Belize–Mexico border crossings.

To **El Salvador** via **Valle Nuevo**, border crossing, with **Ticabus**, 0600 and 1300 daily to San Salvador, US$17 1st class, 5 hrs. From **Ticabus** terminal, Calzada Aguilar Batres 22-25, T2473-0633, www.ticabus.com, clean, safe, with waiting area, café, toilets, no luggage deposit.

Car

Car hire companies **Budget**, at the airport; also at 6 Av, 11-24, Zona 9, www.budget.co.uk. **Hertz**, at the airport, T2470-3800, www.hertz.com. **Tabarini**, 2 Calle "A", 7-30, Zona 10, T2331-2643, airport T2331-4755, www.tabarini.com. **Tally**, 7 Av, 14-60, Zona 1, T2232-0421, very competitive, have pickups. Recommended.

Car and motorcyle repairs **Mike and Andy Young**, 27 Calle, 13-73, Zona 5, T2331-9263, Mon-Fri 0700-1600. Excellent mechanics for all vehicles, extremely helpful. Honda motorcycle parts from **FA Honda**, Av Bolívar, 31-00, Zona 3, T2471-5232. Some staff speak English. Car and motorcycle parts from **FPK**, 5 Calle, 6-75, Zona 9, T2331-9777. **David González**, 32 Calle, 6-31, Zona 11, T5797-2486, for car, bike and bicycle repairs. Recommended.

Shuttle

Shuttles are possible between Guatemala City and all other destinations, but reserve in advance. Contact shuttle operators in Antigua (see Antigua Transport, page 55). Guatemala City to **Antigua**, US$15, **Panajachel** US$30, Chichicastenango US$30, **Copán Ruinas**, US$40, **Cobán**, US$30 and **Quetzaltenango**, US$25.

Taxi

If possible call a taxi from your hotel or get someone to recommend a reliable driver; there are hundreds of illegal taxis in the city that should be avoided.

There are 3 types of taxis: **Rotativos**, **Estacionarios** and the ones that are metered, called **Taxis Amarillos**. *Rotativos* are everywhere in the city cruising the length and breadth of all zones. You will not wait more than a few minutes for one to come along. They are numbered on their sides and on their back windscreen will be written TR (*Taxi Rotativo*) followed by 4 numbers. Most of them have a company logo stamped on the side as well. *Estacionarios* also have numbers on the sides but are without logo. On their back windscreen they have the letters TE (*Taxi Estacionario*) followed by 4 numbers. They are to be found at bus terminals and outside hotels or in other important places. They will always return to these same waiting points (good to know if you leave something in a taxi). Do not get in a taxi that does not have either of these labels on its back windscreen. *Rotativos* and *Estacionarios* are unmetered, but *Estacionarios* will always charge less than *Rotativos*. The fact that both are unmetered will nearly always work to your advantage because of traffic delays. You will be quoted an inflated price by *Rotativos* by virtue of being a foreigner. *Estacionarios* are fairer. It is about US$8 from the airport to Zona 1. From Zona 1 to 4 is about US$4. The metered *Taxi Amarillo* also moves around but less so than the *Rotativos*, as they are more on call by phone. They only take a couple of minutes to come. **Amarillo Express**, T2332-1515, are available 24 hrs.

Antigua
& around

★ Antigua is rightly one of Guatemala's most popular destinations. It overflows with colonial architecture and fine churches on streets that are linked by squat houses, painted in ochre shades and topped with terracotta tiles, basking in the fractured light of the setting sun. Antigua is a very attractive city and is the cultural centre of Guatemala; arts flourish here. Maya women sit in their colourful clothes amid the ruins and in the Parque Central. In the late-afternoon light, buildings such as Las Capuchinas are beautiful, and in the evening the cathedral is wonderfully illuminated as if by candlelight.

If the city was not treasure enough, the setting is truly memorable. Volcán Agua (3766 m) is due south and the market is to the west, behind which hang the imposing peaks of Volcán Acatenango (3976 m) and Volcán Fuego (3763 m), which still emits the occasional column of ash as a warning of the latent power within.

Also around Antigua are a cluster of archaeological sites and highland villages to explore.

Antigua

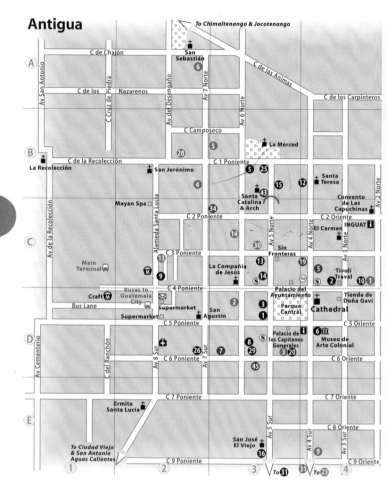

To Chimaltenango & Jocotenango

A
- C de Chajón
- Av San Antonio
- C Cruz de Piedra
- C de los Nazarenos
- Av del Desengaño
- San Sebastián **6**
- Av 7 Norte
- Av 6 Norte
- C de las Ánimas
- C de los Carpinteros

B
- La Recolección
- C de la Recolección
- C Camposeco
- San Jerónimo **4**
- **28**
- **5**
- C 1 Poniente
- La Merced
- **5** **25**
- Santa Teresa
- Convento de Las Capuchinas
- Av 2 Norte
- **15** **12**
- Santa Catalina & Arch **43**
- Mayan Spa
- Alameda Santa Lucía
- **34**
- C 2 Poniente
- C 2 Oriente
- El Carmen
- INGUAT **i**

C
- Av de la Recolección
- Main Terminal
- **14**
- Av 5 Norte
- **30**
- Sin Fronteras
- Av 4 Norte
- Av 3 Norte
- C 3 Poniente
- **13**
- **9**
- La Compañía de Jesús
- **13**
- **14** (S)
- **19**
- **5**
- Tivoli Travel
- **2** (S)
- **10** **1**
- C 4 Poniente
- Craft
- Buses to Guatemala City
- Bus Lane
- Supermarket
- Supermarket
- San Agustín
- **2**
- **3**
- **1**
- Palacio del Ayuntamiento
- Parque Central
- Cathedral
- Tienda de Doña Gavi

D
- Av Cementerio
- C del Ranchón
- C 5 Poniente
- Av 8 Sur
- Av 7 Sur
- **26**
- **7**
- San José
- **8**
- **29**
- (S)
- Palacio de los Capitanes Generales
- **3** **20**
- **i**
- **6** **iii**
- Museo de Arte Colonial
- C 5 Oriente
- C 6 Oriente
- C 6 Poniente
- **45**

E
- Ermita Santa Lucía
- C 7 Poniente
- C 7 Oriente
- C 8 Oriente
- Av 5 Sur
- Av 4 Sur
- Av 3 Sur
- To Ciudad Vieja & San Antonio Aguas Calientes
- C 9 Poniente
- San José El Viejo **16**
- **9**
- C 9 Oriente
- **To 31** **31** **To 23**

1 **2** **3** **4**

N

100 metres

100 yards

Where to stay 🛏
- Aurora **1** C4
- Base Camp **7** D5
- Casa Encantada **31** E4
- Casa Florencia **6** A2
- Casa Rústica **2** D3
- Casa Santo Domingo **8** C6
- Hostel Tropicana **3** D3
- Jungle Party Hostal **14** C3
- Los Encuentros **4** B2
- Mesón de María **30** C3
- Posada del Angel **23** E4

- Posada Juma Ocag **13** C2
- Posada La Merced **5** B3
- San Jorge **9** E4
- Yellow House **28** B2

Restaurants 🍴
- Bagel Barn **1** D3
- Café Condesa **3** D3
- Café Flor **6** D4
- Caffé Mediterráneo **20** D3
- Doña Luisa Xicoténcatl **10** C4

- El Sabor del Tiempo **13** C3
- El Sereno **12** B4
- Fonda de la Calle Real **14** C3
- Frida's **15** B3
- Hector's **5** B3
- La Antigua Viñería **16** E3
- La Casserole **41** C5
- Micho's Gastropub **2** C4
- Quesos y Vinos **25** B3
- Rainbow Café & Travel Center **26** D2
- Sabe Rico **8** D3

To Cerro de la Cruz
To Guatemala City

C de la Candelaria
La Candelaria

C 1 Oriente
Santa Rosa
Plazuela Santa Rosa
C de la Beatas Indias
C de los Duelos
Santo Domingo
Av 1 Norte
C 3 Oriente
8
C 4 Oriente
41
La Concepción
C del Hermano Pedro
7
4
Convento de Santa Clara
Av 1 Sur
San Francisco
C de los Pasos
C del Hermano Pedro
Santa Cruz
To Escuela de Cristo & El Calvario
5
To Santa Isabel, San Juan del Obispo & Santa María de Jesús
6

Típico Antigüeño **9** *C2*
Travel Menu **29** *D3*
Vivero y Café de la Escalonia **31** *E3*

The Snug **7** *D2*

Bars & clubs 🎵
Café No Sé **4** *D5*
Casbah **43** *B3*
La Chiminea **34** *C3*
La Sala **45** *D3*
Ocelot **5** *C4*
Riki's **19** *C4*

Sights

colonial buildings and volcano backdrop

Parque Central and around

In the centre of the city is the Parque Central, the old Plaza Real, where bullfights and markets were held in the early days. The present park was constructed in the 20th century though the fountain dates back to the 18th century. The **cathedral** ⓘ *US$0.40*, to the east, dates from 1680 (the first cathedral was demolished in 1669). Much has been destroyed since then and only two of the many original chapels are now in use. The remainder can be visited. The **Palacio de los Capitanes Generales** is to the south. The original building dates from 1558, was virtually destroyed in 1773, was partly restored in the 20th century, and now houses police and government offices. The **Cabildo**, or **Municipal Palace**, is to the north and an arcade of shops to the west. You can climb to the second floor for a great view of the volcanoes (Monday to Friday 0800-1600). The **Museo de Santiago** ⓘ *Tue-Fri 0900-1600, Sat-Sun 0900-1200, 1400-1600, US$4*, is in the municipal offices to the north of the plaza, as is the **Museo del Libro Antiguo** ⓘ *same hours and price*, which contains a replica of a 1660 printing press (the original is in Guatemala City), old documents and a collection of 16th- to 18th-century books (1500 volumes in the library). The **Museo de Arte Colonial** ⓘ *Tue-Fri 0900-1600, Sat-Sun 0900-1200, 1400-1600, US$6.60*, is half a block from Parque Central at Calle 5 Oriente, in the building where the San Carlos University was first housed. It now has mostly 17th- to 18th-century religious art, well laid out in large airy rooms around a colonial patio.

Hotel Casa Santo Domingo

Hotel Casa Santo Domingo is one of Antigua's most beautiful sights: a converted old Dominican church and also monastery property. Archaeological excavations have turned up some unexpected finds at the site. During the cleaning out of a burial vault in September 1996, one of the greatest finds in Antigua's history was unearthed. The vault had been filled with rubble, but care had been taken in placing stones a few feet away from the painted walls. The scene is in the pristine colours of natural red and blue, and depicts Christ, the Virgin Mary, Mary Magdalene and John the Apostle. It was painted in 1683, and was only discovered with the help of ultraviolet light. Within the monastery grounds are the **Colonial Art Museum**, with displays of Guatemalan baroque imagery and silverware and the **Pre-Columbian Art Museum**, **Glass Museum**, **Museum of Guatemalan Apothecary** and the **Popular Art and Handicrafts of Sacatepequez Museum** ⓘ *3 Calle Ote 28, 0900-1700, US$5.25, 1 ticket covers all admissions.*

Colonial religious buildings

There are many fine religious buildings dating from the colonial era: 22 churches, 14 convents and 11 monasteries, most ruined by earthquakes and in various stages of restoration. Top of the list are the cloisters of the convent of **Las Capuchinas** ⓘ *2 Av Norte y 2 Calle Ote, 0900-1700, US$3.90,* with immensely thick round pillars (1736) adorned with bougainvillea. The church and convent of **San Francisco** ⓘ *1 Av Sur y 7 Calle Ote, 0800-1200, 1400-1700, US$0.40,* with the tomb of Hermano Pedro, is much revered by all the local communities. He was canonized in 2002. The church has been

BACKGROUND
Antigua

Until it was heavily damaged by an earthquake in 1773, Antigua was the capital city. Founded in 1543, after the destruction of an even earlier capital, Ciudad Vieja, it grew to be the finest city in Central America, with numerous great churches, a university (1676), a printing press (founded 1660), and a population of around 50,000, including many famous sculptors, painters, writers and craftsmen.

Antigua has consistently been damaged by earthquakes. Even when it was the capital, buildings were frequently destroyed and rebuilt, usually in a grander style, until the final cataclysm in 1773. For many years it was abandoned, and most of the accumulated treasures were moved to Guatemala City. Although it slowly repopulated in the 19th century, little was done to prevent further collapse of the main buildings until late in the 20th century when the value of the remaining monuments was finally appreciated. Since 1972, efforts to preserve what was left have gained momentum, and it is now a UNESCO World Heritage Site. The major earthquake of 1976 was a further setback, but you will see many sites that are busy with restoration, preservation or simple clearing.

restored and now includes the **Museo de Hermano Pedro** ⓘ *Tue-Sun 0900-1200, 1300-1630, US$0.40*. The convent of **Santa Clara** ⓘ *6 Calle Ote y 2 Av Sur, 0900-1700, US$3.90*, was founded in about 1700 and became one of the biggest in Antigua, until the nuns were forced to move to Guatemala City. The adjoining garden is an oasis of peace. **El Carmen** ⓘ *3 Calle Ote y 3 Av Norte*, has a beautiful façade with strikingly ornate columns, tastefully illuminated at night, but the rest of the complex is in ruins. Likewise **San Agustín** ⓘ *5 Calle Pte y 7 Av Norte*, was once a fine building, but only survived intact from 1761 to 1773; earthquake destruction continued until the final portion of the vault collapsed in 1976, leaving an impressive ruin. **La Compañía de Jesús** ⓘ *3 Calle Pte y 6 Av Norte, 0930-1700*, at one time covered the whole block. The church is today in ruins but the rest of the complex was recently restored by the Spanish government and now houses a cultural centre, **Centro de Formación de la Cooperación Española** ⓘ *www.aecid-cf.org.gt, 0900-1800, free*, with occasional exhibitions and workshops. The church and cloisters of **Escuela de Cristo** ⓘ *Calle de los Pasos y de la Cruz*, a small independent monastery (1720-1730), have survived and were restored between 1940 and 1960. The church is simple and has some interesting original artwork. **La Recolección** ⓘ *Calle de la Recolección, 0900-1700, US$5.25*, despite being a late starter (1700), became one of the biggest and finest of Antigua's religious institutions. It is now the most awe-inspiring ruin in the city. **San Jerónimo** ⓘ *Calle de la Recolección, 0900-1700, US$4*, was a school (early 1600s) for La Merced, three blocks away, but later became the local customs house. There is an impressive fountain in the courtyard. **La Merced** ⓘ *1 Calle Pte y 6 Av Norte, 0800-1700*, with its white and yellow façade dominates the surrounding plaza. The church (1767) and cloisters were built with earthquakes in mind and survived better than most. The church remains in use and the **cloisters** ⓘ *US$0.65*, are being further restored. Antigua's finest fountain is in the courtyard. **Santa Teresa** ⓘ *4 Av Norte*, was a modest convent, but the church walls and the lovely west front have survived. It is now the city's men's prison.

Other ruins including **Santa Isabel**, **Santa Cruz**, **La Candelaria**, **San José El Viejo** and **San Sebastián** are to be found round the edges of the city, and there is an interesting set of the Stations of the Cross, each a small chapel, from San Francisco to **El Calvario** church, which was where Pedro de Betancourt (Hermano Pedro) worked as a gardener and planted an esquisuchil tree. He was also the founder of the **Belén Hospital** in 1661, which was destroyed in 1773. However, some years later, his name was given to the **San Pedro Hospital**, which is one block south of the Parque Central.

There is a fabulous panorama from the **Cerro de la Cruz**, which is 15 minutes' walk from the northern end of town along 1 Avenida Norte. See also, Safety, page 42.

Listings Antigua *map p40*

Tourist information

The monthly magazine *The Revue* is a useful source of tourist information in English with articles, maps, events and advertisements; it's free and widely available in hotels and restaurants.

INGUAT office
2a Calle Ote,11 (between Av 2 and Av 3 Norte), T7832-3782, www.visit guatemala.com. Mon-Fri 0800-1700, Sat and Sun 0900-1700.
Very helpful, with maps and information; occasional exhibitions in rooms around courtyard behind office. Information available about volunteer work. English, Italian and a little German spoken.

Where to stay

In the better hotels, advance reservations are advised for weekends and Dec-Apr. During Holy Week, hotel prices are significantly higher, sometimes double for the more expensive hotels. In the Jul-Aug period, find your accommodation early in the day.

$$$$ Casa Santo Domingo
3 Calle Ote 28, T7820-1220, www.casasantodomingo.com.gt.
This is a beautifully designed hotel with 126 rooms in the ruins of a 17th-century convent with prehispanic archaeological finds. Good service, beautiful gardens, a magical pool, excellent restaurant with breakfast included. Worth seeing just to dream. See also page 42.

$$$$ Posada del Angel
4 Av Sur 24-A, T7832-0260, www.posadadelangel.com.
Bill Clinton is among the former guests of this famous, sumptuous and award-winning hotel. Lodging is in boutique suites and rooms set around a central courtyard, all with own fireplaces and consistently tasteful decor. Amenities include dining room, exercise pool and roof terrace. Romantic, exclusive and private.

$$$ Aurora
4 Calle Ote 16, T7832-0217,
www.hotelauroraantigua.com.
The oldest hotel in the city with old
plumbing (but it works), antique
furnishings and 1970s features. Quieter
rooms face a colonial patio overflowing
with beautiful flowers. Continental
breakfast included, English spoken.

$$$ Casa Encantada
9 Calle Pte1, esq Av 4 Sur, T7832-7903,
www.casa encantada-antigua.com.
This sweet colonial boutique hotel with
10 rooms is a perfect retreat from the
centre of Antigua. It has a small rooftop
terrace where breakfast is served and
a comfortable sitting room with open
fire, books, lilies and textile-lined walls.
2 rooms are accessed by stepping stones
in a pond. The suite, with jacuzzi, enjoys
views of the 3 volcanoes.

$$$ Casa Florencia
7 Av Norte 100, T7832-0261,
www.cflorencia.net.
A sweet little colonial-style hotel
enjoying views towards Volcán Agua.
They offer 10 pleasant rooms set around
a central courtyard with all the usual
mod cons including TV, safe and Wi-Fi.
The 2nd-floor balcony has *cola de quetzal*
plants lining it. Staff are very welcoming.
Recommended.

$$$ Hotel Mesón de María
3 Calle Pte 8, T7832-6068,
www.hotelmesonde maria.com.
Great little place with a wonderful
roof terrace. Their 20 stylish rooms are
decorated with local textiles and earthy
colours. Free internet and breakfast
included at a local restaurant. Friendly
and attentive service. Showers have
large skylights.

$$ Hotel Casa Rústica
6 Av Nte 8, T7832-0694,
www.casarusticagt.com.
Casa Rústica has bright, comfortable
rooms, each equipped with hand-
carved furniture and Guatemalan
textiles; cheaper rooms have shared
bath ($). There are good communal
areas, including kitchen, garden and
sun terrace with views. Pleasant, but on
the pricey side. Ask to see a few rooms
before accepting as size and quality vary.

$$ Hotel Los Encuentros
7 Av Norte 60, T4114-5400, www.
hotelosencuentros.com.
This guesthouse offers quiet,
comfortable and occasionally quirky
rooms with hand-carved wooden
furniture, Guatemalan art, textiles and
antiques. The hostess Irma is very sweet
and helpful. There are cooking facilities
and breakfast is included. Rooms vary,
ask to see a few.

$$ Hotel San Jorge
4 Av Sur 13, Calle del
Conquistador, T7832-3132,
www.hotelsanjorgeantigua.com.
Established in 1989, Hotel San Jorge
has lovely green gardens with wide
lawns and flowery beds. Rooms are
understated but have thoughtful
touches like wall-to-wall carpets, There
is Talavera tilework, fireplaces, cable TV
and handwoven bedspreads.

$$ Posada La Merced
7 Av Nte 43, T7832-3197,
www.posadalamercedantigua.com.
Located 1 block from La Merced church,
this well-established colonial-style
guesthouse features a beautiful patio
with a fountain and plenty of leafy
potted plants. Upstairs, a sun terrace
has fine views. Rooms are smallish and

simple, but comfortable. Quiet, relaxing and central.

$$-$ Hostel Tropicana
6 Calle Pte, between Av 4 and 5, T7832-0462, www.tropicanahostel.com.
This new addition to Antigua's party hostel scene is a cut above the rest with its small but refreshing outdoor pool, a sun deck and a hot tub. There's a well-stocked bar too, and for chilling out, a leafy garden framed by ruined colonial walls. Accommodation includes a range of large and small dorms (**$**), and private rooms (**$$**). Promising and recommended.

$ Base Camp
7 Calle Pte 17, T 7832-0468, www.guatemalavolcano.com.
Nice views of Volcán Agua from the roof terrace at this fun, young, energetic hostel marketed to adventure travellers. Accomodation includes 6 dorm beds and 2 double rooms with lots of shared space and all the usual hostel facilities. Runs adventure tours through **Outdoor Excursions** (see Tour operators, below).

$ Jungle Party Hostal and Café
6 Av Norte 20, T7832-0463, www.junglepartyhostal.com.
Buzzing with backpakers in its onsite bars, this fun and sociable party hostel enjoys a great central location and impressive views of the volcanoes. Accommodation consists of dorm beds with hot water, lockers, small patio, TV, hammocks, swings, bean bags, Wi-Fi, free breakfast and movies. There's an all-you-can-eat barbecue on Sat.

$ Posada Juma Ocag
8 Av Norte 13 (Alameda Santa Lucía), T7832-3109, www.posadajumaocag.com.
This modest, family-run guesthouse is small but very clean, and nicely

decorated using local textiles as bedspreads. It has an enclosed roof terrace and rooms come with or without private bath. Quiet and friendly with Wi-Fi, and free coffee in the morning.

$ Yellow House
1 Calle Pte 24, T7832-6646, www.guatetravel.com.
There are 8 clean rooms in this hostel run by the welcoming Ceci. Breakfast included. Colonial style, laundry service, free internet. 3 rooms with bath, kitchen, patio, parking. Recommended.

Apartments
Look on the notice boards in town. Rooms and apartments are available from about US$25 a week up to US$500 per month. One recommended family is **Estella López**, 1 Calle Pte 41A, T7832-1324, who offer board and lodging on a weekly basis. The house is clean, and the family friendly.

Restaurants

For the cheapest of the cheap go to the stalls on the corner of 4 Calle Pte and 7 Av Norte, and those at the corner of 5 Calle Pte and 4 Av Sur. During the Easter period, the plaza in front of La Merced is transformed into a food market. At all these places you can pick up *elote*, *tortillas*, *tostadas* and *enchiladas*.

$$$ El Sereno
4 Av Norte 16, T7832-0501. Open 1200-1500 and 1800-2300.
International/Italian cuisine. Grand entrance with massive heliconia plants in the courtyard. It has a lovely terrace bar up some stone steps and a cave for romantic dining; it's popular at weekends.

$$$ La Casserole
Callejón de Concepción 7, T7832-0219 close to Casa Santo Domingo. Tue-Sat 1200-1500 and 1900-2200, Sun 1200-1500.
Sophisticated French cooking with fresh fish daily served at tables set in a beautiful courtyard, exclusive. Rigoberta Menchú dined with Jacques Chirac here.

$$$ Micho's Gastropub
4 Calle Ote 10, Edif Jaulon, T7832-3522.
Micho's stands out as one of the city's better establishments with its top-notch international cuisine, creatively prepared and beautifully presented. They serve lunchtime specials, along with breakfast and dinner, good cocktails and wine by the glass. Romantic ambience in the tranquil courtyard. Recommended.

$$$-$$ Caffé Mediterráneo
6 Calle Pte 6A, T7832-7180. Wed-Mon 1200-1500 and 1830-2200.
1 block south of the plaza. Mouth-watering Italian cuisine with great candlelit ambience. Recommended.

$$$-$$ Fonda de la Calle Real
5 Av Norte 5 and No 12, T7832 0507, also at 3 Calle Pte 7 (which wins over the others for the setting).
This place's speciality is *queso fundido*. It also serves local dishes including *pepián* (and a vegetarian version) and *kak-ik*, a Verapaz speciality.

$$ El Sabor del Tiempo
Calle del Arco and 3 Calle Poniente, T7832 0516.
Good steaks, burgers, seafood and pasta in tastefully converted former warehouse, with polished wood and glass cabinets. A bit pricey but full of antiquey character.

$$ Frida's
5 Av Norte 29, Calle del Arco, T7832-0504. Daily 1200-0100.
Ochre and French navy colours decorate this restaurant's tribute to Mexico's famous female artist. It is quite dark inside but Frida memorabilia and colander-like lampshades lighten the interior. Efficient service. 2nd-floor pool table, Wed and Thu ladies' night.

$$ Hector's
1 Calle Poniente No 9, T7832-9867.
Small, busy and welcoming restaurant that serves wonderful food at good prices. Highly recommended.

$$ La Antigua Viñería
5 Av Sur 34A, T7832-7370. Mon-Thu 1800-0100, Fri-Sun 1300-0100.
Owned by Beppe Dángella, next door to San José ruins. Amazing photographic collection of clients in various stages of inebriation, excellent selection of wines and grappa, you name it. Very romantic, feel free to write your comments on the walls, very good food, pop in for a reasonably priced *queso fundido* and glass of wine if you can't afford the whole hog.

$$ Quesos y Vinos
Calle Poniente 1, T7832-7785. Wed-Mon 1200-1600 and 1800-2200.
Authentic Italian food and owners, good selection of wines, wood-fired pizza oven, sandwiches, popular.

$$ Sabe Rico
6 Av Sur No 7, 7832-0648.
Herb garden restaurant and fine food deli that serves healthy, organic food in tranquil surroundings.

$$-$ Café Flor
4 Av Sur 1, T7832-5274. Open 1100-2300.
Full-on delicious Thai/Guatemalan-style and tandoori food. The stir-fries are delicious, but a little overpriced. Discounts sometimes available. Friendly staff.

$$-$ Rainbow Café
7 Av Sur, on the corner of 6 Calle Pte.
Consistently delicious vegetarian food served in a pleasant courtyard surrounded by hanging plants, good filling breakfasts, indulgent crêpes, popular, live music evenings, good book exchange. Bar at night with happy hour and ladies' nights. Recommended.

$$-$ Travel Menu
6 Calle Pte 14.
Buzzing and bohemian, Travel Menu serves fresh, hearty, reasonably priced international fare in large portions, including big fat juicy sandwiches and tofu stir-fry. Candlelit ambience and regular live music. Friendly and sociable.

$ Típico Antigüeño
Alameda Sta Lucía 4, near the PO, T7832-5995.
This locally run place offers an absolute bargain of a *menú del día* (fish, chicken), which includes soup and sometimes a drink. It is extremely popular and can get ridiculously busy, so best to turn up before 1300 for lunch. Recommended.

Cafés and delis

Bagel Barn
5 Calle Pte 2. Open 0600-2200.
Popular, breakfast, snack deals with bagels and smoothies, videos shown nightly, free.

Café Condesa
5 Av Norte 4. Open 0700-2100.
West side of the main plaza in a pretty courtyard, popular, a little pricey for the portions, breakfast with free coffee fill-ups, desserts, popular Sun brunches.

Doña Luisa Xicoténcatl
4 Calle Ote 12, 1½ blocks east of the plaza. Daily 0700-2130.
Popular meeting place with an excellent bulletin board, serving breakfasts, tasty ice cream, good coffee, burgers, large menu, big portions. Good views of Volcán Agua upstairs. Shop sells good selection of wholemeal, banana bread, yogurts, etc. Don't miss the chocolate and orange loaf if you can get it.

Vivero y Café de La Escalonia
5 Av Sur Final 36 Calle, T7832-7074. Daily 0900-1800.
This delightful place is well worth the walk – a café amid a garden centre with luscious flowers everywhere, including bird of paradise flowers and tumbergia, a pergola and classical music. They serve *postres*, herb breads, salads and cold drinks.

Bars and clubs

Café No Sé
1 Av Sur 11 C, www.cafenose.com.
Grungy and bohemian, an interesting place with live music every night, and a range of high-powered mescal cocktails. Good.

Casbah
5 Av Norte 30. Mon-Sat 1800-0100.
Cover charge includes a drink. Gay night Thu. Has a medium-sized dance floor with a podium and plays a mix of good dance and Latin music, the closest place to a nightclub atmosphere in Antigua.

La Chimenea
7 Av Norte 18. Mon-Sat 1700-2430.

ON THE ROAD
Semana Santa

This week-long event in Antigua is a spectacular display of religious ritual and floral design. Through billowing clouds of incense, accompanied by music, processions of floats carried by purple-robed men make their way through the town. The cobbled stones are covered in *alfombras* (carpets) of coloured sawdust and flowers.

The day before the processions leave from each church, Holy Vigils (*velaciones*) are held, and the sculpture to be carried is placed before the altar (*retablo*), with a backdrop covering the altar. Floats (*andas*) are topped by colonial sculptures of the cross-carrying Christ. He wears velvet robes of deep blue or green, embroidered with gold and silver threads, and the float is carried on the shoulders by a team of 80 men (*cucuruchos*), who heave and sway their way through the streets for as long as 12 hours. The processions, arranged by a religious brotherhood (*cofradía*), are accompanied by banner and incense carriers, centurions, and a loud brass band.

The largest processions with some of the finest carpets are on Palm Sunday and Good Friday. Not to be missed are: the procession leaving from La Merced on Palm Sunday at 1200-1300; the procession leaving the church of San Francisco on Maundy Thursday; the 0200 sentencing of Jesus and 0600 processions from La Merced on Good Friday; the crucifixion of Christ in front of the cathedral at noon on Good Friday; and the beautiful, candlelit procession of the crucified Christ which passes the Parque Central between 2300 and midnight on Good Friday.

This is the biggest Easter attraction in Latin America so accommodation is booked far ahead. If you plan to be here and haven't reserved a room, arrive a few days before Palm Sunday. If unsuccessful, commuting from Guatemala City is an option. Don't rush; each procession lasts up to 12 hours. The whole week is a fantastic opportunity for photographs – and if you want a decent picture remember the Christ figure always faces right. Arm yourself with a map (available in kiosks in the Parque Central) and follow the processional route before the procession to see all the carpets while they are still intact. (There are also processions into Antigua from surrounding towns every Sunday in Lent.)

Happy hour every day, seriously cheap, relaxed atmosphere, mixed young crowd, dance floor, salsa, rock.

La Sala
6 Calle Pte, T5671-3008.
One of the most popular salsa dancing and watering holes in town.

Ocelot
4 Av Nte 3.

A splendid watering hole full of interesting characters. They do happy hour, pub quizzes, American grub from the taco cart. Good crowd, popular on the expat scene.

Riki's Bar
4 Av Norte 4, inside La Escudilla.
Usually packed with gringos, but attracts a young Guatemalan crowd as well, and

popular with the gay fraternity. Good place to meet people. A good mix of music, including jazz.

The Snug
6 Calle Pte 14, next to Travel Menu.
The Snug proves good things do come in small packages. A hit with expats and travellers, this intimate and fully authentic Irish bar does cold beer, rum, occasional live music and interesting conversation. Cosy, friendly and fun.

Entertainment

Cinemas
Antigua must be the home of the lounge cinema. All show films or videos in English, or with subtitles.
Café 2000, *6 Av Sur*. Free films daily and the most popular spot in town to watch movies.
Cine Sin Ventura, *5 Av Sur 8*. The only real screen in town, auditorium can get cold, and they need to hit the brightness button.

Festivals

Feb International Culture Festival: dance, music and other top-quality performers from around the globe come to Antigua.
Mar/Apr Semana Santa: see box, page 49.
21-26 Jul The feast of **San Santiago**.
31 Oct-2 Nov All Saints and **All Souls**, in and around Antigua.
7 Dec Quema del Diablo (burning of the Devil) by lighting fires in front of their houses and burning an effigy of the Devil in the Plazuela de La Concepción at night, thereby starting the Christmas festivities.
15 Dec The start of what's known as the **Posadas**, where a group of people leave

from each church, dressed as Mary and Joseph, and seek refuge in hotels. They are symbolically refused lodging several times, but are eventually allowed in.

Shopping

Antigua is a shopper's paradise, with textiles, furniture, candles, fabrics, clothes, sculpture, candies, glass, jade and ceramics on sale. The main municipal market is on Alameda Santa Lucía next to the bus station, where you can buy fruit, clothes and shoes. The *artesanía* market is opposite, next to the bus lane.

Art
Galería de Arte Antigua, *4 Calle Ote 27 y 1 Av. Tue-Sat*. Large art gallery.

Bookshops
Numerous bookshops sell books in English and Spanish, postcards, posters, maps and guides, including **Footprint Handbooks**.
Casa del Conde, *5 Av Norte 4*. Has a full range of books from beautifully illustrated coffee-table books to guides and history books.
Hamlin and White, *4 Calle Ote 12A*. Books on Guatemala are cheaper here than at Casa del Conde.
Rainbow Cafe, *7 Av Sur 18*. Sells second-hand books.
Un Poco de Todo, *near Casa del Conde on the plaza*.

Crafts, textiles, clothes and jewellery
Many other stores sell textiles, handicrafts, antiques, silver and jade on 5 Av Norte between 1 and 4 Calle Pte and 4 Calle Ote.

Casa Chicob, *Callejón de la Concepción 2, www.casachicob.com*. Beautiful textiles, candles and ceramics for sale.

Casa de Artes, *4 Av Sur 11, www.casadeartes.com.gt*. For traditional textiles and handicrafts, jewellery, etc, but very expensive.

Casa de los Gigantes, *7 Calle Ote 18*. For textiles and handicrafts.

Diva, *5 Av Norte 16*. For Western-style clothes and jewellery.

El Telar, *Loom Tree, 5 Av Sur 7*. All sorts of coloured tablecloths, napkins, cushion covers and bedspreads are sold here.

Guate Es, *4 Calle Ote 10, Edif El Jaulón, www.guate-es.com*. Guate Es has an interesting and attractive stock of clothing, shoes, jewellery and handbags which incorporate colourful Mayan textiles and designs. A new concept, fresh and innovative.

Huipil market, *held in the courtyard of La Fuente every Sat 0900-1400*. The display is very colourful and if the sun is out this is an excellent place for photos.

Mercado de Artesanías, *next to the main market at the end of 4 Calle Pte*.

Nativo's, *5 Av Norte, 25 "B", T7832-6556*. Sells some beautiful textiles from places like Aguacatán.

Nim P'ot, *5 Av Norte 29, T7832-2681, www.nimpot.com*. A mega-warehouse of traditional textiles and crafts brought from around the country. Excellent prices.

Textura, *5 Av Norte 33, T7832-5067*. Lots of bedroom accessories.

Food

Doña María Gordillo, *4 Calle Ote 11*. Famous throughout the country. It is impossible to get in the door most days but, if you can, take a peek, to see the *dulces*, as well as the row upon row

of yellow wooden owls keeping their beady eyes on the customers.

La Bodegona, *5 Calle Pte 32, opposite Posada La Quinta, on 5 Calle Pte and with another entrance on 4 Calle Pte*. Large supermarket.

Tienda de Doña Gavi, *3 Av Norte 2, behind the cathedral*. Sells all sorts of lovely potions and herbs, candles and home-made biscuits. Doña Gaviota also sells Guatemala City's most famous ice creams in all sorts of weird and wonderful flavours (see **Helados Marylena**, page 31).

What to do

Horse riding

Ravenscroft Riding Stables, *2 Av Sur 3, San Juan del Obispo, T7830-6669*. You can also hire horses in Santa María de Jesús.

Spas

Antigua Spa Resort, *San Pedro El Panorama, lote 9 and 10 G, T7832-3960. Daily 0900-2100*. Swimming pool, steam baths, sauna, gym, jacuzzi and beauty salon. Reservations advised.

Mayan Spa, *Alameda Sta Lucía Norte 20, T7832-3537. Mon-Sat 0900-1800*. Massages and pampering packages, including sauna, steam baths and jacuzzi, are available.

Swimming

Porta Hotel Antigua, non-residents may use the pool for a charge.

Villas de Antigua, *Ciudad Vieja exit, T7832-0011-15*. For buffet lunch, swimming and marimba band.

Tour operators

Adrenalina Tours, *3a Calle Poniente, T7882 4147, www.adrenalinatours.com*. Xela's respected tour operator has opened up in Antigua too. As well as shuttles all around Guatemala, there are minibuses to San Cristóbal de las Casas, Mexico, US$55. Also customized packages, weekend trips to Xela and discounted Tikal trips. Recommended.

Adventure Travel Center Viareal, *5 Av Norte 25B, T7832-0162.* Daily trips to Guatemalan destinations (including Río Dulce sailing, river and volcano trips), Monterrico, Quiriguá, El Salvador and Honduras.

Antigua Tours, *Casa Santo Domingo, 3 Calle Ote 22, T7832-5821, www. antiguatours.net.* Run by Elizabeth Bell, author of 4 books on Antigua. She offers walking tours of the city (US$20 per person), book in advance, Mon, Thu 1400-1700, Tue, Wed, Fri, Sat 0930-1230. During Lent and Holy Week there are extra tours, giving insight into the processions and carpet making. Highly recommended.

Aventuras Naturales, *Col El Naranjo No 53, Antigua, T5381-6615, http:// aventuras naturales.tripod.com.* Specialized trips including guided birding tours.

Aventuras Vacacionales, *T5306-3584, www.sailing-diving-guatemala.com.* Highly recommended sailing trips on *Las Sirenas* owned by Captain John Clark and sailed by Captain Raúl Hernández (see also under Río Dulce, page 149).

Language schools

Footprint has received favourable reports from students for the following language schools:

Academia Antigüeña de Español, *1 Pte 10, T7832-7241, www.spanishacademyantiguena.com.*

Alianza Lingüística 'Cano', *Av El Desengaño 21A, T7832-0370.* Private classes are also available.

Amerispan, *6 Av Norte 40 and 7 Calle Ote, T7832-0164, www.amerispan.com.* In the US, 1334 Walnut St, 6th floor, Philadelphia PA 19107.

Centro Lingüístico Maya, *5 Calle Pte 20, T7832-1342, www.clmmaya.com.*

CSA (Christian Spanish Academy), *6 Av Norte 15, Aptdo Postal 320, T7832-3922, www.learncsa.com.*

Don Pedro de Alvarado, *6 Av Norte 39, T5872-2469, www.donpedrospanishschool.com.* 25 years' experience.

Proyecto Bibliotecas Guatemala (PROBIGUA), *6 Av Norte 41B, T7832-2998, www.probigua.org.* Gives a percentage of profits towards founding and maintaining public libraries in rural towns; frequently recommended.

Proyecto Lingüístico Francisco Marroquín, *6 Av Norte, www.plfm-antigua.org.*

Sevilla Academia de Español, *1 Av Sur 8, T7832-5101, www.sevillantigua. com.*

Tecún Umán, *6 Calle Pte 34A, T7832-2792, www.tecunuman.centramerica.com.*

For private lessons check the ads in Doña Luisa's and others around town and the tourist office. Recommended teachers are: Julia Solís, 5 Calle Pte 36, T7832-5497, julisar@hotmail. com (she lives behind the tailor's shop); and Armalia Jarquín, Av El Desengaño 11 (there are, unbelievably, numerous No 11s on this road), T7832-2377. Armalia's has a sign up and is opposite No 75, which has a tiled plaque.

ON THE ROAD

Learning the lingo

Antigua is overrun with language students and so some say it is not the most ideal environment in which to learn Spanish. There are about 70-plus schools, open year round. At any one time there may be 300-600 overseas students in Antigua. Not all schools are officially authorized by INGUAT and the Ministry of Education. INGUAT has a list of authorized schools in its office. Rates depend on the number of hours of tuition per week, and vary from school to school. As a rough guide, the average fee for four hours a day, five days a week is US$120-200, at a reputable school, with homestay, though many are less and some schools offer cheaper classes in the afternoon. You will benefit more from the classes if you have done a bit of study of the basics before you arrive. There are guides who take students around the schools and charge a high commission (make sure this is not added to your account). They may approach tourists arriving on the bus from the capital.

All schools offer one-to-one tuition; if you can meet the teachers in advance, so much the better, but don't let the director's waffle distract you from asking pertinent questions. Paying more does not mean you get better teaching and the standard of teacher varies within schools as well as between schools. Beware of 'hidden extras' and be clear on arrangements for study books. Some schools have an inscription fee. Several schools use a portion of their income to fund social projects and some offer a programme of activities for students such as dance classes, Latin American film, tours, weaving and football. Before making any commitment, find somewhere to stay for a couple of nights and shop around at your leisure. Schools also offer accommodation with local families, but check the place out if possible before you pay a week in advance. Average accommodation rates with a family with three meals a day are US$75-100 per week. In some cases the schools organize group accommodation; if you prefer single, ask for it.

CA Tours, *6 Calle Oriente Casa 14, T7832-9638, www.catours.co.uk.* British-run motorbike tour company. Recommended.

Eco-Tour Chejo's, *3 Calle Pte 24, T832-5464, ecotourchejos@hotmail.com.* Well-guarded walks up volcanoes. Interesting tours also available to coffee fincas, flower plantations, etc, shuttle service, horse riding, very helpful.

Gran Jaguar, *4 Calle Pte 30, T7832-2712, www.guacalling.com/jaguar/.* Well-organized fun volcano tours with official security. Also shuttles and trips to Tikal and Río Dulce. Very highly recommended for the Pacaya trip.

Guatemala Reservations.com, *3 Av Norte 3, T7832-3293, www. guatemalareservations.com. Closed Sun.* A wide range of tours and transport services. Frequently recommended. Also has guidebooks for reference or to buy, along with a water bottle-filling service to encourage recycling. Cheap phone call service. Shuttles and tours.

Old Town Outfitters, *5 Av Sur 12 "C",
T7832-4171, www.adventureguatemala.
com*. Action adventure specialists, with
mountain bike tours (½-day tour, US$39),
kayak tours hiking and climbing, outdoor
equipment on sale, maps, very helpful.
Outdoor Excursions, *1 Av Sur 4b,
T7832-0074, www.guatemalavolcano.
com*. Professional, knowledgeable and
fun volcano tour company with private
security. Overnight tours to Fuego (US$79),
Acatenango (US$79) and Pacaya (US$59).
Rainbow Travel Center, *7 Av Sur 8, T7931-
7878, www.rainbowtravelcenter.com*. Full
local travel service, specialists in student
flights and bargain international flights,
will attempt to match any quote. It also
sells ISIC, Go25 and teachers' cards. English,
French, German and Japanese spoken.
Sin Fronteras, *5a Av Norte 15 "A", T7720-
4400, www.sinfront.com*. Local tours,
shuttles, horse riding, bicycle tours,
canopy tours, national and international
air tickets including discounts with
ISIC and Go25 cards. Also sells travel
insurance. Agents for rafting experts
Maya Expeditions. Reliable and highly
recommended.
Tivoli Travel, *4 Calle Ote 10, T7832-
4274, antigua@tivoli.com.gt. Closed Sun*.
Helpful with any travel problem, English,
French, Spanish, German, Italian spoken,
reconfirm tickets, shuttles, hotel bookings,
good-value tours. Useful for organizing
independent travel as well as tours.
ViaVenture, *2 Calle Ote 2, T7832-2509,
www.viaventure.com*. Professional tour
operator offering special interest and
tailor-made tours.

Transport

Bus
To **Guatemala City**: buses leave when
full between 0530 and 1830, US$1,
1-1½ hrs, depending on the time of
day, from the Alameda Santa Lucía near
the market, from an exit next to **Pollo
Campero** (not from behind the market).
All other buses leave from behind the
market. To **Chimaltenango**, on the
Pan-American Hwy, from 0600-1600,
every 15 mins, US$0.65, for connections
to **Los Encuentros** (for Lake Atitlán
and **Chichicastenango**), **Cuatro
Caminos** (for **Quetzaltenango**) and
Huehuetenango (for the Mexican
border). It is possible to get to
Chichicastenango and back by bus in a
day, especially on Thu and Sun, for the
market. Get the bus to Chimaltenango
and then change. It's best to leave early.
See Chimaltenango for connections. The
only direct bus to **Panajachel** is **Rebuli**,
leaving at 0700, from 4 Calle Pte, in front
of **La Bodegona** supermarket, US$5,
2½ hrs, returning 1100. Other buses to
Pana via Chimaltenango with **Rebuli** and
Carrillo y Gonzalez, 0600-1645, US$2.50.
To **Escuintla**, 0530-1600, 1 hr, US$1.25.

To **Ciudad Vieja**, US$0.30, every
30 mins, 20 mins. **San Miguel de las
Dueñas**. Take a bus marked 'Dueñas',
every 30 mins, 20 mins, US$0.30. To
San Antonio Aguas Calientes, every
30 mins, 30 mins, US$0.30. To **Santa
María de Jesús** every 30 mins, 45 mins,
US$0.50.

International To **Copán** and other cities
in Honduras, including **Tegucigalpa**,
with **Hedman Alas**, www.hedmanalas.
com, from Posada de Don Rodrigo
to its terminal in Guatemala City for a
connection to Copán. Leaves at 0330 and
0630 from Antigua, US$41, US$77 return
and 0500 and 0900 from Guatemala City,
US$35, US$65 return. Return times are
1330 and 1800 to Guatemala City; the

earlier bus continues to Antigua. See also box, page 213.

Shuttles Hotels and travel agents run frequent shuttle services to and from **Guatemala City** and the **airport** (1 hr) from 0400 to about 2000 daily, US$10-15 depending on the time of day: details from any agency in town. There are also shuttles to **Chichicastenango**, US$5-18, **Panajachel**, US$5-12, **Quetzaltenango**, US$16, **Monterrico**, US$15, **Flores**, US$20-40, **Copán**, US$8-25 and other destinations, but check for prices and days of travel. **Plus Travel** (www.plustravelguate.com) has some of the best prices and range of destinations, with offices in Antigua (6a Calle Pte No 19, T7832-3147) and Copán Ruinas. Recommended.

Around Antigua

former colonial capital, village fiestas and coffee farm

Ciudad Vieja – the former capital – is 5.5 km southwest of Antigua at the foot of Volcán Agua. Today Ciudad Vieja is itself a suburb of Antigua, but with a handsome church, founded in 1534, and one of the oldest in Central America. There's a fiesta on December 8.

In 1527, Pedro de Alvarado moved his capital, known then as Santiago de Los Caballeros, from Iximché to San Miguel Escobar, now a suburb of Ciudad Vieja. On 11 September 1541, after days of torrential rain, an immense mudslide came down the mountain and swallowed up the city. Alvarado's widow, Doña Beatriz de la Cueva, newly elected governor after his death, was among those drowned.

Between Ciudad Vieja and San Miguel de las Dueñas is the **Valhalla macadamia nut farm** ⓘ *T7831-5799, www.exvalhalla.net, free visits and nut tasting, 0800-1700*.

About 3 km northwest of Ciudad Vieja is **San Antonio Aguas Calientes**. The hot springs unfortunately disappeared with recent earthquakes, but the village has many small shops selling locally made textiles. **Carolina's Textiles** is recommended for a fine selection, while on the exit road **Alida** has a shop. You can watch the weavers in their homes by the roadside. Local fiestas are 16-21 January, **Corpus Christi** (a moveable feast celebtrated around June) and 1 November.

Beyond San Juan del Obispo, beside Volcán Agua, is the charming village of **Santa María de Jesús**, with its beautiful view of Antigua. In the early morning there are good views of all three volcanoes from 2 km back down the road towards Antigua. Colourful *huipiles* are worn, made and sold from a couple of stalls, or ask at the shops on the plaza. The local fiesta is on 10 January.

Just north of Antigua is **Jocotenango**. The music museum, **Casa K'ojom** ⓘ *Mon-Fri 0830-1630, Sat 0830-1600, US$4*, is in the **Central Cultural La Azotea**, with displays of traditional Maya and colonial-era instruments. The village also has public saunas at the **Fraternidad Naturista Antigua**.

Five kilometres beyond San Lucas Sacatepéquez, at Km 29.5, Carretera Roosevelt (the Pan-American Highway), is **Santiago Sacatepéquez**, whose fiesta on 1 November, **Día de los Muertos** (All Souls' Day), is characterized by colourful kite-flying (*barriletes*). They also celebrate 25 July. Market days are Wednesday and Friday.

Visiting a **coffee farm** is an interesting short excursion. **Tour Finca Los Nietos** ⓘ *on the outskirts of Antigua, near the Iglesia San Felipe de Jesús, T7728-0812, www.filadelfiaresort.com,* runs two-hour tours (US$18) three times a day. They are very informative and interesting with expert multilingual guides, in beautiful manicured grounds and restored colonial buildings; also with restaurant and shop.

North of Guatemala City is **Mixco Viejo**, the excavated site of a post-Classic Maya fortress, which spans 14 hilltops, including 12 groups of pyramids. Despite earthquake damage it is worth a visit and is recommended. It was the 16th-century capital of the Pokomam Maya. There are a few buses a day between Mixco Viejo and the Zona 4 terminal, Guatemala City. The bus goes to Pachalum; ask to be dropped at ruins entrance.

Volcanoes

active volcanoes, lava fields and spectacular views

Each of the four volcanoes that are immediately accessible from Antigua provides a unique set of challenges and rewards. Agua, Fuego and Acatenango volcanoes directly overlook Antigua whilst Volcan Pacaya is about an hour's drive away. All of these volcanoes can be experienced either as part of a day trip (a cheaper and faster option that requires only lightweight packs) or with an overnight excursion (heavier packs making climbing times longer, but with better light conditions for lava viewing and enhancing already spectacular views with beautiful sunset and sunrises).

Whatever option you choose, it is important to prepare properly for the unique features of each volcano (Pacaya is a relatively quick climb in a secure national park, while the three volcanoes on Antigua's perimeter are longer climbs with much greater risk of robberies and attacks). At a minimum, ensure that you have appropriate clothing and footwear (as summits are cold and volcanic ash is sharp bring fleeces and ideally use climbing boots), enough water (very important) and snacks for the trip and make informed decisions about safety. Although you can climb each of these volcanoes independently, you will significantly decrease your risks of getting lost, attacked or not finding shelter by using a professional guiding service; **Outdoor Excursions** (see Tour operators, page 54), which runs trips with expert guides and armed security, is particularly recommended. Remember that altitude takes its toll and for the longer hikes it is important to start early in the morning to allow enough time to ascend and descend in daylight. As a general rule, descents take from a third to a half of the ascent time.

Volcán Pacaya

Tours are available for US$6 upwards and are sold by most tour companies in Antigua. The popular and best time for organized trips is to leave Antigua at 1300 and return at 2100. Departures also 0600 returning 1300. There is also a US$3.50 fee to be paid at the entrance to the Volcán Pacaya National Park in San Francisco de Sales (toilets available).

At 2552 m, the still-active Volcán Pacaya can't be missed and is the most exciting volcano to climb. Pacaya has erupted about 20 times since 1565, but since the mid-1960s it has been continuously active, meaning it can reward climbers with some spectacular lava flows. The cone – now split in two since the most recent eruption, in 2010 – is covered in black basaltic rock, shed from the crater. The rocks get warm and are lethally sharp. One of the results of the eruption is that shallow tunnels have formed, creating natural open-air saunas. They offer quite a spectacular experience, though for obvious safety reasons you should only enter these at the advice of an experience guide.Take a torch/flashlight refreshments and water and – it may sound obvious – wear boots or trainers, not sandals. Walking sticks are also offered at the park entrance – don't be too proud, on the steeper slopes, the crumbly lava screes can be very tricky to climb up or down. If you bring marshmallows to toast on the lava, make sure you have a long stick – lava is (rather unsurprisingly) very hot! Security officers go with the trips and police escorts ensure everyone leaves the area after dark. Check the situation in advance for **camping** (well below the crater lip). Sunrise comes with awesome views over the desolate black lava field to the distant Pacific (airborne dust permitting) and the peaks of Fuego, Acatenango and Agua. And as the sun sets on the horizon, Agua is silhouetted in the distance, a weak orange line streaked behind it.

Volcán Agua
Most organized tours with Antigua tour operators are during the day; you should enure that costs include both a guide and security. Trips normally leave Antigua about 0500.

At 3760 m, Agua is the easiest but least scenic of the three volcanoes overlooking Antiqua. The trail, which can be quite littered, begins at **Santa María de Jesús**. Speak to Aurelio Cuy Chávez at the **Posada El Oasis**, who offers a guide service or take a tour with a reputable agency. You have to register first at the Municipalidad; guides are also available in the main square, about US$50 a day per guide. For Agua's history, see Ciudad Vieja above. The crater has a small shelter (none too clean), which was a shrine, and about 10 antennae. There are great views of Volcán Fuego. It's a three- to five-hour climb if you are fit, and at least two hours down. To get the best views before the clouds cover the summit, it is best to stay at the radio station at the top. Agua can also be climbed from **Alotenango**, a village between Agua and Fuego, south of Ciudad Vieja. It's 9 km from Antigua and its name means 'place surrounded by corn'. Alotenango has a fiesta from 18-20 January.

Volcán Acatenango
If you do this climb independently of a tour agency, ask for a guide in La Soledad. However, it is strongly recommended that you use a professional guiding service, ideally with security.

Acatenango is classified as a dormant volcano and is the third tallest in the country (3975 m) with two peaks to its name. Its first recorded eruption was in 1924. Two other eruptions were reported in 1924-1927 and 1972. The best trail heads south at

La Soledad, 2300 m (15 km west of Ciudad Vieja), which is 300 m before the road (Route 5) turns right to Acatenango (see Where to stay, below). A small plateau, La Meseta on maps, known locally as **El Conejón**, provides a good camping site half way up (three or four hours). From here it is a further three or four hours' harder going to the top. The views of the nearby (lower) active crater of Fuego are excellent.

Volcán Fuego

This is an active volcano with trails that are easy to lose; it is recommended that you use a guiding service and do not venture up to the crater.

This volcano (3763 m) can be climbed via Volcán Acatenango, sleeping between the two volcanoes, then climbing for a further two to three hours before stopping a safe distance from the crater. This one is for experienced hikers only. Do not underestimate the amount of water needed for the climb. It is a seven-hour ascent with a significant elevation gain; it's a very hard walk, both up and down. There are steep, loose cinder slopes, which are very tedious, in many places. It is possible to camp about three-quarters of the way up in a clearing. Fuego has regular eruptions that shoot massive boulders from its crater, often without warning. Check in Antigua before attempting to climb. If driving down towards the south coast you can see the red volcanic rock it has thrown up.

Listings Volcanoes

Where to stay

$ Pensión
Volcán Acatenango.
Basic, with good cheap meals.

Transport

Volcán Agua
Bus
From Antigua to **Alotenango** from 0700-1800, 40 mins.

Volcán Acatenango
Bus
To reach **La Soledad**, take a bus heading for Yepocapa or Acatenango village and get off at La Soledad.

Car
Tabarini, 6 Av Sur 22, T7832-8107, also at the **Hotel Radisson Villa Antigua**, T7832-7460, www.tabarini.com.

Horse-drawn carriage
Available at weekends and during fiestas around the plaza.

Motorcycle hire
La Ceiba, 6 Calle Pte 15, T7832-0077.

Taxi
Servicio de Taxi 'Antigua', Manuel Enrique Gómez, T5417-2180, has been recommended.

Tuk-tuk
Motorbike taxis with a seat for 2 will whizz you around town for US$1.50.

Lake Atitlán
& around

★ In the Central Highlands volcano landscapes are dotted with colourful markets and the Maya wearing traditional clothes in the towns and villages. Aldous Huxley called Lake Atitlán "the most beautiful lake in the world" and attractive villages flank its shores. Further north you can explore the streets of Chichicastenango as the town fills with hawkers and vendors at the weekly markets serving tourists and locals alike. North of Chichicastenango, the Quiché and Ixil Triangle regions have small and very traditional hamlets set in beautiful countryside and are easily explored by bus.

Towards Lake Atitlán
beautiful scenery stretching west of the capital

The Pan-American Highway heads west out of the capital passing through Chimaltenango and on to Los Encuentros where it turns north for Chichicastenango, Santa Cruz del Quiché, Nebaj and the Ixil Triangle, and south for Sololá and the Lake Atitlán region. It continues to the western highland region of Quetzaltenango, Totonicapán, Huehuetenango and the Cuchumatanes Mountains.

Chimaltenango and around
Chimaltenango is busy with traffic. Here, another road runs south for 20 km to Antigua. This tree-lined road leads to Parramos where it turns sharp left. Straight on through the village, in 1.5 km, is a well known inn and restaurant, **La Posada de Mi Abuelo** (see Where to stay, below). This road continues through mountains to Pastores, Jocotenango and finally to Antigua. Some 6 km south of Chimaltenango, **San Andrés Itzapa** is well worth a visit; there is a very interesting **chapel to Maximón** ⓘ *open till 1800 daily*. Shops by the chapel

sell prayer pamphlets and pre-packaged offerings. Beyond Chimaltenango is **Zaragoza**, a former Spanish penal settlement, and beyond that a road leads 13 km north to the interesting village of **Comalapa**. This is the best place to see *naíf* painting and there are plenty of galleries. The **tourist information office** ⓘ *Av 3-76, T5766-3874*, is in the house of Andrés Curuchich, a popular artist. There's a colourful market on Monday and Tuesday.

Routes west: La Mesilla, Tecpán and Los Encuentros

Returning to the Pan-American Highway the road divides 6 km past Zaragoza. The southern branch, the old Pan-American Highway, goes through Patzicía and Patzún (see below) to Lake Atitlán, then north to Los Encuentros. The northern branch, the new Pan-American Highway, which is used by all public transport, goes past Tecpán (see below) and then to Los Encuentros. From Los Encuentros there is only the one road west to San Cristóbal Totonicapán, where it swings northwest to La Mesilla/ Ciudad Cuauhtémoc, at the Mexican border; see box, page 210.

From Zaragoza the Pan-American Highway runs 19 km to near **Tecpán**, which is slightly off the road at 2287 m. It has a particularly fine church with silver altars,

Lake Atitlán

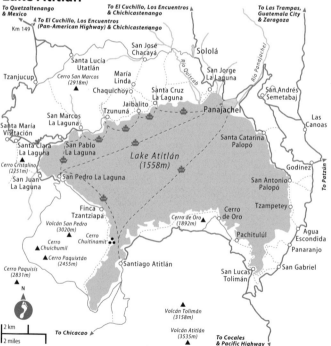

To Quetzaltenango & Mexico

To El Cuchillo, Los Encuentros & Chichicastenango

To Las Trampas, Guatemala City & Zaragoza

To El Cuchillo, Los Encuentros (Pan-American Highway) & Chichicastenango

Km 149

Tzanjucup

Santa Lucía Utatlán

Cerro San Marcos (2918m)

María Linda

Chaquichoy

San José Chacayá

Sololá

Santa Cruz La Laguna

Jaibalito

San Jorge La Laguna

Río Quiscab

Río Panajachel

San Andrés Semetabaj

San Marcos La Laguna

Tzununá

Panajachel

Las Canoas

Santa María Visitación

Santa Clara La Laguna

San Pablo La Laguna

Santa Catarina Palopó

Cerro Cristalino (2251m)

San Juan La Laguna

San Pedro La Laguna

Lake Atitlán (1558m)

Godínez

San Antonio Palopó

To Patzún

Finca Tzantziapa

Volcán San Pedro (3020m)

Cerro Chuitinamit

Cerro de Oro (1892m)

Cerro de Oro

Tzampetey

Agua Escondida

Cerro Chuichumil

Cerro Paquixtán (2455m)

Pachitulúl

Panaranjo

Cerro Paquisís (2831m)

Santiago Atitlán

San Lucas Tolimán

San Gabriel

N

2 km
2 miles

To Chicacao

Volcán Tolimán (3158m)

Volcán Atitlán (3535m)

To Cocales & Pacific Highway

carved wooden pillars, odd images and a wonderful ceiling that was severely damaged by the 1976 earthquake. There is accommodation, restaurants and banks. Near Tecpán are the important Maya ruins of **Iximché** ⓘ *5 km of paved road south of Tecpán, 0800-1700, US$3.25*, once capital and court of the Cakchiqueles. The first capital of Guatemala after its conquest was founded near Iximché; followed in turn by Ciudad Vieja, Antigua and Guatemala City. The ruins are well presented with three plazas, a palace and two ball courts on a promontory surrounded on three sides by steep slopes.

The old and new Pan-American highways rejoin 11 km from Sololá at the **El Cuchillo** junction. About 2 km east is **Los Encuentros**, the junction of the Pan-American Highway and the paved road 18 km northeast to Chichicastenango.

To Lake Atitlán along the old Pan-American Highway

With amazing views of Lake Atitlán and the surrounding volcanoes, travellers of the southern road from Zaragoza to Lake Atitlán encounter a much more difficult route than the northern option, with several steep hills and many hairpin bends. Nevertheless, if you have both the time and a sturdy vehicle, it is an extremely rewarding trip. Note that there is no police presence whatsoever along the old Pan-American Highway.

The route goes through **Patzicía**, a small Maya village founded in 1545 (no accommodation). Market days are Wednesday and Saturday and the local fiesta is 22-27 July. The famous church, which had a fine altar and beautiful silver, was destroyed by the 1976 earthquake. Beyond is the small town of **Patzún**; its church, dating from 1570, is severely damaged and is not open to the public. There is a Sunday market, which is famous for the silk (and wool) embroidered napkins and for woven *fajas* and striped red cotton cloth; other markets are on Tuesday and Friday and the town fiesta is 17-21 May. For accommodation, ask at the *tiendas*.

The road leaves Patzún and goes south to Xepatán and on to **Godínez**, the highest community overlooking the lake. From Godínez, a good paved road turns off south to the village of San Lucas Tolimán and continues to Santiago Atitlán.

The main (steep, paved) road continues straight on for Panajachel. The high plateau, with vast wheat and maize fields, now breaks off suddenly as though pared by a knife. From a viewpoint here, there is an incomparable view of Lake Atitlán, 600 m below. The very picturesque village of **San Antonio Palopó** is right underneath you, on slopes leading to the water. It is about 12 km from the viewpoint to Panajachel. For the first 6 km you are close to the rim of the old crater and, at the point where the road plunges down to the lakeside, is **San Andrés Semetabaj** which has a beautiful ruined early 17th-century church. Market day is Tuesday. Buses go to Panajachel.

Sololá

On the road down to Panajachel is Sololá (altitude 2113 m), which has superb views across Lake Atitlán. Outside the world of the tourist, this is the most important town in the area. A fine, modern, white church, with bright stained-glass windows and an attractive clocktower dominates the west side of the plaza. Sololá is even more special for the bustling market that brings the town to life every Tuesday and Friday, when the Maya gather from surrounding commuties to buy and sell local produce. Women and particularly men wear traditional dress. While it is primarily a produce market, there is also a good selection of used *huipiles*. Even if you're not in the market to buy, it is a colourful sight. Markets are mornings only; Friday market gets underway on Thursday. There's a fiesta 11-17 August.

From Sololá the old Pan-American Highway weaves and twists through a 550-m drop in the 8 km to Panajachel. The views are impressive at all times of day, but particularly in the morning. Time allowing, it is quite easy to walk down direct by the road (two hours); you also miss the unnerving bus ride down (US$0.40).

Listings Towards Lake Atitlán

Where to stay

Chimaltenango and around

$$ La Posada de Mi Abuelo
Carretera a Yepocapa, Parramos, T7849-5930, see Facebook.
A delightful inn, formerly a coffee farm, with a good restaurant. Packages with horse riding, biking and meals are available.

$ Pixcayá
0 Av, 1-82, Comalapa, T7849-8260.
Hot water, parking.

Sololá

$ Del Viajero
7 Av, 10-45, on Parque Central (also annexe around the corner on Calle 11), T7762-3683.
Rooms with bath, cheaper without, spacious, clean and friendly, good food in restaurant on the plaza (**El Cafetín**).

$ El Paisaje
9 Calle, 5-41, 2 blocks from Parque Central, T7762-3820.
Pleasant colonial courtyard, shared baths and toilets, clean, hot water, restaurant, good breakfast, family-run, laundry facilities.

Transport

Chimaltenango and around
Bus
Any bus heading west from Guatemala City stops at Chimaltenango. To **Antigua** buses leave from the corner of the main road and the road south to Antigua where there is a lime green and blue shop, Auto Repuestos y Frenos Nachma, 45 mins, US$0.34. To **Chichicastenango**, every 30 mins, 0600-1700, 2 hrs, US$2. To **Cuatro Caminos**, 2½ hrs, US$2.50. To **Quetzaltenango**, every 45 mins, 0700-1800, 2½ hrs, US$2.80. To **Tecpán** every 30 mins, 0700-1800, 1 hr.

Routes west: La Mesilla, Tecpán and Los Encuentros
Bus
From Tecpán to **Guatemala City**, 2¼ hrs, buses every hour, US$2.20; easy day trip from **Panajachel** or **Antigua**.

To Lake Atitlán along the old Pan-American Highway
Bus
To and from **Godínez** there are several buses to Panajachel, US$0.45 and 1 bus daily Patzún–Godínez. To **San Andrés Semetabaj**, bus to Panajachel, US$0.40.

Sololá

Bus

To **Chichicastenango**, US$0.50, 1½ hrs; to **Panajachel**, US$0.38, every 30 mins, 20 mins, or 1½-2 hrs' walk.

To **Chimaltenango**, US$1.20. To **Quetzaltenango**, US$1.8. *Colectivo* to **Los Encuentros**, US$0.20. To **Guatemala City** direct US$2.50, 3 hrs.

Panajachel
charming old town, busy shopping street and starting point for lake ferries

The old town of Panajachel is pretty and quiet but the newer development, strung along a main road, is a tucker and trinket emporium. It's busy and stacked cheek by jowl with hundreds of stalls and shops along the principal street. Some of the best bargains are here and textiles and crafts from across the country can be found. Panajachel is a gringo magnet, and if you want to fill up on international cuisine and drink then it's a good place to stay for a few days. There are also stunning views from the lakeshore.

The town centre is the junction of Calle Principal and Calle (or Avenida) Santander. The main bus stop is here, stretching south back down Calle Real, and it marks the junction between the old and the modern towns. It takes about 10 minutes to walk from the junction to the lakeshore. Calle Rancho Grande is sometimes called Calle del Balneario and other streets have variants. The **tourist information office**, INGUAT ① *Calle Real Principal and Av Los Arboles, T7762-1106, daily 0900-1300 and 1400-1700*, is helpful with information about buses and boats and offer good local knowledge. Also see www.atitlan.com.

Safety There have been reports from travellers who have suffered robbery walking around the lake between San Juan and San Pablo and between San Marcos and Tzununá. Seek local advice from INGUAT, other travellers and local hotels/hostels before planning a trip.

Sights
The old town is 1 km from the lake and dominated by the **church**, originally built in 1567, but now restored. It has a fine decorated wooden roof and a mixture of Catholic statues and Maya paintings in the nave. A block up the hill is the daily market, worth a visit on Sunday mornings especially for embroideries. The local fiesta runs from 1-7 October; the main days are at the weekend and on 4 October.

In contrast, the modern town, almost entirely devoted to tourism, spreads out towards the lake. Calle Santander is the principal street, leading directly to the short but attractive **promenade** and boat docks. The section between Calle Santander and Calle Rancho Grande has been turned into a park, which delightfully frames the traditional view across the lake to the volcanoes. Near the promenade, at the

Tip...
Bartering is the norm. There are better bargains than in Chichicastenango. The main tourist shops are on Calle Santander.

Hotel Posada de Don Rodrigo, is the **Museo Lacustre Atitlán** ⓘ *daily 0900-1200, 1400-1800, US$4.40*, created by Roberto Samayoa, a prominent local diver and archaeologist, to house some of the many items found in the lake. The geological

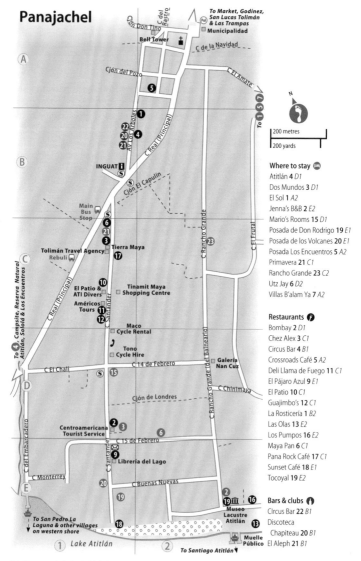

Panajachel

Where to stay 🛏

Atitlán **4** *D1*
Dos Mundos **3** *D1*
El Sol **1** *A2*
Jenna's B&B **2** *E2*
Mario's Rooms **15** *D1*
Posada de Don Rodrigo **19** *E1*
Posada de los Volcanes **20** *E1*
Posada Los Encuentros **5** *A2*
Primavera **21** *C1*
Rancho Grande **23** *C2*
Utz Jay **6** *D2*
Villas B'alam Ya **7** *A2*

Restaurants 🍴

Bombay **2** *D1*
Chez Alex **3** *C1*
Circus Bar **4** *B1*
Crossroads Café **5** *A2*
Deli Llama de Fuego **11** *C1*
El Pájaro Azul **9** *E1*
El Patio **10** *C1*
Guajimbo's **12** *C1*
La Rosticería **1** *B2*
Las Olas **13** *E2*
Los Pumpos **16** *E2*
Maya Pan **6** *C1*
Pana Rock Café **17** *C1*
Sunset Café **18** *E1*
Tocoyal **19** *E2*

Bars & clubs 🎶

Circus Bar **22** *B1*
Discoteca
  Chapiteau **20** *B1*
El Aleph **21** *B1*

Panajachel

The original settlement of Panajachel was tucked up against the steep cliffs to the north of the present town, about 1 km from the lake. Virtually all traces of the original Kaqchikel village have disappeared, but the early Spanish impact is evident with the narrow streets, public buildings, plaza and church. The original Franciscan church was founded in 1567 and used as the base for the Christianization of the lake area. Later, the fertile area of the river delta was used for coffee production, orchards and many other crops, some of which are still grown today and can be seen round the back of the tourist streets or incorporated into the gardens of the hotels.

Tourism began here in the early 20th century with several hotels on the waterfront, notably the Tzanjuyú and the Monterrey, the latter originally a wooden building dating from about 1910, rebuilt in 1975. In the 1970s came an influx of young travellers, quite a few of whom stayed on to enjoy the climate and the easy life. Drugs and the hippy element eventually gave Panajachel a bad name, but rising prices and other pressures have encouraged this group to move on, some to San Pedro across the lake. Others joined the commercial scene and still run services today.

history is explained and there is a fine display of Maya classical pottery and ceremonial artefacts classified by period. A submerged village has been found at a depth of 20 m, which is being investigated. It has been named **Samabaj** in honour of Don Roberto. For those interested in local art, visit **La Galería** (near **Rancho Grande Hotel**), where Nan Cuz, an indigenous painter, sells her pictures evoking the spirit of village life. She has been painting since 1958 and has achieved international recognition.

On the road past the entrance to **Hotel Atitlán** is the **Reserva Natural Atitlán** ⓘ *T7762-2565, www.atitlanreserva.com, daily 0800-1800, US$8.30 entrance, US$29-45 zip-line (including entrance)*, a reserve with a bird refuge, butterfly collection, monkeys and native mammals in natural surroundings, with a picnic area, herb garden, waterfall, visitor centre, café, zip-lines and access to the lakeside beach. Camping and lodging are available ($).

Listings Panajachel *map p64*

Where to stay

$$$$ Villas B'alam Ya
Outside Panajachel, Carretera a Catarina Palopó Km 2, T7762-2522, www.panzaverde.com.

The sister property of the swish Meson Panza Verde in Antigua, Villas B'alam Ya includes 4 luxury villas on the hillside and lakeshore, all tastefully attired and equipped with all mod cons. Guests can enjoy plentiful services and facilities including kayaks, gourmet room service, tours and yoga classes. Very peaceful, secluded and romantic.

$$$ Atitlán
1 km west of centre on lake, 2nd turning off the road to Sololá, T7762-1441, www.hotelatitlan.com.
Full board available, colonial style, excellent rooms and service, beautiful gardens with views across lake, pool, private beach and top-class restaurant.

$$$ Posada de Don Rodrigo
Final Calle Santander, overlooks the lake, T7762-2326, www.posadadedonrodrigo.com.
Pool, sauna, terrace, gardens, good restaurant, excellent food and service, comfortable and luxurious bathrooms, and fireplaces.

$$$ Rancho Grande
Calle Rancho Grande, Centro, T7762-1554, www.ranchogrande inn.com.
Cottages in charming setting, 4 blocks from beach, popular for long stay, good, including breakfast with pancakes. Pool with café in spacious gardens which have good children's play equipment. Staff are helpful. Recommended.

$$$-$$ Jenna's B&B
Casa Loma, Calle Rancho Grande, T5458-1984, www.jennasriverbedandbreakfast.com.
This quirky B&B has 7 cosy guest rooms decorated with local antiques, Guatemalan art and textiles. There is also a basement apartment available by the week or month and, for those seeking something different, a yurt ($$$). Amenities include garden, TV, Wi-Fi, living room and full bar. Breakfast included, additional meals on request.

$$ Dos Mundos
Calle Santander 4-72, Centro, T7762-2078, www.hoteldosmundos.com.
Pool, cable TV, some rooms surround pool, good Italian restaurant (**La Lanterna**). Breakfast included.

$$ Posada de los Volcanes
Calle Santander, 5-51, Centro, T7762-0244, www.posadadelosvolcanes.com.
12 rooms with bath, hot water, clean, comfortable, quiet, friendly owners, Julio and Jeanette Parajón.

$$ Posada Los Encuentros
Barrio Jucany, a 15-min walk from town, T7762-1603, www.losencuentros.com.
Off-the-beaten track in Panajachel, Los Encuentros boasts a lovely medicinal herb garden, wood-fuelled sauna, thermally heated mineral pool, and a well-equipped fitness centre. They have links to local healers and offer Mayan cultural tours. Accommodation includes 7 pleasant rooms.

$$ Primavera
Calle Santander, Centro, T7762-2052, www.primaveratitlan.com.
Clean, bright rooms, with TV, cypress wood furniture, gorgeous showers, washing machine available, friendly. Recommended. **Chez Alex** next door serves French food in a lovely patio setting at the back. Don't get a room overlooking the street at weekends.

$$ Utz Jay
5 Calle, 2-50, Zona 2, T7762-0217, www.hotelutzjay.com.
This small hotel has 13 rooms overlooking a lush tropical garden replete with leafy foliage and birds. Rooms are clean and tranquil, equipped with hot water and decorated with Mayan textiles. Services available at extra

cost include breakfast, laundry, sauna, jacuzzi and packed lunch.

$ Hotel El Sol
Barrio Jucanya, a 15-min walk from town, T7762-6090, www.hotelelsolpanajachel.com.
Hotel El Sol is a Japanese-owned hostel, which is quiet, good value, economical and suitable for backpackers or families. Lodgings include immaculately clean private rooms and an 8-bed dorm. There is a small garden outside and a sun terrace with views of the hills. Inside there is a restaurant and lounges for watching DVDs. Pleasant and restful.

$ Mario's Rooms
Calle Santander esq Calle 14 de Febrero, Centro, T7762-1313.
Cheaper without bath, with garden, clean, bright rooms, hot showers, good breakfast (extra), popular and friendly.

Apartments
Ask around for houses to rent; available from US$125 a month for a basic place, to US$200, but almost impossible to find in Nov and Dec. Break-ins and robberies of tourist houses are not uncommon. Water supply is variable. **Apartamentos Bohemia**, Callejón Chinimaya, rents furnished bungalows.

Camping
Possible in the grounds of **Hotel Visión Azul** and **Tzanjuyú**.

Restaurants

$$$ Chez Alex
Calle Santander, centre, T7762-0172. Open 1200-1500 and 1800-2000.
French menu, good quality, mainly tourists, credit cards accepted.

$$$ Tocoyal
Annexe to Hotel del Lago.
A/c, groups welcome, buffet on request but tourist prices.

$$ Circus Bar
Av Los Arboles 0-62, T7762-2056. Open 1200-2400.
Italian dishes including delicious pasta and pizzas, good coffee, popular. Live music from 2030, excellent atmosphere. Recommended.

$$ Crossroads Café
Calle de Campanario 0-27. Tue-Sat 0900-1300 and 1500-1900.
Global choice of quality coffee, but you can't go wrong with Guatemalan! Excellent cakes.

$$ El Patio
Calle Santander.
Good food, very good large breakfasts, quiet atmosphere but perfect for people-watching from the garden. Try the amaretto coffee.

$$ Guajimbo's
Calle Santander.
Good atmosphere, excellent steaks, fast service, popular, live music some evenings. Recommended.

$$ La Rosticería
Av Los Arboles 0-42, T7762-2063. Daily 0700-2300.
Good food, try eggs 'McChisme' for breakfast, good fresh pasta, excellent banana cake, good atmosphere, popular, a bit pricey. Live piano music at weekends, friendly service.

$$ Los Pumpos
Calle del Lago.
Varied menu, bar, good fish and seafood dishes.

$$ Pana Rock Café
With Pana Arte upstairs, Calle Santander 3-72.
Buzzing around happy hour (2 for 1), salsa music, very popular, international food, pizza.

$$ Sunset Café
Superb location on the lake. Open 1100-2400.
Excellent for drinks, light meals and main dishes, live music evenings, but you pay for the view.

$$-$ Bombay
Calle Santander near Calle 15 Febrero, T7762-0611. Open 1100-2130.
Vegetarian recipes, including spicy curries, German beer, Mexican food, good food and wines, set lunch popular, good service. Very highly recommended.

$$-$ El Pájaro Azul
Calle Santander 2-75, T7762-2596. Open 1000-2200.
Café, bar, crêperie with gorgeous stuffed sweet or savoury crêpes, cakes and pies. Vegetarian options available. Reasonable prices, good for late breakfasts. Recommended.

$ Deli Llama de Fuego
Calle Santander, T7762-2586. Thu-Tue 0700-2200.
Sweet little café with a giant cheese plant as its focus. Breakfasts, muffins, bagels, pizzas, pasta, Mexican food and vegetarian sandwiches.

$ Restaurante Las Olas
Overlooking the lake at the end of Calle Santander, down by the dock.
Serves the absolute best nachos, great for just before catching the boat.

Bakeries

Maya Pan
Calle Santander 1-61.
Excellent wholemeal breads and pastries, banana bread comes out of the oven at 0930, wonderful, cinnamon rolls and internet too. Recommended.

Bars and clubs

Circus Bar
Av los Arboles. Daily 1200-0200.
Good live music from 2030.

Discoteca Chapiteau
Av los Arboles 0-69.
Nightclub Thu-Sat 1900-0100.

El Aleph
Av los Arboles. Thu-Sat 1900-0300.
One of a number of bars.

Shopping

Librería del Lago, *Calle Santander Local A-8, T7762-2788. Daily 0900-1800.* Great bookshop selling a good range of quality English-language and Spanish books.
Tinamit Maya Shopping Centre, *Calle Santander.* Bargain for good prices. Maya sell their wares cheaply on the lakeside; varied selection, bargaining is easy/expected.

What to do

Cycling
There are several rental agencies on Calle Santander, eg **Maco Cycle Rental** and **Tono Cycle Rental**. Also **Alquiler de Bicicletas Emanuel**, on Calle 14 de Febrero. Prices start at US$2 per hr or about US$10 for a day.

Diving

ATI Divers, *round the back of El Patio, Calle Santander, T5706-4117, www. laiguana perdida.com*. A range of options including PADI Open Water US$220, fun dive US$30, 2 for US$50. PADI Rescue and Dive Master also available. Altitude speciality, US$80. Dives are made off Santa Cruz La Laguna and are of special interest to those looking for altitude diving. Here there are spectacular walls that drop off, rock formations you can swim through, trees underwater and, because of its volcanic nature, hot spots, which leaves the lake bottom sediment boiling to touch. Take advice on visibility before you opt for a dive.

Fishing

Lake fishing can be arranged, black bass (*mojarra*) up to 4 kg can be caught. Boats for up to 5 people can be hired for about US$15. Check with INGUAT, see page 63, for latest information.

Hang-gliding

Rogelio, *contactable through Americo's Tours, Calle Santander, and other agencies will make arrangements, at least 24 hrs' notice is required.* Jumps are made from San Jorge La Laguna or from above Santa Catarina, depending on weather conditions.

Kayaking and canoing

Kayak hire is around US$2 per hr. Ask at the hotels, INGUAT and at lakeshore. Watch out for strong winds that occasionally blow up quickly across the lake; these are potentially dangerous in small boats.
Diversiones Acuáticos Balán, *in a small red and white tower on the lakeshore.* Rent out kayaks.

Tour operators

All offer shuttle services to Chichicastenango, Antigua, the Mexican borders, etc, and some to San Cristóbal de las Casas (see Transport, below) and can arrange most activities on and around the lake. There are a number of tour operators on Calle Santander, including those listed below.
Americo's Tours, *T7762-2021*.
Centroamericana Tourist Service, *T7832-5032*.
Tierra Maya, *T7725-7320*. Friendly and reliable tour operator, which runs shuttles to San Cristóbal de las Casas as well as within Guatemala.
Toliman Travel, *T7762-1275*.

Waterskiing

Arrangements can be made with **ATI Divers** at **Iguana Perdida** in Santa Cruz.

Transport

Boat

There are 2 types of transport – the scheduled ferry service to Santiago Atitlán and the *lanchas* to all the other villages. The tourist office has the latest information on boats. The boat service to **Santiago Atitlán** runs from the dock at the end of Calle Rancho Grande (Muelle Público) from 0600-1630, 8 daily, 20 mins in launch, US$3.10, 1 hr in the large **Naviera Santiago** ferry, T7762-0309 or 20-35 mins in the fast *lanchas*. Some *lanchas* to all the other villages leave from here, but most from the dock at the end of Calle Embarcadero run by **Tzanjuyú** from 0630-1700 every 45 mins or when full (minimum 10 people). If you set off from the main dock the *lancha* will pull in at the Calle Embarcadero dock as well. These *lanchas* call in at **Santa Cruz**, **Jaibalito**,

Tzununá, San Marcos, San Pablo, San Juan and San Pedro, US$1.20 to US$2.50 to San Marcos and beyond. To San Pedro US$3.10. There are no regular boats to Santa Catarina, San Antonio or San Lucas: pickups and buses serve these communities, or charter a *lancha*, US$30 return to Santa Catarina and San Antonio.

The first boat of the day is at 0700. If there is a demand, there will almost always be a boatman willing to run a service but non-official boats can charge what they like. Virtually all the dozen or so communities round the lake have docks, and you can take a regular boat to any of those round the western side. The only reliable services back to Panajachel are from Santiago or San Pedro up to about 1600. If you wait on the smaller docks round the western side up to this time, you can get a ride back to Panajachel, flag them down in case they don't see you, but they usually pull in if it's the last service of the day.

Note that, officially, locals pay less. Only buy tickets on the boat; if you buy them from the numerous ticket touts on the dockside, you will be overcharged. Bad weather can, of course, affect the boat services. Crossings are generally rougher in the afternoons, worth bearing in mind if you suffer from sea-sickness.

Boat hire and tours *Lanchas* can be hired to go anywhere round the lake, about US$100 for 5 people for a full day. For round trips to San Pedro and Santiago and possibly San Antonio Palopó, with stopovers, go early to the lakefront and bargain. Trip takes a full day, eg 0830-1530, with stops of 1 hr or so at each, around US$6-7, if the boat is full. If on a tour, be careful not to miss

the boat at each stage; if you do, you will have to pay again.

Bus
Rebuli buses leave from opposite Hotel Fonda del Sol on Calle Real, otherwise, the main stop is where Calle Santander meets Calle Real. Rebuli to Guatemala City, 3½ hrs, US$3.30, crowded, hourly between 0500 and 1500. To Guatemala City via Escuintla south coast, 8 a day plus 3 Pullman a day. Direct bus to Quetzaltenango, 7 a day between 0530 and 1415, US$2.70, 2½ hrs. There are direct buses to Los Encuentros on the Pan-American Hwy (US$0.75). To Chichicastenango direct, Thu and Sun, 0645, 0700, 0730 and then hourly to 1530. Other days between 0700-1500, US$2, 1½ hrs. There are 4 daily direct buses to Cuatro Caminos, US$1.60 from 0530, for connections to Totonicapán, Quetzaltenango, Huehuetenango, etc. To Antigua take a bus up to Los Encuentros through Sololá. Change for a bus to Chimaltenango US$3.10, and change there for Antigua. There is also a direct bus (Rebuli) to Antigua leaving 1030-1100, daily, US$4.40. To Sololá, US$0.40, 20 mins, every 30 mins. You can wait for through buses by the market on Calle Real. The fastest way to southern Mexico is probably by bus south to Cocales, 2½ hrs, 5 buses between 0600 and 1400, then many buses along the Pacific Highway to Tapachula on the border. For La Mesilla, take a bus up to Los Encuentros, change west for Cuatro Caminos. Here catch a bus north to La Mesilla; see also box, page 210. Some travel agencies go direct to San Cristóbal de las Casas via La Mesilla, daily at 0600. See Tour operators, above.

Shuttles Services are run jointly by travel agencies, to **Guatemala City**, **Antigua**, **Quetzaltenango**, **Chichi** and more. Around 4 a day. **Antigua**, US$14, **Chichicastenango**, on market days, US$15, **Quetzaltenango** US$20 and the **Mexican border** US$40. **Atitrans**, Calle Santander, next to Hotel Regis, T7762-0146, is recommended.

Motorcycle
Motorcycle hire About US$6 per hour, plus fuel and US$100 deposit. Try **Maco Cycle** near the junction of Calle Santander and 14 de Febrero, T7762-0883.

Motorcycle parts David's Store, opposite Hotel Maya Kanek, has good prices and also does repairs.

Around Lake Atitlán

thriving Mayan villages and colourful traveller hang-outs

Villages around the lake are connected to Panajachel by boat services. Some are served by buses. Travelling round the lake is the best way to enjoy the stunning scenery and the effect of changing light and wind on the mood of the area. The slower you travel the better, and walking round the lake gives some fantastic views (but take advice on safety). With accommodation at towns and villages on the way, there is no problem finding somewhere to bed down for the night if you want to make a complete circuit. Here and there the cliffs are too steep to allow for easy walking and private properties elsewhere force you to move up 'inland'.

> Tip...
> The lake is 50 km in circumference and you can walk on or near the shore for most of it.

For boat information see Transport, page 69. At almost any time of year, but especially between January and March, strong winds (*El Xocomil*) occasionally blow up quickly across the lake. This can be dangerous for small boats.

Santa Catarina Palopó
The town, within easy walking distance (4 km) of Panajachel, has an attractive adobe church. Reed mats are made here, and you can buy *huipiles* (beautiful, green, blue and yellow) and men's shirts. Watch weaving at **Artesanías Carolina** on the way out towards San Antonio. Bargaining is normal. There are hot springs close to the town and an art gallery. Houses can be rented and there is at least one superb hotel (see Where to stay, below). The town fiesta is 25 November.

San Antonio Palopó
Six kilometres beyond Santa Catarina, San Antonio Palopó has another fine 16th-century church. Climbing the hill from the dock, it lies in an amphitheatre created by the mountains behind. Up above there are hot springs and a cave in the rocks used for local ceremonies. The village is noted for the clothes and head dresses of the men, and *huipiles* and shirts are cheaper than in Santa Catarina. A good hike is to take the bus from Panajachel to Godínez; take the path toward the lake 500 m south along the road to Cocales, walk on down from there to San Antonio Palopó (one

hour) and then along the road back to Panajachel via Santa Catarina Palopó (three hours). You can walk on round the lake from San Antonio, but you must eventually climb steeply up to the road at Agua Escondida. The local fiesta is 12-14 June.

San Lucas Tolimán

San Lucas is at the southeastern tip of the lake and is not as attractive as other towns. It is known for its fiestas and markets especially Holy Week with processions, arches and carpets on the Thursday and Friday, and 15-20 October. Market days are Tuesday, Friday and Sunday (the best). There are two banks and an internet centre. **Comité Campesino del Altiplano** ① *T5804-9451, www.ccda.galeon.com*, is based in the small village of Quixaya, 10 minutes from San Lucas. This Campesino Cooperative now produces fairtrade organic coffee buying from small farmers. You can visit its organic processing plant on a small coffee finca and learn about its *café justicia*, and political work. Long-term volunteers welcome, Spanish required.

Volcán Atitlán and Volcán Tolimán

Ask Father Gregorio at the Parroquia church, 2 blocks from the Central Plaza, or at the Municipalidad for information and for available guides in San Lucas. Father Greg has worked in the area for more than 40 years so has a vested interest in recommending safe and good guides. One guide is Carlos Huberto Alinan Chicoj, leaving at 2400 with torches to arrive at the summit by 0630 to avoid early cloud cover.

From San Lucas the cones of Atitlán, 3535 m, and Tolimán, 3158 m, can be climbed. The route leaves from the south end of town and makes for the saddle (known as Los Planes, or Chanán) between the two volcanoes. From there it is south to Atitlán and north to the double cone (they are 1 km apart) and crater of Tolimán. Though straightforward, each climb is complicated by many working paths and thick cover above 2600 m. If you are fit, either can be climbed in seven hours, five hours down. Cloud on the volcano is common, but least likely from November to March. There have been reports of robbery so consider taking a guide, and ask local advice before setting out.

Santiago Atitlán

Santiago is a fascinating town, as much for the stunningly beautiful embroidered clothing of the locals, as for the history and character of the place with its mix of Roman Catholic, evangelical and Maximón worship. There are 35 evangelical temples in town as well as the house of the revered idol Maximón. The Easter celebrations here rival Antigua's for interest and colour. These are some of the most curious and reverential ceremonies in the world. If you only visit Guatemala once in your lifetime and it's at Easter and you can't bear to leave Antigua, come to Santiago at least for Good Friday. Commemorative events last all week and include Maximón as well as Christ.

You will be taken to the house of Maximón for a small fee. The fine church, with a wide nave decorated with colourful statues, was founded in 1547. The original roof was lost to earthquakes. There is a plaque dedicated to priest Father

Francis Aplas Rother who was assassinated by the government in the church on 28 August 1981. At certain times of the year, the square is decked with streamers gently flapping in the breeze. The Tz'utujil women wear fine clothes and the men wear striped, half-length embroidered trousers (the most beautiful in Guatemala). There is a daily market, best on Friday and all sorts of artwork and crafts can be bought. **Asociación Cojol ya weaving centre** ① *T5499-5717, Mon-Fri 0900-1600, Sat 0900-1300, free, weaving tours also*. As well as Holy Week, the local fiesta takes place 23-27 July.

Near town is the hill, **Cerro de Oro**, with a small village of that name on the lake. The summit (1892 m) can be reached from the village in 45 minutes.

For more information on the **Lake Atitlán Medical Project** and volunteer opportunities, see www.puebloapueblo.org.

San Pedro La Laguna

San Pedro is a small town set on a tiny promontory with coffee bushes threaded around tracks lined with hostels and restaurants on the lakeside fringes. The tourists and long-term gringos have colonized the lakeside while the **Tz'utujil Maya** dominate the main part of the town up a very steep hill behind. San Pedro is now the favourite spot to hang out in for a couple of days or longer. It's a place to relax, to soak in hot baths, learn a bit of Spanish, horse ride and trek up Nariz de Maya. Some of the semi-permanent gringo inhabitants run bars and cafés or sell home-made jewellery and the like. The cobbled road from the dock facing Panajachel (known as the *muelle*) climbs up to the centre and another goes down, more or less at right angles, to the other dock (known as the *playa* or beach) facing Santiago with the town arranged around. There's a mazy network of *callejones* and paths that fringe the shoreline between the two ferries. Market days are Thursday and Sunday (better) and there's a fiesta 27-30 June with traditional dances.

The town lies at the foot of the **Volcán San Pedro** (3020 m), which can be climbed in four to five hours, three hours down. It is now in the Parque Ecológico Volcán San Pedro, and the US$15 entrances includes the services of a guide. **Politur** also work in the park and there have been no incidents of robbery since the park's inauguration. Camping is possible. Go early (0530) for the view, because after 1000 the top is usually smothered in cloud; also you will be in the shade all the way up and part of the way down.

Descubre San Pedro has set up a museum of local culture and coffee, with natural medicine and Maya cosmovision tours.

Evangelical churches are well represented in San Pedro, and you can hardly miss the yellow and white **Templo Evangélico Bautista Getsemaní** in the centre. A visit to the rug-making cooperative on the beach is of interest and backstrap weaving is taught at some places. A session at the **thermal baths** ① *about US$10, Mon-Sat 0800-1900, best to reserve in advance*, is a relaxing experience. Note that the water is solar heated, not chemical hot springs. Massage is also available, US$10.

Canoes are made in San Pedro and hire is possible.

San Juan La Laguna and Santa Clara La Laguna

The road north from San Pedro passes around a headland to San Juan La Laguna
(2 km), a traditional lakeside town. Look for **Los Artesanos de San Juan** ⓘ *8 Av,*

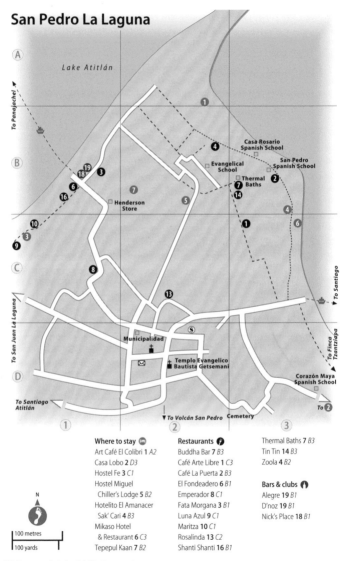

San Pedro La Laguna

Lake Atitlán

To Panajachel

To San Juan La Laguna

Casa Rosario
Spanish School

Evangelical
School

San Pedro
Spanish School

Thermal
Baths

Henderson
Store

To Santiago

To Finca
Tzantziapa

Municipalidad

Templo Evangelico
Bautista Getsemani

Corazón Maya
Spanish School

To Santiago
Atitlán

To Volcán San Pedro   Cemetery   To

N

100 metres
100 yards

Where to stay 🛏	Restaurants 🍴	Thermal Baths **7** *B3*
Art Café El Colibri **1** *A2*	Buddha Bar **7** *B3*	Tin Tin **14** *B3*
Casa Lobo **2** *D3*	Café Arte Libre **1** *C3*	Zoola **4** *B2*
Hostel Fe **3** *C1*	Café La Puerta **2** *B3*	
Hostel Miguel	El Fondeadero **6** *B1*	**Bars & clubs** 🍸
Chiller's Lodge **5** *B2*	Emperador **8** *C1*	Alegre **19** *B1*
Hotelito El Amanacer	Fata Morgana **3** *B1*	D'noz **19** *B1*
Sak' Cari **4** *B3*	Luna Azul **9** *C1*	Nick's Place **18** *B1*
Mikaso Hotel	Maritza **10** *C1*	
& Restaurant **6** *C3*	Rosalinda **13** *C2*	
Tepepul Kaan **7** *B2*	Shanti Shanti **16** *B1*	

6-20, Zona 2, T5963-9803, and another image of Maximón displayed in the house opposite the Municipalidad. **Rupalaj Kistalin** ⓘ *close to the textile store, LEMA, T5964-0040, daily 0800-1700*, is a highly recommended organization run by local guides. **LEMA** ⓘ *T2425-9441, lema@sanjuanlalaguna.com*, the women weavers' association that uses natural dyes in their textiles, is also in town. Weaving classes (T7759-9126) are possible too. On the road towards San Pablo there's a good viewpoint from the hilltop with the cross; a popular walk. A more substantial walk, about three hours, is up behind the village to Santa Clara La Laguna, 2100 m, passing the village of **Cerro Cristalino** with its attractive, white church with images of saints around the walls.

Santa María Visitación and San Pablo La Laguna

A short distance (500 m) to the west, separated by a gully, is a smaller village, Santa María Visitación. As with Santa Clara La Laguna, this is a typical highland village, and unspoilt by tourism. San Juan is connected to San Pablo by the lakeshore road, an attractive 4-km stretch mainly through coffee plantations. San Pablo, a busy village set 80 m above the lake, is known for rope making from *cantala* (maguey) fibres, which are also used for bags and fabric weaving.

San Marcos La Laguna

San Marcos' location is deceptive with the main part of the community 'hidden' up the hill. The quiet village centre is set at the upper end of a gentle slope that runs 300 m through coffee and fruit trees down to the lake, reached by two paved walkways. If arriving by boat and staying in San Marcos, ask to be dropped at the Schumann or the Pirámides dock. The village has grown rapidly in the last few years with a focus on the spiritual and energy; there is a lot of massage, yoga, and all sorts of other therapies. It is the ideal place to be pampered. Beyond the centre 300 m to the east is the main dock of the village down a cobbled road. Down the two main pathways are the hotels; some with waterfront sites have their own docks. There is a slanting trail leaving the village up through dramatic scenery over to Santa Lucía Utatlán, passing close to Cerro San Marcos, 2918 m, the highest point in the region apart from the volcanoes.

San Marcos to Santa Cruz

From the end of San Marcos where the stone track goes down to the dock, a rough track leads to **Tzununá**, passable for small trucks and 4WD vehicles, with views across the lake all the way. The village of Tzununá is along the tree-lined road through coffee plantations with a few houses up the valley behind. There is also a hotel with wonderful views (see Where to stay, below). There is a dock on the lakeside but no facilities. From here to Panajachel there are no roads or vehicular tracks and the villages can only be reached by boat, on horse or on foot. Also from here are some of the most spectacular views of the lake and the southern volcanoes. **Jaibalito** is smaller still than Tzununá, and hemmed in by the mountains with wonderful accommodation (see Where to stay, below). Arguably the best walk in the Atitlán area is from Jaibalito to Santa Cruz.

Santa Cruz La Laguna

Santa Cruz village is set in the most dramatic scenery of the lake. Three deep ravines come down to the bay separating two spurs. A stone roadway climbs up the left-hand spur, picks up the main walking route from Jaibalito and crosses over a deep ravine (unfortunately used as a rubbish tip) to the plaza, on the only flat section of the right spur, about 120 m above the lake. The communal life of the village centres on the plaza. The hotels, one of them overflowing with flowers, are on the lakeshore. Behind the village are steep, rocky forested peaks, many too steep even for the locals to cultivate. The fiesta takes place 7-11 May.

There is good walking here. Apart from the lake route, strenuous hikes inland eventually lead to the Santa Lucía Utatlán–Sololá road. From the left-hand (west) ravine reached from the path that runs behind the lakeshore section, a trail goes through fields to an impossible looking gorge, eventually climbing up to Chaquijchoy, **Finca María Linda** and a trail to San José Chacayá (about four hours). In the reverse direction, the path southwest from San José leads to the Finca María Linda, which is close to the crater rim from where due south is a track to Jaibalito, to the left (east) round to the trail to Santa Cruz. Others follow the ridges towards San José and the road. These are for experienced hikers, and a compass (you are travelling due north) is essential if the cloud descends and there is no one to ask. From Santa Cruz to Panajachel along the coast is difficult, steep and unconsolidated, with few definitive paths. If you do get to the delta of the Río Quiscab, you may find private land is barred. The alternatives are either to go up to Sololá, about 6 km and 800 m up, or get a boat.

Listings Around Lake Atitlán *map p74*

Where to stay

Santa Catarina Palopó

You can stay in private houses (ask around) or rent rooms (take a sleeping bag).

$$$$ Casa Colibri
Carretera a San Antonio Palopó Km 6.7, entrada a Tzampoc Casa 4, T5353-5823, www.lacasacolibri.com.
Beautifully designed and decorated, this plush vacation rental boasts an extravagant infinity pool overlooking the lake, sauna, fireplaces, and 5 luxurious guestrooms, all with en suite bathrooms. Tasteful and tranquil with space for 12 people.

$$$$ Casa Palopó
Carretera a San Antonio Palopó, Km 6.8, less than 1 km beyond Santa Catarina, on the left up a steep hill, T5773-7777, www.casapalopo.com.
One of the finest hotels in the country, 9 beautiful rooms all richly furnished, flowers on arrival, excellent service, heated pool, spa, gym and a top-class restaurant overlooking the lake. Reservations necessary.

$$$$ Tzam Poc Resort
Vía Rural Km 6.5, T7762-2680, www.atitlanresort.com.
Resort on the slopes above Santa Catarina with an amazing infinity pool.

Lovely villas and spa. There's also an archery range.

$$$ Villa Santa Catarina
T7762-1291,
www.villasdeguatemala.com.
36 comfortable rooms with balconies around the pool, most with view of the lake. Good restaurant.

$$ Hotel Terrazas del Lago
T7762-0157,
www.hotelterrazasdellago.com.
On the lake with view, bath, clean, restaurant, a unique hotel built up over the past 30 plus years.

San Lucas Tolimán

$$$ Toliman
Av 6, 1 block from the lake, T7722-0033.
18 rooms and suites in colonial style washed in terracotta colours with some lovely dark wood furniture. Suite No 1 is very romantic with lit steps to a sunken bath, good but expensive restaurant (reservations), fine gardens, pool, partial lake views. Recommended.

$ Casa Cruz Inn
Av 5 4-78, a couple of blocks from the park.
Clean, comfortable beds, run by an elderly couple, garden, quiet, good value.

$ Hotel y Restaurante Don Pedro
Av 6, on lakeside, T7722-0028.
An unattractive building in a sort of clumsy rustic style, a little rough around the edges, with 12 rooms, restaurant, bar.

$ La Cascada de María
Calle 6, 6-80, T7722-0136.
With bath, TV, parking, garden, restaurant, good.

Santiago Atitlán
Book ahead for Holy Week.

$$$$ Lake Villa Guatemala
Between Santiago and Cerro de Oro, 5 km from Santiago Atitlán, T5050-0767, www.lakevillaguatemala.com.
This private villa with just 2 cosy guestrooms would particularly suit those seeking a spiritual retreat. With hilltop and lakeside views, the property offers numerous meditation spaces, including rooms, terraces and gardens. The food is gourmet vegan and the owners can arrange Mayan ceremonies and consultations with local healers. Minimum 2-night stay.

$$$-$$ Posada de Santiago
1.5 km south of town, T7721-7366, www.posadade santiago.com.
Relaxing lakeside lodge with comfortable stone cottages (some cheaper accommodation), restaurant with home-grown produce and delicious food, tours and a pool. Massage and language classes arranged. Friendly and amusing management – David, Susie and his mum, Bonnie – quite a trio. Has its own dock or walk from town. Highly recommended.

$$ Bambú
On the lakeside, 500 m by road towards San Lucas, T7721-7332, www.ecobambu.com.
10 rooms, 2 bungalows and 1 *casita* in an attractive setting with beautifully tended gardens, restaurant, a secluded pool, a few minutes by *lancha* from the dock. Kayaks available.

$$ Mystical Yoga Farm
Bahía de Atitlán, a 5-min boat ride from Santiago, T4860-9538, www.mysticalyogafarm.com.
There are surely few better places to practice asanas than on the shores of

Lake Atitlán. Part of the **School Yoga Institute**, which has properties and yoga schools all over the world, the Mystical Yoga Farm offers all-inclusive packages which cover lodging, food, meditation, workshops, ceremonies and more. 3-night minimum stay.

$ Chi-Nim-Ya
Walk up from the dock, take the 1st left, walk 50 m and it's there on the left, T7721-7131.
Clean, comfortable and friendly, cheaper without bath, good value, good café, cheap, large helpings.

$ Tzutuhil
On left up the road from the dock to centre, above Ferretería La Esquina, T7721-7174.
With bath and TV, cheaper without, restaurant, great views, good.

Camping
Camping is possible near **Bambú**.

San Pedro La Laguna
Accommodation is mostly cheap and laid back; it's worth bringing your own sleeping bag.

$$$ Casa Lobo
6 Av, Callejon B, on the lakeshore, 200 m after Villa Cuba, 15 mins' walk out of town, www.casalobo.org.
Set in verdant grounds overlooking the lake, German-owned Casa Lobo is a secluded colonial-style property with a range of bungalows, apartments and houses, all tastefully furnished and fully equipped with Wi-Fi, stove, fridge and cable TV. 2-night minimum stay.

$$-$ Mikaso Hotel Resto
Callejon A, I-82, T7721-8232, www.mikasohotel.com.

Owned and managed by a family from Quebec, Mikaso has great lake views and a good restaurant serving wood-fired pizzas and crêpes. Private rooms are clean and cosy (**$$**) and for the thrifty there's 6 and 8-bed dorms (**$**). Facilities include a hot tub, roof terrace, pool table, shared kitchen and Swedish massage. Occasional live music.

$ Art Café El Colibri
Behind Colegio Bethel, in front of the museum Tzununya, T7721-8378, www.colibrisanpedro.com.
Colibri offers Spanish and painting classes and is also home to an art gallery, restaurant-cafe and a small B&B with 3 quiet, no-frills rooms, all equipped with hot showers. Owned by a local artist, very chilled place, simple and down to earth, lovely atmosphere complete with friendly dogs.

$ Hostel Fe
Calle Principal, turn right from the boat dock, then 60 m along the lake on the left, T3486-7027, www.hostelfe.com.
If you're in San Pedro to party, try Hostel Fe. Perched on the edge of the water, their restaurant-bar is buzzing with action every most evening; Tue is Ladies' Night, Fri is quiz night. Other sources of entertainment include a diving platform, board games, darts and live music. Accommodation is in basic dorms and private rooms.

$ Hostel Miguel Chiller's Lodge
Opposite Yo Mama Hostel.
Managed by the friendly Miguel and his family, this quiet, low-key hostel has a handful of simple private rooms and dorm accommodation. Amenities include Wi-Fi, shared kitchen, lounge and barbecue. There are great views of San Pedro volcano from the roof

terrace. Relaxed and hospitable. Good breakfast included.

$ Hotelito El Amanacer Sak' Cari
T7721-8096, www.hotelsakcari.com.
With bath, hot water, lovely rooms with great garden, ask for those with fabulous lake views. Extremely good value. Recommended.

$ Tepepul Kaan
6 Calle 5-10, take the 2nd left heading up from the Pana boat dock, T4301-2271, www.hoteltepepulkaan.com.
This ultra-economical hotel offers basic rooms with bath for about US$10 a night and donates 25% of the rates to scholarship funds for local students. Facilities include kitchen, hammocks, lawn and lake view. They claim to offer the 'best deal' in San Pedro and they may be right.

San Juan La Laguna

$$$-$$ Hotel Uxlabil
T5990-6016/2366-9555 (in Guatemala City), www.uxlabil.com.
This is an eco-hotel set up on the hill with its own dock (flooded, like all the village shore, in 2010), a short walk from the town centre. It's run by very friendly people with a small restaurant, and beautiful views from its rooftop terrace. It is a perfect, relaxing getaway, with a Maya sauna and tended gardens, in this most unassuming and interesting of towns. It has links with the ecotourism association in town. Recommended.

San Marcos La Laguna

$$$-$$ Aaculaax
Las Pirámides dock, on a path from the Centro Holístico, T5287-0521, www.aaculaax.com.
A Hansel-and-Gretel affair on the lakeshore, run by German Niels. It is a blend of cave work with Gaudí-type influence from the stained-glass work down to the sculptures and lamp shades. A corner of artistic nirvana on Lake Atitlán. Each of the 7 rooms with private bathroom is different, with quirky decor. It is run on an eco-basis, with compost toilets and all. There is a restaurant, bar, bakery and massage room, as well as glass and papier mâché workshops. Highly recommended.

$$ Posada del Bosque Encantado
Barrio 3, T4146-1050, www.hotel posadaencantado.com.
Rustic and arty, this colonial-style guesthouse features spacious, earthy, brick-built rooms with solid wood doors, red tile roofs, terracotta floors, Mayan textiles and stonework. The garden is so verdant and lush it is like a mini-jungle. Their restaurant serves *comida típica*.

$ Hotel Jinava
2nd dock, left at the top of 1st pathway, T5299-3311, www.hoteljinava.com.
This is heaven on a hill. With fabulous views, this German-owned place clings to a steep slope with lovely rooms, restaurants, terraces and a patio. There are books and games or solitude if you want it. It's close to the lakeshore with its own dock where launches will drop you. There are only 5 rooms, breakfast included. Recommended.

$ Hotel Paco Real
Barrio 3, T4688-3715, www.pacorealatitlan.com.
Located 50 m from the lake, Paco Real has simple but comfortable rooms inside wood and stone-built *cabañas*, with or without private bath. Also on site is a *temazcal* sauna, lush garden, Wi-Fi,

bar-restaurant, movie projector and book exchange.

$ Las Pirámides del Ka
Las Pirámides dock, www. laspiramidesdelka.com.
A residential meditation centre. See also What to do, below.

$ Unicornio
Las Pirámides dock, 2nd pathway.
With self-catering, bungalows, shared kitchen and bathrooms. It also has a little post office.

San Marcos to Santa Cruz

$$$ Lomas de Tzununá
Tzununá, T7820-4060, www.lomasdetzununa.com.
This hotel enjoys a spectacular position high up above the lake. The views from the restaurant terrace are magnificent. The 10 spacious rooms, decorated with local textiles, have 2 beds each with lake views and a balcony. The hotel, run by a friendly Belgian family, offers walking, biking, kayaking and cultural tours. The restaurant (**$$-$**) uses home-made ingredients, the hotel is run on solar energy and the pool does not use chlorine. Board games, internet, bar and giant chess available. The family are reforesting a hill. Breakfast and taxes included.

$$ La Casa del Mundo
Jaibalito, T5218-5332, www.lacasadelmundo.com.
Enjoys one of the most spectacular positions on the entire lake. Room No 15 has the best view followed by room No 1. Cheaper rooms have shared bathrooms. Many facilities, standard family-style dinner, lakeside hot tub, a memorable place with fantastic views. Repeatedly recommended.

Santa Cruz La Laguna

$$$$ Laguna Lodge
1 Tzantizotz, Santa Cruz La Laguna, T4066-8135, www.thelagunalodge.com.
Overlooking the lake, this luxury boutique hotel features tasteful suites beautifully decorated with hand-made furniture and antiques. A stunning setting, exquisite design and impeccably executed. Spa services available. Romantic and restful. Recommended.

$$$ La Fortuna
Patzisotz Bay, between Panajachel and Santa Cruz, T5203-1033, www.lafortunaatitlan.com.
A truly green venture with solar energy and all natural building materials, this self-described 'nano boutique hotel' is a very romantic option with its 4 luxury bungalows set in beautifully landscaped grounds. Secluded and tranquil, the perfect getaway.

$$$-$$ Villa Sumaya
Paxanax, beyond the dock, about 15 mins' walk, T5810-7199, www.villasumaya.com.
With its own dock, this comfortable, peaceful place has a sauna, massage and healing therapies and yoga. Rates include breakfast.

$$-$ Arca de Noé
To the left of the dock, T5515-3712.
Bungalows, cheaper rooms with shared bathrooms, good restaurant, barbecue, lake activities arranged, nice atmosphere, veranda overlooking a really beautiful flower-filled gardens and the lake. Low-voltage solar power.

$$-$ La Casa Rosa
To the right as you face the dock from the water, along a path, T5416-1251, www.atitlanlacasarosa.com.

Bungalows and rooms, with bath, cheaper without, home-made meals, attractive garden, sauna. Candlelit dinners at weekends.

$$-$ La Iguana Perdida
Opposite dock, T5706-4117, www.laiguanaperdida.com.
Rooms with and without bathroom and dorm ($ per person) with shared bath, lively, especially weekends, delicious vegetarian food, barbecue, popular, friendly, great atmosphere. **ATI Divers** centre (see What to do, below), waterskiing; kayaks and snorkelling. Bring a torch.

Restaurants

San Lucas Tolimán

$ La Pizza de Sam
Av 7, 1 block down from the plaza towards the lake.
Pizzas and spaghetti.

$ Restaurant Jardín
Orange building on corner of plaza. Comida típica and *licuados.*

Santiago Atitlán
There are many cheap *comedores* near the centre. The best restaurants are at the hotels.

$$$ El Pescador
On corner 1 block before Tzutuhil.
Full menu, good but expensive.

$$$ Posada de Santiago
1.5 km south of town, T7721-7167.
Delicious, wholesome food and excellent service in lovely surroundings. Highly recommended.

$ Restaurant Wach'alal
Close to Gran Sol. Daily 0800-2000.

A small yellow-painted café serving breakfasts, snacks and cakes. Airy and pleasant.

San Pedro La Laguna
Be careful of drinking water in San Pedro; both cholera and dysentery exist here.

$$-$ Café Arte Libre
Up the hill from Hotel San Pedro.
All meals, vegetarian dishes, good value.

$$-$ Luna Azul
Along shore.
Popular for breakfast and lunch, good omelettes.

$$-$ Restaurant Maritza
With commanding views over lake. Chilled place to hang out with reggae music. Service is slow though. 5 rooms also to rent with shared bath ($).

$$-$ Tin Tin.
Good value. Thai food, delightful garden. Recommended.

$ Buddha Bar
Shows movies every night and has a rooftop and sports bar.

$ Café La Puerta
On the north shore coastal path. Daily 0800-1700.
Cheap, tasty dishes, with tables in a quirky garden, or looking out over the lake. Beautiful setting.

$ Comedor Sta Elena
Near Nick's Italian.
Seriously cheap and filling breakfasts.

$ El Fondeadero
Good food, lovely terraced gardens, reasonable prices.

$ Emperador
Up the hill.
Comedor serving good local dishes.

$ Fata Morgana
Near the Panajachel dock.
Great focaccia bread sandwiches, with pizza and fine coffee too.

$ Rosalinda
Near centre of village.
Friendly, breakfasts (eg *mosh*), local fish and good for banana and chocolate cakes.

$ Shanti Shanti
Run by Israelis, Italian dishes.

$ Thermal Baths
Along shore from playa.
Good vegetarian food and coffee, but it's expensive.

$ Zoola
Close to the north shore. Open 0900-2100.
A quiet, hideaway with pleasant garden. A great spot.

Language schools

San Pedro is a popular place for learning Spanish. Students may make their own accommodation arrangements but homestays are possible.
Casa Rosario, www.casarosario.com. Offers classes from US$70 a week for 20 hrs' tuition.
Corazón Maya, T7721-8160, www.corazonmaya.com. Classes from US$49 a week. Tz'utujil classes also. Run by the welcoming Marta Navichoc.
San Pedro, T5715-4604, www.sanpedrospanishschool.org. Classes from US$75 per week. The school has a great location with gardens close to the lakeshore.

San Marcos La Laguna
All hotels and hostels offer food.

$$-$ Il Giardino
Up the 2nd pathway.
Attractive garden, Italian owners, good breakfasts.

Bars and clubs

San Pedro La Laguna
Nick's Place, overlooking the main dock, is popular, and well frequented in the evening. Nearby are **Bar Alegre**, a sports bar (www.thealegrepub.com) and **D'noz**. **Ti Kaaj** is another popular spot.

What to do

Santiago Atitlán
Aventura en Atitlán, *Jim and Nancy Matison, Finca San Santiago, T7811-5516. 10 km outside Santiago.* Riding and hiking tours.
Francisco Tizná *from the* **Asociación de Guías de Turismo**, *T7721-7558.* Extremely informative. Ask for him at the dock or at any of the hotels. Payment is by way of donation.

San Pedro La Laguna
There is a growing list of activities available in San Pedro, from hiking up the Nariz de Maya (5 hrs, US$13) and other local trips, through to local crafts. Yoga for all levels is available down towards the shore (US$5 for 1½ hrs).

San Juan La Laguna
Rupalaj Kistalin, *T5964-0040, rupalajkistalin@yahoo.es.* Offers interesting cultural tours of the town visiting painters, weavers, *cofradías* and traditional healers. As well as this cultural circuit there is an adventure

circuit taking in Panan forest and a canopy tour at Park Chuiraxamolo' or a nature circuit taking in a climb up the Rostro de Maya and fishing and kayaking. Some of the local guides speak English. Highly recommended.

San Marcos La Laguna
Body and soul
Casa Azul Eco Resort, *T5070-7101, www. casa-azul-ecoresort.com*. A gorgeous little place offering yoga and reiki, among other therapies and writers' workshops hosted by Joyce Maynard. There's also a sauna, campfire and café/restaurant serving vegetarian food. You can reach it from the first dock, or from the centre of the village.
Kaivalya Yoga and Ashram, *50 m on the left after the Lion's gate at the entrance to San Marcos, T3199-1344, www.yogaretreatguatemala.com.* Spiritual seekers may find illumination at this interesting ashram which offers everything from yoga and meditation classes to 'dark retreats'.
Las Pirámides del Ka, *www.laspiramides delka.com.* The month-long course costs US$420, or US$15 by the day if you stay for shorter periods, accommodation included. Courses are also available for non-residents. In the grounds are a sauna, a vegetarian restaurant with freshly baked bread and a library. This is a relaxing, peaceful place.
San Marcos Holistic Centre, *up the 2nd pathway, beyond Unicornio, www. sanmholisticcentre.com. Mon-Sat 1000-1700.* Offers iridology, acupuncture, kinesiology, Indian head massage, reflexology and massage. Classes in various techniques can also be taken.

Santa Catarina Palopó
There are frequent pickups from Panajachel and boat services.

San Antonio Palopó
Frequent pickups from Panajachel. Enquire about boats.

San Lucas Tolimán
Boat
Enquire about boats. Private *lancha*, US$35.

Bus
To **Santiago Atitlán**, hourly and to **Guatemala City** via **Panajachel**.

Santiago Atitlán
Boat
4 sailings daily to Pana with *Naviera*, 1¼ hrs, US$1.80, or by *lancha* when full, 20-35 mins, US$1.30-2. To **San Pedro** by *lancha* several a day, enquire at the dock for times, 45 mins, US$1.80.

Bus
To **Guatemala City**, US$2.60 (5 a day, first at 0300). 2 **Pullmans** a day, US$3.40. To **Panajachel**, 0600, 2 hrs, or take any bus and change on main road south of San Lucas.

San Pedro La Laguna
Boat
Up to 10 *lanchas* to **Panajachel**. To **Santiago**, leave when full (45 mins, US$2.50). To **San Marcos**, every 2 hrs. Private *lanchas* (10 people at US$2 each).

Bus
There are daily buses to **Guatemala City**, several leave in the early morning and early afternoon, 4 hrs, US$4.50, to

Antigua and to **Quetzaltenango**, in the morning, 3½ hrs, US$3.

San Marcos La Laguna
Boat
Service roughly every ½ hr to **Panajachel** and to **San Pedro**. Wait on any dock. Fare US$1.80 to either.

Bus
San Pedro to Pan-American Hwy can be boarded at San Pablo. **Pickup** Frequent pickups from the village centre and anywhere along the main road. To **San Pedro**, US$0.50, less to villages en route.

Chichicastenango

famous for its market where hundreds come for a bargain

★Chichicastenango (altitude 2071 m) is a curious blend of mysticism and commercialism. On market mornings the steps of the church are blanketed in flowers as the women, in traditional dress, fluff up their skirts, amid baskets of lilies, roses and blackberries. But, with its mixture of Catholic and indigenous religion readily visible, it is more than just a shopping trolley stop. On a hilltop peppered with pine, villagers worship at a Mayan shrine; in town, a time-honoured tradition of brotherhoods focuses on saint worship. Coupled with the mist that encircles the valley in the late afternoon, you can sense an air of intrigue.

A large plaza is the focus of the town, with two white churches facing one another: **Santo Tomás** the parish church and **Calvario**. Santo Tomás, founded in 1540, is

Chichicastenango

Where to stay		
Chalet House **3**	Salvador **6**	La Villa de los Cofrades **4**
Chugüilá **4**	Santo Tomás **11**	Las Brasas Steak House **5**
Mayan Inn **8**	Tuttos **2**	Tu Café **3**
Pensión Girón **9**		Tziguan Tinamit **6**
Posada Belén **1**	**Restaurants**	
Posada El Arco **5**	La Fonda de Tzijolaj **4**	
	La Parrillada **2**	

200 metres
200 yards

BACKGROUND
Chichicastenango

Often called 'Chichi' but also known as Santo Tomás, Chichicastenango is the hub of the Maya-K'iche' highlands. The name derives from the *chichicaste*, a prickly purple plant-like a nettle, which grows profusely, and *tenango*, meaning 'place of'. Today the locals call the town 'Siguan Tinamit' meaning 'place surrounded by ravines'. The townsfolk are also known as Masheños, which comes from the word Max, also meaning Tomás. About 1000 ladinos live in the town, but 20,000 Maya live in the hills nearby and flood the town for the Thursday and Sunday markets. The town itself has winding streets of white houses roofed with bright red tiles, which wander over a little knoll in the centre of a cup-shaped valley surrounded by high mountains.

The men's traditional outfit is a short-waisted embroidered jacket and knee breeches of black cloth, a woven sash and an embroidered kerchief around the head. The cost of this outfit, now over US$200, means that fewer and fewer men are wearing it. Women wear *huipiles* with red embroidery against black or brown and their *cortes* skirts have dark blue stripes.

open to visitors, although photography is not allowed, and visitors are asked to be discreet and enter by a side door (through an arch to the right). Next to Santo Tomás are the cloisters of the Dominican monastery (1542). Here the famous *Popol Vuh* manuscript of the Maya creation story was found. A human skull wedged behind a carved stone face, found in Sacapulas, can be seen at the **Museo Arqueológico Regional** ① *main plaza, Tue, Wed, Fri, Sat 0800-1200, 1400-1600, Thu 0800-1600, Sun 0800-1400, closed Mon, US$0.70, photographs and video camera not permitted*. There's also a jade collection once owned by 1926-1944 parish priest Father Rossbach. The **tourist office** ① *5 Av and Teatro Municipalidad, 1 block from church, T7756-2022, daily 0800-2000*, is helpful and provides a free leaflet with map, and local tour information.

The Sunday and Thursday markets are both very touristy, and bargains are harder to come by once shuttle-loads of people arrive mid-morning. Articles from all over the Highlands are available: rugs, carpets and bedspreads; walk one or two streets away from the main congregation of stalls for more realistic prices, but prices are cheaper in Panajachel for the same items and you won't find anything here that you can't find in Panajachel.

The idol, **Pascual Abaj**, a god of fertility, is a large black stone with human features on a hill overlooking the town. Crosses in the ground surrounding the shrine are prayed in front of for the health of men, women and children, and for the dead. Fires burn and the wax of a thousand candles, flowers and sugar cover the shrine. One ceremony you may see is that of a girl from the town requesting a good and sober husband. If you wish to undergo a ceremony to plead for a partner, or to secure safety from robbery or misfortune, you may ask the *curandero* (US$7 including photographs). To reach the deity, walk along 5 Avenida, turn right on 9 Calle, down the hill, cross the stream and take the second track from the left going steepest uphill, which passes directly through a farmhouse and buildings. The farm now belongs to a mask-maker whom you can visit and buy masks from. Follow the path to the top of the pine-topped hill where you may well see a Maya ceremony in progress. It's about 30 minutes' walk. The site can be easily visited independently (in a small group), or an INGUAT-approved guide arranged through the local tourist committee can take you there and explain its history and significance (US$6.50, one or two hours, identified by a license in town).

Listings Chichicastenango map p84

Where to stay

As soon as you get off the bus, boys will swamp you and insist on taking you to certain hotels.

$$$ Mayan Inn
Corner of 8 Calle, 1-91, T7756-1176,
www.mayaninn.com.gt.
A classic, colonial-style courtyard hotel, filled with plants, polished antique furniture, beautiful dining room and bar with fireplaces. Gas-heated showers and internet. The staff are very friendly and wear traditional dress. Secure parking.

$$$ Santo Tomás
7 Av, 5-32, T7756-1061.
A very attractive building with beautiful colonial furnishings and parrots in patios. There's a pool, sauna, good restaurant and bar. It is often full at weekends. Buffet lunch (US$14) is served on market days in the stylish dining room, with attendants in traditional dress.

$$ Posada El Arco
4 Calle, 4-36, T7756-1255.
Clean, very pretty, small, friendly, garden, washing facilities, negotiate lower rates for stays longer than a night, some large rooms, good view, parking, English spoken.

$$-$ Chalet House
3 Calle, 7-44, T7756-1360,
www.chalethotelguatemala.com.
A clean, guesthouse with family atmosphere, hot water. Don't be put off by the dingy street.

$ Chugüilá
5 Av, 5-24, T7756-1134,
hotelchuguila@yahoo.com.
Some rooms have fireplaces. Avoid the front rooms, which are noisy. There's also a restaurant.

$ Pensión Girón
Edif Girón on 6 Calle, 4-52, T7756-1156.
Clean rooms with bath, cheaper without, hot water, parking.

$ Posada Belén
12 Calle, 5-55, T7756-1244.
With bath, cheaper without, hot water, clean, will do laundry, fine views from balconies and hummingbirds in attractive garden, good value. Recommended.

$ Salvador
10 Calle, 4-47.
Large rooms with bath, a few with fireplaces (you can buy wood in the

Tip...
You won't find accommodation easily on Sat evening, when prices are increased.

ON THE ROAD

Markets

Market days in Guatemala are alive with colour and each community is characterized by unique clothes and crafts. Simply wandering through the labyrinthine stalls amid the frenetic throng of colour, noise, aromas and movement is a potent and memorable experience.

Markets run the gamut from low-key indoor bazaars to massive, sprawling outdoor events that draw traders from across the country. The most famous takes place in the town of **Chichicastenango**, an hour north of Lake Atitlán, where Maya and visitors converge in a twice-weekly frenzy of produce and textile shopping. It is a superb venue for souvenir purchases and the quintessential Guatemala market experience. **Sololá**, 20 minutes from Panajachel, hosts a Friday market that is always crowded with locals but rarely visited by foreigners, so it's an authentic slice of Mayan culture. For sheer size and scope, don't miss the Friday market at **San Francicso de Alto**, the largest, busiest and best stocked open-air market in Central America.

When shopping, bartering is the norm and almost expected; sometimes, unbelievable discounts can be obtained. You won't do better anywhere else in Central America, but getting the discount is less important than paying a fair price. Woven goods are normally cheapest bought in the town of origin. Try to avoid middlemen and buy direct from the weaver. Guatemalan coffee is highly recommended, although the best is exported; coffee sold locally is not vacuum-packed.

market), good views over town, parking. Cheaper, smaller rooms without bath available.

$ Tuttos
12 Calle, near Posada Belén, T7756-7540.
Reasonable rooms.

Restaurants

The best food is in the top hotels, but is expensive. On market days there are plenty of good food stalls and *comedores* in the centre of the plaza that offer chicken in different guises or a set lunch for US$1.50.

There are several good restaurants in the Centro Comercial Santo Tomás, on the north side of the plaza (market).

$$ La Fonda de Tzijolaj
On the plaza.
Great view of the market below, good meals, pizza, prompt service, reasonable prices.

$$ Las Brasas Steak House
6 Calle 4-52, T7756-2226.
Nice atmosphere, good steak menu, accepts credit cards.

$$-$ La Villa de los Cofrades
On the plaza.
Café downstairs, breakfasts, cappuccinos, espressos, good value. There is a 2nd restaurant 2 blocks up the street towards Arco Gucumatz, which is more expensive but has a great people-watching upstairs location. An

escape during market days, and popular for breakfast.

$$-$ Tziguan Tinamit
On the corner of 5 Av, esq 6 Calle.
Some local dishes, steaks, tasty pizzas, breakfasts, good pies but a little more expensive than most places, good.

$ Caffé Tuttos
See Where to stay. Daily 0700-2200.
Good breakfast deals, pizzas, and *menú del día*, reasonable prices.

$ La Parrillada
6 C 5-37, Interior Comercial Turkaj.
Escape the market bustle, courtyard, reasonable prices, breakfast available.

$ Tu Café
5 Av 6-44, on market place, Santo Tomás side. Open 0730-2000.
Snacks, budget breakfast, sandwiches, set lunch, good value.

Festivals

1 Jan Padre Eterno.
20 Jan San Sebastián.
19 Mar San José.
Feb/Apr Jesús Nazareno and María de Dolores (both Fri in Lent).
Mar/Apr Semana Santa (Holy Week).
29 Apr San Pedro Mártir.
3 May Santa Cruz.
29 Jun Corpus Christi.
18 Aug Virgen de la Coronación.
14 Sep Santa Cruz.
29 Sep San Miguel.
30 Sep San Jerónimo Doctor.
1st Sun of Oct Virgen del Rosario.
2nd Sun in Oct Virgen de Concepción.
1 Nov San Miguel.
13-22 Dec Santo Tomás, with 21 Dec being the main day. There are processions, traditional dances, the *Palo Volador* (19, 20, 21 Dec) marimba music, well worth a visit – very crowded.

Shopping

Chichicastenango's markets are on Sun and Thu. See box, page 87.
Ut'z Bat'z, *5a Avenida and 5a Calle, T5008-5193.* Women's Fair Trade weaving workshop, with free demonstrations; high-quality clothes and bags for sale.

What to do

Chichicastenango
Maya Chichi Van, *6 Av, 6-45, T7756-2187, mayachichivan@yahoo.com.* Shuttles and tours ranging from US$10-650.

Transport

Bus
Buses passing through Chichi all stop at 5 Av/5 Calle by the **Hotel Chugüilá**, where there are always police and bus personnel to give information. To **Guatemala City**, every 15 mins 0200-1730, 3 hrs, US$3.70. To **Santa Cruz del Quiché**, every ½ hr 0600-2000, US$0.70, 30 mins or 20 mins, if the bus driver is aiming for honours in the graduation from the School of Kamikaze Bus Tactics. To **Panajachel**, ½ hr, US$2, several until early afternoon or take any bus heading south and change at Los Encuentros. Same goes for **Antigua**, where you need to change at Chimaltenango. To **Quetzaltenango**, 5 between 0430-0830, 2½ hrs, US$3.80. To **Mexico**, and all points west, take any bus to Los Encuentros and change. To **Escuintla** via Santa Lucía Cotzumalguapa, between 0300 and 1700, 3 hrs, US$2.80. There are additional buses to local villages especially on market days.

Santa Cruz del Quiché and around

a quaint, friendly town, with a bustling daily market

Santa Cruz del Quiché (population 7750, altitude 2000 m), often simply called Quiché, attracts few tourists here and prices are consequently reasonable. Its main attraction is Utatlán, the remains of the Maya K'iche' capital. The large Parque Central has a military garrison on the east side with a jail on the lower floor and a sinister military museum with reminders of recent conflicts above. The date of the town's fiesta varies around the Assumption but is usually held around 14-20 August.

Three kilometres away are the remains of temples and other structures of the former Quiché capital, **Gumarcaj**, sometimes spelt **K'umarkaaj**, and now generally called **Utatlán** ① *0800-1700, US$1.30, from the bus station, walk west along 10 Calle for 40 mins until you reach a small junction with a blue sign (SECP), take the right lane up through gates to the site*. The city was largely destroyed by the Spaniards, but the stonework of the original buildings can be seen in the ruins, which can be reached on foot; the setting is very attractive and well maintained. There are two subterranean burial chambers (take a torch, as there are unexpected drops) still used by the Maya for worship and chicken sacrifices. The seven plazas, many temples, ball court, gladiator's archway and other features are marked.

There is a paved road east from Quiché to (8 km) **Santo Tomás Chiché**, a picturesque village with a fine, rarely visited Saturday market (fiesta 25-28 December). There is also a road to this village from Chichicastenango. Although it is a short-cut, it is rough and virtually impassable in any vehicle. It makes a good, three- to four-hour walk, however. Further east (45 km) from Chiché is **Zacualpa**, where beautiful woollen bags are woven. The church has a remarkably fine façade and there is an unnamed *pensión* near the plaza. Market days are Sunday and Thursday.

At **Joyabaj** women weave fascinating *huipiles* and there is a colourful Sunday market, followed by a procession at about noon from the church led by the elders with drums and pipes. This was a stopping place on the old route from Mexico to Antigua. There is good walking in the wooded hills around, for example north to Chorraxaj (two hours), or across the Río Cocol south to Piedras Blancas to see blankets being woven. During fiesta week (9-15 August) Joyabaj has a *Palo Volador* and other traditional dances. There is a restaurant next to the Esso station on the Santa Cruz end of the plaza with a bank opposite (will change US dollars cash).

The road east to Cobán

The road east from **Sacapulas** is one of the most beautiful mountain roads in all Guatemala, with magnificent scenery in the narrow valleys. There is accommodation in **Uspantán** and this is the place to stay for the night enroute to Cobán. The road is not paved beyond Uspantán.

It's a five-hour walk from Uspantán south to **Chimul**, the birthplace of **Rigoberta Menchú**, Nobel Peace Prize winner in 1992. The village was virtually wiped out during the 1980s, but the settlement is coming to life again. Only pickups go to the village.

Listings Santa Cruz del Quiché and around

Where to stay

There are several very basic options around the bus arrival/departure area.

$ Rey K'iché
8 Calle, 0-9, 2 blocks from bus terminal.
Clean, comfortable, hot water, parking, restaurant, TV.

$ San Pascual
7 Calle, 0-43, 2 blocks south of the central plaza, T5555-1107.
Good location, with bath, cheaper without, quiet, locked parking.

The road east to Cobán
There are a couple of *hospedajes* in Uspantán.

$ Galindo
4 blocks east of the Parque Central.
Clean, friendly, recommended.

Restaurants

Try *sincronizadas*, hot tortillas baked with cubed ham, spiced chicken and cheese.

$ La Cabañita Café
1 Av, 1-17.
Charming, small café with pinewood furniture, home-made pies and cakes, excellent breakfasts (pancakes, cereals, etc), eggs any way you want 'em, and great snacks, such as *sincronizadas*.

$ La Toscan
1 Av just north of the church, same road as La Cabañita.
A little pizza and *pastelería* with checked cloth-covered tables. Lasagne lunch a bargain with garlic bread and pizza by the slice also.

Transport

Bus
Terminal at 10 Calle y 1 Av, Zona 5.
To **Guatemala City**, passing through **Chichicastenango**, at 0300 until 1700, 3 hrs, US$4.50. To **Nebaj** and **Cotzal**, 8 a day, US$3.20, 2 hrs. Buses leave, passing through Sacapulas (1 hr, US$2.50), roughly every hour from 0800-2100. To **Uspantán**, via **Sacapulas**, for **Cobán** and **San Pedro Carchá** every hour, 2 hrs, US$3.90. To **Joyabaj**, several daily, via Chiché and Zacualpa, US$1.80, 1½ hrs. 1st at 0800 with buses going on to the capital. Last bus back to Quiché at 1600. It is possible to get to **Huehuetenango** in a day via Sacapulas, then pickup from bridge to **Aguacatán** and bus from there to Huehuetenango. Last bus to Huehue from Aguacatán, 1600. Daily buses also to **Quetzaltenango**, **San Marcos**, and to **Panajachel**. To **Joyabaj**, **Joyita** bus from Guatemala City, 10 a day between 0200 and 1600, 5 hrs, US$1.80. There are buses from Quiché to **San Andrés Sajcabaja**.

The road east to Cobán
Bus and truck
Several trucks to Cobán, daily in the morning from **Sacapulas**; 7 hrs if you're lucky, usually much longer. Start very early if you wish to make it to Cobán the same day. **Transportes Mejía** from Aguacatán to **Cobán** stops in Sacapulas on Tue and Sat mornings. Also possible to take Quiché–Uspantán buses (0930, 1300, 1500), passing Sacapulas at about 1030, 1400, 1600. Then take the early morning buses at 0300 and 0500 from Uspantán to Cobán or the **Transportes Mejía** buses. After that, pickups leave when full. Hitchhiking to Cobán is also possible. Buses to **Quiché** 0300, 2200, other early morning departures.

The Ixil Triangle
spectacular forested mountainous scenery with great walking

The Ixil Triangle is made of up of the highland communities of Nebaj, Chajul and Cotzal set in the beautiful Cuchumatanes mountains, although sadly, out of local necessity, many of the slopes have been badly deforested and the wood burnt for fires. The traditional dress of the Nebaj women – an explosion of primary colours – is spectacular. Much of this area was decimated during the Civil War and then repopulated with the introduction of 'model villages' established by the government. Evidence of wartime activities can still be seen and more remote Maya Ixil-speaking villages are gradually opening up to visitors with the introduction of hostel and trekking facilities.

Nebaj and around
The town of Nebaj is high in the Cuchumatanes Mountains and its green slopes are often layered with mist. It is coloured by the beautiful dress worn by the local women, in an extravaganza of predominantly green, with red, yellow, orange, white and purple. The *corte* is mainly maroon with vertical stripes of black and yellow; some are bright red, and the *huipil* is of a geometric design. The women also wear a headdress with colourful bushy pom-poms on them. The men hardly ever wear the traditional costume; their jacket is red and embroidered in black designs. The main plaza is dominated by a large, simple white church. At the edge of the plaza there are weaving cooperatives selling *cortes, huipiles* and handicrafts from the town and the surrounding area – bargaining is possible. When you arrive, boys will meet you from incoming buses and will guide you to a *hospedaje* – they expect a tip. Nebaj has Sunday and Thursday markets and a fiesta on 12-15 August with traditional dancing. There is an excellent website for Nebaj, www.nebaj.com, run by **Solidaridad Internacional**, with useful phrases in Ixil and your daily Maya horoscope. There's a **tourist office** ① *6a Av and 8a Calle Cantón Vitzal, T7755-8337.*

La Tumba de la Indígena Maya is a shrine a 15-minute walk outside Nebaj where some of those massacred during the war were buried. Take the same route as to Ak'Tzumbal, but at the bottom of the very steep hill, immediately after the bridge over the river, take a left, walk straight on over a paved road, then you come to a small junction – carry straight on until you see a minor crossroads on a path with an orange house gate to your left. Look up and you will see a small building. This is the shrine. Walk to your right where you will see a steep set of stairs leading to the shrine.

There is a walk to **Ak'Tzumbal**, through fields with rabbits, and through long, thin earth tunnels used by the military and guerrillas during the war. You need a guide to walk this cross-country route. Alternatively, you can take the road to Ak'Tzumbal, where the new houses still display signs warning of the danger of land mines. Walk down 15 Avenida de Septiembre away from the church, and take a left just before **El Triangulo** gas station past **El Viajero Hospedaje**, then left and then right down a very steep hill and keep walking (1½ hours). When you reach a small yellow tower just before a fork take the right (the left goes to Salquil Grande) to reach the model village. Above the village of Ak'Tzumbal is **La Pista**, an airstrip used during the war. Next to it bomb craters scar the landscape. Only a few avocado trees, between the bomb holes, survive, and the *gasolinera* to refuel planes, is still there, although it is now covered in corrugated iron. Ask around for directions.

Chajul and Cotzal

Chajul, the second largest village in the Ixil Triangle, is known for its part in the Civil War, where Rigoberta Menchú's brother was killed in the plaza, as relayed in her book *I, Rigoberta Menchú*. According to the Nobel Peace Prize winner, on 9 September 1979 her 16-year-old brother Petrocinio was kidnapped after being turned in for 15 quetzales. He was tortured in the plaza by the army along with numerous others. Villagers were forced to watch the torture under threat of being branded communists. People were set on fire, but the onlookers had weapons and looked ready to fight. This caused the army to withdraw. Chajul's main fiesta is the second Friday in Lent. There is also a pilgrimage to Christ of Golgotha on the second Friday in Lent, beginning the Wednesday before (the image is escorted by 'Romans' in blue police uniforms). Market day is Tuesday and Friday. It is possible to walk from Chajul to Cotzal. It's a six-hour walk from Nebaj to Chajul.

Cotzal is spread over a large area on a number of steep hills. The village's fiesta is 22-25 June, peaking on the day of St John the Baptist (24 June). Market days are Wednesday and Saturday. You can hire bikes from **Maya Tour** on the plaza next to the church. Nebaj to Cotzal is a pleasant four-hour walk. There's no accommodation or restaurants in other small villages and it is difficult to specify what transport is available in this area as trucks and the occasional pickup or commercial van are affected by road and weather conditions. For this reason, be prepared to have to spend the night in villages.

Where to stay

$ Solidaridad Internacional
Supports 6 hostels in the villages of
Xexocom, **Chortiz**, **Xeo**, **Cocop**, **Cotzol**
and **Párramos Grande** where there
is room for 5 people. Contact them
at the PRODONT-IXIL office, Av 15 de
Septiembre, Nebaj.

Nebaj and around

$$-$ Hotel Turansa
1 block from plaza down 5 Calle,
T7755-8219.
Tiny rooms, but very clean, soap, towels,
2nd-floor rooms are nicer, cable TV
and parking, little shop in entrance,
phone service.

$ Hospedaje Esperanza
6 Av, 2-36.
Very friendly, clean, hot showers
in shared bathroom, noisy when
evangelical churches nearby have
activities, hotel is cleaner than it looks
from the outside.

$ Hostal Ixil Don Juan
0 Av A, 1 Calle B, Canton Simocol. Take
Av 15 de Septiembre and take a left at
Comedor Sarita, opposite grey office of
PRODONT-IXIL, then it's 100 m to the
right, on the right, T7755-4014/1529.
Part of **Programa Quiché**, run with
the support of the EU, there are 6 beds
in 2 rooms, each bed with a locked
strongbox, and hot showers. The colonial
building has a traditional sauna, *chuj*.

$ Hotel Mayan Ixil
On north side of main square,
T7755-8168.
Just 5 rooms with private bath and gas
hot water. Small restaurant overlooking
the plaza, internet service downstairs.

$ Ilebal Tenam
Cantón Simecal, bottom of Av 15 de
Septiembre, road to Chajul, T7755-8039.
Hot water, shared and private bath,
very clean, friendly, parking inside,
attractive decor.

$ Media Luna MediaSol
T5749-7450, www.nebaj.com/hostel.htm.
A backpackers' hostel close to **El**
Descanso restaurant with dorms and
private rooms. The hostel's also got a
little kitchenette, DVD player and Wi-Fi.

Chajul
There are a couple of very basic
hospedajes in town.

Cotzal

$ Hostal Doña Teresa.
Has a sauna, patio and honey products
for sale.

Restaurants

Nebaj and around
Boxboles are squash leaves rolled
tightly with *masa* and chopped meat
or chicken, boiled and served with salsa
and fresh orange juice.

$ El Descanso
Popular volunteer hang-out, good food
and useful information about their other
community-based projects (see www.
nebaj.com).

$ Maya Ixil
On the Parque Central.
Substantial food, local and international dishes, pleasant family atmosphere.

$ Pizza del César
Daily 0730-2100.
Breakfasts, mouth-wateringly good strawberry cake, and hamburgers as well as pizzas.

Cotzal

$ Comedor and Hospedaje El Maguey.
Bland meals, but a decent size, plus drink, are served up for for US$1.70. Don't stay here though, unless you're desperate.

What to do

Nebaj and around
Guías Ixiles *(El Descanso Restaurant), www.nebaj.com.* ½- to 3-day hikes, bike rental. There's also a 3-day hike to Todos Santos.
Solidaridad Internacional, *Av 15 de Septiembre, www.nebaj.org. Inside the PRODONT-IXIL (Proyecto de Promoción de Infraestructuras y Ecoturismo) office, in a grey building on the right 1 block after the Gasolinera El Triángulo on the road to Chajul.* For further information call in to see the director Pascual, who is very helpful. 2-, 3- and 4-day hikes, horses available. Options to stay in community *posadas*, with packages available, from 1 to 4 days, full board, from about US$100-200 per person.

Chajul and Cotzal
Ask Teresa at **Hostal Doña Teresa** about trips from the Cotzal or ask for Sebastián Xel Rivera who leads 1-day camping trips.

Transport

Nebaj and around
Bus
The bus ride to Quiché is full of fabulous views and hair-raising bends but the road is now fully paved. Buses to **Quiché** (US$3.20, 2½ hrs) passing through **Sacapulas** (1¾ hrs from Nebaj, US$1.30) leave hourly from 0500-1530. Bus to **Cobán** leaves Gazolinera Quetzal at 0500, 4-5 hrs, US$6.50. Cobán to Nebaj at 1300. Alternatively get to Sacapulas on the main road, and wait for a bus.

Chajul and Cotzal
Bus
Buses to Chajul and Cotzal do not run on a set schedule. It is best to ask the day before you want to travel, at the bus station. There are buses and numerous pickups on Sun when villagers come to Nebaj for its market, which would be a good day to visit the villages. Alternatively, bargain with a local pickup driver to take you on a trip.

Western
highlands

Just before the volcanic highlands reach their highest peaks, this part of the western highlands takes the form of scores of small market towns and villages, each with its own character: the loud animal market at San Francisco El Alto, the extra-planetary landscape at Momostenango, and its Maya cosmovision centre, and the dancing extravaganzas at Totonicapán. The modern *ladino* town of Huehuetenango sits at the gateway to the Sierra de los Cuchumatanes, within which hides, in a cold gash in a sky-hugging valley, the indigenous town and weaving centre of Todos Santos Cuchumatán.

North to Huehuetenango

highland Mayan towns with colourful markets

Nahualá and Cuatro Caminos

Before the major four-way junction of Cuatro Caminos, the Pan-American Highway runs past Nahualá, a Maya village at 2470 m. The traditional *traje* is distinctive and best seen on market days on Thursday and Sunday, when finely embroidered cuffs and collars are sold, as well as very popular *huipiles*. The **Fiesta de Santa Catalina** is on 23-26 November (25th is the main day).

There is an unpaved all-weather road a little to the north and 16 km longer, from Los Encuentros (on the Pan-American Highway) through Totonicapán (40 km) to San Cristóbal Totonicapán. The route from Chichicastenango to Quiché, Xecajá and Totonicapán takes a day by car or motorcycle, but is well worth taking and recommended by cyclists. There are no buses. There is also a scenic road from Totonicapán to Santa Cruz del Quiché via San Antonio Ilotenango. It takes one hour by car and two hours by pickup truck. There are no buses on this route either.

Cuatro Caminos is a busy junction with roads, east to Totonicapán, west to Los Encuentros, north to Huehuetenango and south to Quetzaltenango. Buses stop here every few seconds so you will never have to wait long for a connection. There is a petrol station and lots of vendors to keep you fed and watered. Just north of Cuatro Caminos is **San Cristóbal Totonicapán**, noted for its *huipiles*.

Totonicapán

The route to San Miguel Totonicapán (altitude 2500 m), the capital of its department, passes through pine-forested hillsides, pretty red-tiled roofs and *milpas* of maize on the roadside. The 18th-century beige church stands on one of the main squares, unfortunately now a car park, at 6 y 7 Avenida between 3 and 4 Calle. The market is considered by Guatemalans to be one of the cheapest, and it is certainly very colourful. Saturday is the main market noted for ceramics and cloth, with a small gathering on Tuesdays. There is a traditional dance fiesta on 12-13 August, music concerts and a chance to see *cofradía* rituals. The annual **feria** is on 24-30 September in celebration of the Archangel San Miguel, with the main fiesta on 29 September. The **Casa de Cultura** ① *8 Av, 2-17, T5630-0554, www. larutamayaonline.com/aventura.html*, run by Carlos Humberto Molina, displays an excellent collection of fiesta masks, made on site at the mask factory, and for sale. It has a cultural programme with a number of tour options, cultural activities and bicycle adventures. You need to reserve in advance.

San Francisco El Alto

San Francisco stands high on a great big mound in the cold mountains at 2640 m above the great valley in which lie Totonicapán, San Cristóbal and Quetzaltenango. It is famous for its market, which is stuffed to capacity, and for the animal market held above town, where creatures from piglets to kittens to budgies are for sale. The town's fiesta is on 1-6 October, in honour of St Francis of Assisi.

The market is packed to bursting point on Fridays with locals buying all sorts, including woollen blankets for resale throughout the country. It's an excellent place for buying woven and embroidered textiles of good quality, but beware of pickpockets. Go early to see as much action as possible. Climb up through the town for 10 minutes to see the animal market (ask for directions all the time as it's hard to see 5 m ahead, the place is so packed).

The **church** on the main square is magnificent; notice the double-headed Hapsburg eagle. It is often full on market days with locals lighting candles, and their live purchases ignoring the 'Silencio' posters. The white west front of the church complements the bright colours of the rest of the plaza, especially the vivid green and pink of the Municipalidad.

Momostenango

Momostenango is set in a valley with ribbons of houses climbing higgledy-piggledy out of the valley floor. Momostenango, at 2220 m, represents *Shol Mumus* in K'iche', meaning 'among the hills', and on its outlying hills are numerous altars and a hilltop image of a Maya god. Some 300 medicine men are said to practise in the town. Their insignia of office is a little bag containing beans and quartz crystals. Momostenango is the chief blanket-weaving centre in the country, and locals can be seen beating the blankets (*chamarras*) on stones, to shrink them. There are also weird stone peaks known as the *riscos* – eroded fluted columns and draperies formed of volcanic ash – on the outskirts of town.

The town is quiet except on Wednesday and Sunday market days, the latter being larger and good for weaving, especially the blankets. On non-market days try **Tienda Manuel de Jesús Agancel** ① *1 Av, 1-50, Zona 4, near bank*, for good bargains, especially blankets and carpets. There is also **Artesanía Paclom** ① *corner of 1 Calle and 3 Av, Zona 2*, just five minutes along the road to Xela. This family have the weaving looms in their back yard and will show you how it's all done if you ask.

The **Feast of Wajshakib Batz' Oj** (pronounced 'washakip'), is celebrated by hundreds of *Aj Kij* (Maya priests) who come for ceremonies. New priests are initiated on this first day of the ritual new year; the initiation lasting the year. The town's very popular fiesta is between 21 July and 4 August, with the town's patron saint of Santiago Apóstol celebrated on 25 July. The **Baile de Convites** is held in December with other dances on 8, 12 and 31 December and 1 January. At **Takilibén Maya Misión** ① *3 Av 'A', 6-85, Zona 3, T7736-5537, wajshakibbatz13@yahoo.es*, just after the Texaco garage on the right on the way in from Xela, Chuch Kajaw (day keeper/senior priest) Rigoberto Itzep welcomes all interested in learning more about Maya culture and cosmology. He offers courses in culture and does Maya horoscope readings. He also has a **Maya sauna** (*Tuj*).

Just outside town are three sets of *riscos* (eroded columns of sandstone with embedded quartz particles), creating a strange eerie landscape of pinnacles that look like rocket lollipop ice creams. To get there, take the 2 Calle, Zona 2, which is the one to the right of the church, for five minutes until you see a sign on a building pointing to the left. Follow the signs until you reach the earth structures (five to 10 minutes).

Listings North to Huehuetenango

Where to stay

Totonicapán

$ Hospedaje San Miguel
3 Calle, 7-49, Zona 1, T7766-1452.
Rooms with or without bath, hot water, communal TV.

$ Pensión Blanquita
13 Av and 4 Calle.
20 rooms, hot showers, good. Opposite this *pensión* is a Shell station.

San Francisco El Alto

$ Hotel Vásquez
4 Av, 11-53, T7738-4003.
Rooms all with private bathroom.
Parking.

$ Vista Hermosa
2 Calle, 2-23, T7738-4010.
36 rooms, cheaper without bathroom, hot water, TV.

Momostenango

$ Estiver Ixcel
1 Calle, 4-15, Zona 4, downhill away from plaza, T7736-5036.
12 rooms, hot water, cheaper without bath, clean.

$ Hospedaje y Comedor Paclom
Close to central plaza, at 1 Calle, 1-71, Zona 4.
Pretty inner courtyard with caged birds and plants, hot water in shared bathrooms.

$ La Villa
1 Av, 1-13, Zona 1, below bank,
T7736-5108.
6 rooms, warm water only, clean and
nicely presented.

Restaurants

Totonicapán

$ Comedor Brenda 2
9 Av, 3-31.
Good, serving local food.

$ Comedor Letty
3 Calle, 8-18.
Typical Guatemalan fare.

Momostenango

$ Comedor Santa Isabel
Next door to Hospedaje y Comedor
Paclom.
Friendly, cheap and good breakfasts.

$ Flipper
1 Calle y 2 Av A.
Good *licuados* and a range of fruit juices.

$ Hospedaje y Comedor Paclom
Close to the central plaza and where
buses arrive from Xela, 1 Calle, 1-71,
Zona 4.
Cheap meals, including snacks in a
pretty inner courtyard.

Transport

Totonicapán
Bus Every 15 mins to **Quetzaltenango**,
US$0.40, 45 mins. To **Los Encuentros**,
US$2.20. To **Cuatro Caminos**, 30 mins,
US$0.30.

San Francisco El Alto
Bus 2 km along the Pan-American
Hwy heading north from Cuatro
Caminos is a paved road, which runs
to San Francisco El Alto (3 km) and
then to Momostenango (19 km). Bus
from **Quetzaltenango**, 50 mins on Fri,
US$0.75. The last bus back is at 1800.

Momostenango
Bus From **Cuatro Caminos** (US$0.50)
and **Quetzaltenango**, 1-1½ hrs. Buses to
Xela every 30 mins from 0430-1600.

Huehuetenango and around

a pleasant, large town and a busy transport hub

Huehuetenango (altitude 1905 m) – colloquially known as Huehue – offers
little to detain you. However, it is an important transport centre serving the
Cuchumatanes Mountains and the Mexican border. Its bus terminal, 2 km from
town, is one of the busiest in the country. There are Maya ruins near the town,
which were badly restored by the infamous United Fruit Company, and new
adventure tourism opportunities opening up nearby. Trips, including horse rides,
to more remote spots in the Huehuetenango region to see forests, haciendas and
lakes are organized by Unicornio Azul. A useful website is www.interhuehue.com.

The neoclassical **cathedral** was built between 1867 and 1874, destroyed by
earthquake in 1902, and took 10 years to repair. In 1956, the image of the patron
saint, the Virgen de la Concepción was burnt in a fire. Then, during the 1976
earthquake, 80% of it was damaged, save the bells, façade and cupola. The skyline

to the north of the city is dominated by the Sierrra de los Cuchumatanes, the largest area over 3000 m in Central America.

The ruins of **Zaculeu** ⓘ *0800-1800, US$6.40*, the old capital of the Mam Maya, are 5 km west of Huehuetenango on top of a rise with steep drops on three sides – a site chosen because of these natural defence measures. Its original name in Mam was *Xinabajul*, meaning 'between ravines'. In K'iche' it means 'white earth'. It was first settled in the Early Classic period (AD 250-600), but it flourished during the late post-Classic (AD 1200-1530). In July 1525, Gonzalo de Alvarado, the brother of Guatemala's conqueror, Pedro de Alvarado, set out for Zaculeu with 80 Spaniards, 40 horses and 2000 indigenous fighters, passing Mazatenango and Totonicapán on the way. The battle lasted four months, during which time the soldiers and residents of Zaculeu were dying of hunger, and eating their dead neighbours. The weakened Kaibil Balam, the Zaculeu *cacique* (chief), called for a meeting with Gonzalo. Gonzalo told the Mam chief that peace was not on the cards. Negotiations followed with the outcome being that Kaibil Balam be instructed in Christianity, obey the Spanish king and leave the city, whereupon Gonzalo de Alvarado would take possession of the Mam kingdom settlement in the name of the Spanish crown.

Aguacatán

The women of Aguacatán (altitude 1670 m) wear the most stunning headdresses in the country. On sale in *tiendas* in town, they are a long, slim belt of woven threads using many colours. The women also wear beautiful clothes: the *cortes*

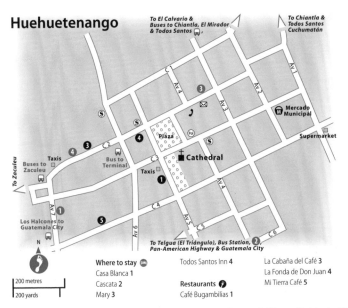

Huehuetenango

To El Calvario &
Buses to Chiantla, El Mirador
& Todos Santos

To Chiantla &
Todos Santos
Cuchumatán

Mercado
Municipal

Supermarket

Plaza

Cathedral

To Zaculeu
Buses to
Zaculeu

Taxis

Bus to
Terminal

Taxis

Los Halcones to
Guatemala City

To Telgua (El Triángulo), Bus Station,
Pan-American Highway & Guatemala City

N

200 metres

200 yards

Where to stay
Casa Blanca 1
Cascata 2
Mary 3

Todos Santos Inn 4

Restaurants
Café Bugambilias 1

La Cabaña del Café 3
La Fonda de Don Juan 4
Mi Tierra Café 5

are dark with horizontal stripes of yellow, pink, blue and green. The town fiesta is 40 days after Holy Week, Virgen de la Encarnación.

Towards Todos Santos Cuchumatán

To get to Todos Santos, you have to climb the front range of the Cuchumatanes Mountains above Chiantla by a steep road from Huehuetenango. **Chiantla** has the **Luna Café** with art gallery and the nearby paleontological site of **El Mamutz**. Looking down on a clear day the cathedral at Huehuetenango resembles a blob of orange blancmange on the plain. At the summit, at about 3300 m, there is **El Mirador**.

The paved road continues over bleak moorland to Paquix where the road divides. The unpaved road to the north continues to Soloma. The other to the west goes through Aldea Chiabel, noted for its outhouses, more obvious than the small dwellings they serve. Here, giant agave plants appear to have large pom-poms attached, reminiscent of the baubles on Gaudí's Sagrada Familia in Barcelona. On this journey you often pass through cloud layer, eventually surfacing above it. On cloudier days you will be completely submerged until descending again to Huehuetenango. The road crosses a pass at 3394 m before a difficult long descent to Todos Santos, about 50 km from Huehuetenango.

The walk northwest from Chiantla to Todos Santos Cuchumatanes can be done in around 12-14 hours, or better, two days, staying overnight at **El Potrillo** in the barn owned by Rigoberto Alva. This route crosses one of the highest parts of the sierra at over 3500 m. Alternatively, cycle the 40-km part-gravel road, which is steep in places, but very rewarding.

Listings Huehuetenango and around *map p99*

Where to stay

Huehuetenango

$$ Casa Blanca
7 Av, 3-41, T7769-0777.
Comfortable, good restaurant in a pleasant garden, buffet breakfast, set lunch, very popular and good value, parking.

$$ Cascata
Lote 4, 42, Zona 5, Col Alvarado, Calzada Kaibil Balam, close to the bus station, T7769-0795, www.hotelcascata.ya.st.
Newish hotel with 16 rooms with Wi-Fi and private bathrooms. It is owned by

Dutch, French and English folk and the service is excellent.

$ Mary
2 Calle, 3-52, T7764-1618.
With bath, cheaper without, good beds, hot water, cable TV, parking, clean, quiet, safe, well-maintained, good value. Recommended.

$ Todos Santos Inn
2 Calle, 6-74, T7764-1241.
Shared bath and private bath available, hot water, TV, helpful, clean, laundry, some rooms a bit damp, luggage stored. Recommended.

Restaurants

Huehuetenango

$$-$ La Cabaña del Café
2 Calle, 6-50.
Log cabin café with to-die-for cappuccino, snack food and good *chapín* breakfasts, good atmosphere. Recommended.

$ Café Bugambilias
5 Av 3-59, on the plaza.
Large, unusual 4-storey building, most of which is a popular, cheap, restaurant, very good breakfasts, *almuerzos*, sandwiches. Recommended.

$ La Fonda de Don Juan
2 Calle, 5-35.
Italian restaurant and bar (try the *cavatini*), sandwiches, big choice of desserts, *licuados*, coffees, good pizzas, also *comida típica*, with reasonable prices all served in a bright environment with red and white checked tablecloths.

$ Mi Tierra Café
4 Calle, 6-46, T7764-1473.
Good drinks and light meals, Mexican offerings; try the *fajitas*, nice setting, popular with locals and travellers. Recommended.

What to do

Unicornio Azul, *based in Chancol, T5205-9328, www.unicornioazul.com.* Horse-riding trips, trekking, mountain biking and birdwatching in the Cuchumatanes.

Transport

Huehuetenango
Bus and taxi
Local From the terminal to town, take 'Centro' minibus, which pulls up at cathedral, 5 mins. Taxis from behind the covered market. Walking takes 20-25 mins. Bus leaves Salvador Osorio School, final Calle 2, every 30 mins, 15 mins, to **Zaculeu**, last return 1830. Taxi, US$8, including waiting time. To walk takes about 1 hr; either take 6 Av north, cross the river and follow the road to the left, through Zaculeu modern village to the ruins, or go past the school and turn right beyond the river. The signs are barely visible.

Long distance To **Guatemala City**, 5 hrs, US$11, **Los Halcones**, 7 Av, 3-62, Zona 1 (they do not leave from the terminal) at 0430, 0700, 1400, reliable. From the bus terminal there are numerous services daily to the capital from 0215-1600 via **Chimaltenango**, 5 hrs, US$4. Via **Mazatenango** there are 5 daily.

North To **Todos Santos Cuchumatán**, 10 daily until 1630, 2-3 hrs, US$3.60. To **Barillas**, via **San Juan Ixcoy** (2½ hrs), **Soloma** (3 hrs), and **San Mateo Ixtatan** (7 hrs), 10 daily from 0200-2330, US$7. There are also buses to **San Rafael la Independencia** passing through Soloma and **Sta Eulalia**.

Northwest To **La Mesilla** for Mexico, frequent buses between 0530-1800, US$3.50, 2½ hrs, last bus returning to Huehue, 1800. To **Nentón**, via La Mesilla twice a day. To **Gracias a Dios**, several times a day.

South To **Quetzaltenango**, 13 a day from 0600-1600, US$3, 2-2¼ hrs. To **Cuatro Caminos**, US$2, 2 hrs. To **Los Encuentros**, for Lake Atitlán and Chichicastenango, 3 hrs.

East To **Aguacatán**, 12 daily, 0600-1900, 1 hr 10 mins, US$1.20. To **Nebaj** you have to get to Sacapulas via Aguacatán. To **Sacapulas**, 1130, 1245.

To **Cobán**, take the earliest bus/pickup to Aguacatán and then Sacapulas and continue to Uspantán to change for Cobán.

Aguacatán
Bus
From **Huehue**, 1 hr 10 mins. It is 26 km east of Huehuetenango on a semi-paved route (good views). Returning between 0445 and 1600. Buses and pickups for **Sacapulas** and for onward connections to Nebaj and Cobán leave from the main street going out of town. Wait anywhere along there to catch your ride. It is 1½ hrs from Aguacatán to Sacapulas. To **Guatemala City** at 0300, 1100.

Todos Santos Cuchumatán and around

indigenous village in a spectacular mountain setting

★High in the Cuchumatanes, the Mam-speaking Todos Santeros maintain a traditional way of life with their striking, bright, indigenous dress and their adherence to the 260-day Tzolkin calendar. Todos Santos (altitude 2470 m) is hemmed in by 3800-m-high mountains either side that squeeze it into one long, 2-km street down the valley. The town is famous for its weaving, and even more famous for the horse race, see box, page 103.

Some of Guatemala's best weaving is done in Todo Santos. Fine *huipiles* may be bought in the cooperative on the main street and direct from the makers. The men wear the famous red-and-white striped trousers. Some wear a black wool over-trouser piece. Their jackets are white, pink, purple and red-striped with beautifully coloured, and intricately embroidered, collars and cuffs. Their straw hat is wrapped with a blue band. You can buy the embroidered cuffs and collars for men's shirts, the red trousers, and gorgeous colourful crocheted bags made by the men. The women wear navy blue *cortes* with thin, light blue, vertical stripes.

There is a colourful Saturday market and a smaller one on Wednesday. The **church** near the park was built in 1580.

Around Todos Santos
The closest walk is to **Las Letras**, where the words 'Todos Santos' are spelt out in white stone on a hillside above the town. The walk takes an hour. To get there take the path down the side of **Restaurant Cuchumatlán**. The highest point of the Cuchumatanes, and the highest non-volcanic peak in the country, **La Torre** at 3837 m, is to the northeast of Todos Santos and can be reached from the village of **Tzichem** on the road to Concepción Huista. When clear, it's possible to see the top of Volcán Santa María, one of the highest volcanoes in the country. The hike takes about five hours. The best way to do it is to start in the afternoon and spend the night near the top. It is convenient for camping, with wood but no water. A compass is essential in case of mist. From Todos Santos, you can also hike south to **San Juan Atitán**, four to five hours, where the locals wear an interesting *traje típico*. Market days are on Mondays and Thursdays. From there you can hike to the Pan-American Highway; it's a one day walk. The local fiesta is 22-26 June.

ON THE ROAD

Todos Santos festival

The horse racing festival of Todos Santos is one of the most celebrated and spectacular in Central America – it is also a frenzied day that usually degenerates into a drunken mess. Quite simply riders race between two points, having a drink at each turn until they fall off.

According to Professor Margarito Calmo Cruz, the origins of the fiesta lie in the 15th or 16th century with the arrival of the conquistadores to Todos Santos. They arrived on horses wearing large, colourful clothes with bright scarves flowing down their backs and feathers in their hats. The locals experimented, imitating them, enjoyed it and the tradition was born.

When the day begins, the men are pretty tipsy, but sprightly and clean. The race is frantic and colourful with scarves flying out from the backs of the men. As the day wears on, they get completely smashed, riding with arms outstretched – whip in one hand and beer bottle in the other. They are mudspattered, dishevelled and are moaning and groaning from the enjoyment and the alcohol which must easily have reached near comatose level. At times the riders fall, and look pretty lifeless. They are dragged by the scruff of the neck, regardless of serious injury or death, to the edge of the fence as quickly as possible, to avoid trampling.

The men guzzle gallons of beer and the aim is to continue racing all day. A fall means instant dismissal from the race. There are wardens on the side lines with batons, whose primary job is the welfare of the horses, changing them when they see necessary. But they also deal with protesting fallen riders, who try and clamber back onto their horses. By the end of the day the spectacle is pretty grotesque. The horses are drenched with sweat and wild-eyed with fear. The men look hideous and are paralytic from booze. The edge of the course and the town is littered with bodies.

The race takes place on the road that winds its way out of town, not the incoming road from Huehue. It starts at 0800. There are about 15 riders on the course at any one time. It continues until noon, stops for *cerveza* guzzling and begins again at 1400, ending at 1700.

Jacaltenango to the Mexican border

The road from Todos Santos continues northwest through **Concepción Huista**. Here the women wear towels as shawls and Jacalteco is spoken. The fiesta, 29 January-3 February, has fireworks and dancing. The hatmaker in Canton Pilar supplies the hats for Todos Santos, he welcomes viewers and will make a hat to your specifications (but if you want a typical Todos Santos leather *cincho*, buy it there).

Beyond Jacaltenango is **Nentón**, and **Gracias a Dios** at the Mexican border. When the road north out of Huehue splits at Paquix, the right fork goes to **San Mateo Ixtatán**, with ruins nearby. The road from Paquix crosses the roof of the Cuchumatanes, before descending to **San Juan Ixcoy, Soloma** and **Santa Eulalia**, where the people speak O'anjob'al as they do in Soloma. East along a scenic route is **Barillas**. There are several *pensiones* in these places and regular buses from Huehue.

Where to stay

Reservations are necessary in the week before the Nov horse race, but even if the town is full, locals offer their homes.

$ Casa Familiar
Up the hill, close to central park, T7783-0656.
Run by the friendly family of Santiaga Mendoza Pablo. Hot shower, sauna, breakfast, dinner, delicious banana bread, spectacular view, popular. The Mendoza family give weaving lessons.

$ Hotel La Paz
Friendly, great view of the main street from balconies, excellent spot for the 1 Nov fiesta, shared showers not great, enclosed parking.

$ Hotel Mam
Above the central park, next to Hotelito Todos Santos.
Friendly, clean, hot water, but needs 1 hr to warm up, not too cold in the rooms as an open fire warms the building, good value.

$ Hotelito Todos Santos
Above the central park.
Hot water, clean, small café, but beware of boys taking you to the hotel quoting one price, and then on arrival, finding the price has mysteriously gone up.

Around Todos Santos

$ Hospedaje San Diego
San Juan Atitán.

Only 3 beds, basic, friendly, clean, food available.

Restaurants

There are *comedores* on the 2nd floor of the market selling very cheap meals.

$ Comedor Katy
Will prepare vegetarian meals on request, good-value *menú del día*.

$ Cuchumatlán
Has sandwiches, pizza and pancakes, and is popular at night.

Festivals

1 Nov Horse race. The festival begins on 21 Oct. See box, page 103.
2 Nov Day of the Dead, when locals visit the cemetery and leave flowers and food.

Shopping

The following shops all sell bags, trousers, shirts, *huipiles*, jackets and clothes. The best bargains are at **Tienda Maribel**, up the hill from Casa Familiar, and **Cooperativa Estrella de Occidente**, on the main street. **Casa Mendoza**, just beyond Tienda Maribel, is where Telésforo Mendoza makes clothes to measure. **Domingo Calmo** also makes clothes to measure. His large, brown house with tin roof is on the main road to the Ruinas (5 mins); follow the road up from Casa Familiar. Ask for **Casa de Domingo**.

Bus

To **Huehuetenango**, 2-3 hrs, crowded Mon and Fri, 0400, 0500, 0600, 0615-0630, 1145, 1230, 1300. Possible changes on Sat so ask beforehand. For petrol, ask at **El Molino**.

Jacaltenango to the Mexican border

Bus

From **Huehuetenango** at 0330, 0500, returning at 1130 and 1400; also pickups.

Quetzaltenango
& around

★ Quetzaltenango (commonly known as Xela, pronounced 'shayla') is the most important city in western Guatemala. It is set among a group of high mountains and volcanoes, one of which, Santa María, caused much death and destruction after an eruption in 1902. The bulk of the city is modern, but its 19th-century downtown revamp and its narrow streets give the centre more of a historic feel. There is a pleasant park with its beautifully restored façade of the colonial church. It is an excellent base from which to visit nearby hot springs, religious idols, volcanoes and market towns.

Quetzaltenango
Guatemala's second city, with a colonial cathedral and breathtaking views

The central park, Parque Centro América, is the focus of Quezaltenango (altitude 2335 m). It is surrounded by the cathedral, with its beautifully restored original colonial façade, and a number of elegant neoclassical buildings, constructed during the late 19th and early 20th century.

The modern cathedral, **Catedral de la Diócesis de los Altos**, was constructed in 1899 and is set back behind the original. The surviving façade of the 1535 **Catedral del Espíritu Santo** is beautiful, intricately carved and with restored portions of murals on its right side. On the south side of the park is the **Casa de la Cultura**. Inside are the **Museo de la Marimba** with exhibits and documents relating to the 1871 Liberal Revolution. On the right-hand side of the building is the totally curious **Museo de Historia Natural** ① *Mon-Fri 0800-1200, 1400-1800, US$0.90.* Deformed stuffed animals are cheek by jowl with pre-Columbian pottery, sports memorabilia, fizzy drink bottles, a lightning-damaged mirror and dinosaur remains. It satisfies the most morbid of curiosities with displays of a two-headed calf, Siamese twin pigs, an eight-legged goat, and a strange sea creature that looks like an alien, known as *Diabillo del Mar* (little sea devil). On the park's southwest side is the **Museo de Arte**, with a collection of contemporary Guatemalan art, and the **Museo del Ferrocarril Nacional de los Altos** ① *7 Calle and 12 Av, Mon-Fri 0800-1200, 1400-1800, US$0.90*, recounting the story of an electric railway between Xela and the Pacific slope. The **Banco de Occidente**, founded in 1881, and the first bank to opened in Guatemala, dominates the northern edge of the park. The overly wired-up **Municipalidad** straddles the eastern edge of the park with its neoclassical columns. Its first building blocks were laid in 1881, but it wasn't completed until 1897.

The stately **Teatro Municipal** (1892-1896) is on 14 Avenida y 1 Calle and can be visited outside of performance hours. Restored at a cost of four million quetzales, it has an imposing presence. To its left, on Avenida 14 "A", is the **Teatro Roma**. Building began in 1898, but was not completed until 1931, when it became the first cinema to open in Guatemala. It was restored in 2000 as a theatre with a capacity for 1400 and is open for performances.

There is a sickly green modern church, the **Sagrado Corazón**, on the Parque Benito Juárez near the market. Inside is a gigantic, freestanding, Chagall-influenced painting with swooping angels, and Christ in a glass box, built into the picture. The church of **La Transfiguración** ① *near the corner of 11 Calle and 5 Av, Zona 1*, houses the largest crucified Christ figure (San Salvador del Mundo) to be found in Central America – it is almost 3 m in height and now housed behind glass. At 20 Avenida and 4 Calle is the city's **Cementerio** ① *0700-1900*. Inside are the remains of the Quetzalteco President, Estrada Cabrera (1898-1920) in a small cream neoclassical temple. Behind his tomb are the unmarked graves of a large number of cholera victims wiped out in a 19th-century epidemic. Manuel Lisandra Barillas (Guatemalan President 1885-1892) is also entombed here. There is a small patio area known as Colonia Alemana lined with graves

Essential
Quetzaltenango

Best places to stay
Casa Seibel, page 113
Casa Xelajú, page 113
Orejas Hostal, page 112

Getting around

The town centre is compact and all sites and most services are within walking distance. The Santa Fe city bus goes between the terminal, the rotonda and the town centre. Out of town destination buses stop at the rotonda and it is quicker to get here from the town centre than to the Minerva Terminal. City buses for the terminal leave from 4 Calle and 13 Avenida, Zona 1, and those straight for the rotonda leave from 11 Avenida and 10 Calle, Zona 1, US$0.15.

A taxi within Zona 1, or from Zona 1 to a closer part of Zona 3, is about US$3.20.

Best restaurants
Cardinali, page 114
Restaurante Royal París, page 114
Restaurante Tertulianos Villa Lesbia, page 114
Sabor de India, page 114

BACKGROUND
Quetzaltenango

The most important battle of the Spanish conquest took place near Quetzaltenango when the great K'iche' warrior Tecún Umán was slain. In October 1902 the Volcán Santa María erupted, showering the city with half a metre of dust. An ash cloud soared 8.6 km into the air and some 1500 people were killed by volcanic fallout and gas. A further 3000 people died a short while later from malaria due to plagues of mosquitoes which had not been wiped out by the blast. Some 20 years on, a new volcano, born after the 1902 eruption, began to erupt. This smaller volcano, Santiaguito, spews clouds of dust and ash on a daily basis and is considered one of the most dangerous volcanoes in the world. The city's prosperity, as seen by the grand neoclassical architecture in the centre, was built on the back of the success of the coffee fincas on the nearby coastal plain. This led to the country's first bank being established here.

of German residents; a large area where those that died as martyrs in the civil war lie; and a memorial to those that perished in the September Revolution of 1897. The town's fiestas are 9-17 September, Holy Week and the October fiesta of La Virgen del Rosario.

North of Quetzaltenango

Between Quetzaltenango and Cuatro Caminos is the small *ladino* town of **Salcajá**, where *jaspé* skirt material has been woven since 1861. If you fancy a taste or a whiff of some potent liquor before bracing yourself for an entry into Quetzaltenango, then this is the place to halt. It is worth a visit not only for the booze but its famous church – the oldest in Central America – and for its textiles, often seen being produced in the streets. In 1524 the first church in Central America was founded by the conquering Spaniards. **San Jacinto** is a small church on 6 Avenida y 2 Calle; it may not always be open. *Caldo de frutas*, a highly alcoholic drink with quite a kick, is not openly sold but is made in the town and drunk on festive occasions. It is illegal to drink it in public places. It is a concoction of nances, cherries, peaches, apples and quinces and is left to ferment in rum. There is also *rompope*, a drink made with eggs. Salcajá is a town that also revolves around textiles, with shops on every street. Yarn is tied and dyed, untied, and wraps are then stretched around telephone poles along the road or on the riverside. One of these can be seen outside San Jacinto church. Market day is Tuesday.

San Andrés Xecul is a small village in stunning surroundings with an extraordinarily lurid-coloured church, 8 km north of Xela. Painted a deep-mustard yellow in 1900, its figurines, including angels, have been given blue wings and pastel-pink skirts. Climb the hill a bit above the town and catch a glimpse of the fantastic dome – mulitcoloured like a beach ball. With your back to the church climb the cobbled street leading up the right-hand side of the plaza to

Quetzaltenango

To Estado Mario Camposeco
& Olintepeque

Calzado
Rodolfo Robles

La Democracia Market
& Sagrado Corazón

To Transportes Alamo

C Oa

Parque
Gabriel
Pinillos

To 12,
Transportes Galgos,
Mont Blanc Shopping
Centre, Templo de
Minerva, Market &
Minerva Bus Terminal

Teatro
Roma

ZONA 1

Teatro
Municipal

C 0C

Agencia de
Viajes SAB

C 1

To Rotonda,
To Líneas América Buses
Cuatro Caminos & Guatemala City

La Rotonda,
& Guatemala City

To Cementerio

Vrisa

Museo de Ferrocarril
Nacional de los Altos
& Museo de Arte

Parque
Centro
América

Municipalidad

Cine

Despensa Familiar
Supermarket

Cathedral

Diagonal 13

Casa de
la Cultura

Centro
Comercial
Municipal

Buses to
Almolonga
& Zunil

N

| 100 metres |
| 100 yards |

Where to stay
7 Orejas Hostal **1** A1
Black Cat Hostel **10** B2
Casa Doña Mercedes **4** C1
Casa Mañen **6** C3
Casa Renaissance **5** D2
Casa San Bartolomé **14** C3

Casa Seibel **7** D3
Casa Xelajú **8** D1
Hostel Nim Sut **9** B3
Kiktem-Ja **11** C2
Modelo **12** B1
Villa del Centro **13** B2

Restaurants
Asados Puente **17** C2
Bakeshop **12** A1
Blue Angel Café **2** C1
Café Baviera **1** C2

Café y Chocolate
  La Luna **8** C3
Cardinali **20** B2
Chocolate Doña
  Pancha **18** D1
El Apaste **4** C2
El Deli Crepe **5** B2
La Chatia Artesana **3** C1
Las Calas **9** B1
Royal París & Guatemaya
  Intercultural Travel
  Agency **10** B1

Sabor de India **7** B1
Salón Tecún **16** C2
Tertulianos Villas Lesbia **6** B2
Ut'z Hua **11** B2

Bars & clubs
El Duende **14** A1
El Zaguán **13** A1
La Taberna de Don
  Rodrigo **15** A2
Ojalá **19** B1

a yellow and maroon chapel peering out across the valley. The view from here is spectacular. Market day is Thursday, opposite the church. The town's fiestas are on 21 November, 30 November and 1 December.

South of Quetzaltenango

Souteast of Xela is Cantel which has the largest and oldest textile factory in the country. Sunday is market day and the town's fiesta is 12-18 August (main day 15 August). At Easter a passion play is performed. A little further on, on the outskirts of town, on the right-hand side (one minute on the bus), is the white **Copavic glass factory** ① *T7763-8038, www.copavic.com, Mon-Fri 0500-1300, Sat 0500-1200*, where you can watch and photograph the workers blow the recycled glass.

Zunil Pinned in by a very steep-sided valley is the town of Zunil, 9 km from Quetzaltenango. It is visited for the nearby hot thermal baths that many come to wallow in, and for its worship of its well-dressed idol San Simón (Maximón). The market is held on Mondays. The town's fiesta is 22-26 November (main day 25) and there is a very colourful Holy Week. The **church** is striking both inside and out. It has a large decorated altarpiece and a small shrine to murdered Bishop Gerardi at the altar. The façade is white with serpentine columns wrapped in carved ivy.

San Simón (Maximón) is worshipped in the town and is often dressed in different clothes at different times. A small charge is made for the upkeep and to take photos; ask anyone in the town to escort you to his house. To the left of the church is the **Santa Ana Cooperative**, which sells beautiful *huipiles*, shirt and skirt materials, as well as bags and bookmarks.

The nearby extinct **Volcán Pico Zunil**, rises to 3542 m to the southeast of the town. On its slopes are the **thermal baths of Fuentes Georginas** ① *0700-1900, US$2.70*, which you'll know you're approaching by the wafts of sulphurous fumes that come your way. There are several different-sized pools set into the mountainside surrounded by thick, luscious vegetation and enveloped in the steam that continuously rises up in wafts from the hot pools. There are spectacular views on the way to the baths.

The thermal baths of **Aguas Amargas** ① *0800-1700, US$2, children, US$1.30*, are on Zunil Mountain below Fuentes Georginas. They are reached by following the road south and heading east (left) by Estancia de La Cruz. This road passes fields of flowers and would make a great trip on a bike.

El Viejo Palmar This is Guatemala's Pompeii. The river that cuts through here flows directly down from the active Santiaguito volcanic cone following a series of serious lahars (mudflows of water and volcanic material) that took place in the 1990s. The small town of 10,000 was evacuated, leaving an extraordinary legacy. In August 1998, the whole south end of the ghost town was destroyed by a massive lahar that crushed the church. This also shifted the course of the Río Nimá I, which began to flow directly through the centre of the church remains. Very heavy erosion since has left the west front and the altar separated by a 30-m-deep ravine – an unbelievable sight.

Volcán Santa María and Santiaguito Santiaguito's mother, Santa María (3772 m), is a rough 5½-hour climb (1500 m). You can see Santiaguito (2488 m) below, erupting mostly with ash blasts and sometimes lava flows from a mirador. It is possible to camp at the summit of Santa María, or on the saddle west of the summit, but it is cold and windy, but worth it because dawn provides views of the entire country's volcanic chain and an almighty shadow is cast across the area by Santa Maria's form. Santiaguito is a fairly new volcano that formed after the eruption of Santa María out of its crater. Do not attempt to climb Santiaguito: it erupts continuously on a daily basis throwing up ash and is considered one of the most dangerous volcanoes in the world. To see it erupting you need to climb Santa María, where you can look down on this smaller volcano. See Tour operators, page 116.

Laguna Chicabal **San Martín rangers' station** ⓘ *0700-1800, US$2*, is where the two-hour climb to Laguna Chicabal starts. This is a lime-green lake, at 2712 m, in the crater of the extinct volcano (2900 m) of the same name, with wild white lilies, known as *cartucho,* growing at the edges. The Maya believe the waters are sacred and it is thought that if you swim in the lake you will become ill. The highlight of a trip here is the sight of the clouds tumbling down over the circle of trees that surround the lake, and then appearing to bounce on the surface before dispersing. Ceremonies of Maya initiation are held at the lake in early May, known as *Jueves de la Ascensión*. The walk from San Martín takes about two hours.

West of Quetzaltenango
It takes 30 minutes to reach **San Juan Ostuncalco**, 15 km away. It's a pleasant, prosperous town with a big white church noted for its good weekly market on Sunday and beautiful sashes worn by men. Its fiesta, Virgen de la Candelaria, is held on 29 January to 2 February. The road, which is paved, switchbacks 37 km down valleys and over pine-clad mountains to a plateau looking over the valley in which are San Pedro and San Marcos. **San Marcos** has a few places to stay and eat. It is a transport hub with little to see. **San Pedro Sacatepéquez** has a huge market on Thursday. The Maya women wear golden and purple skirts.

The extinct **Volcán Tajumulco**, at 4220 m, is the highest in Central America. Start very early in the day if you plan to return to San Marcos by nightfall. It's about a five-hour climb and a three-hour descent. Once you have reached the ridge on Tajumulco, turn right along the top of it; there are two peaks, the higher is on the right. The peak on the left (4100 m) is used for shamanistic rituals.

Dormant **Volcán Tacaná** (4093 m) on the Mexican border may be climbed from the village of Sibinal. Its last eruption was 1949, but there was activity in 2001, so check before climbing. It is the second highest volcano in Guatemala with a 400-m-wide crater and fumaroles on its flanks. Take a bus to Sibinal from San Marcos. It is a six-hour difficult climb to the summit and it's recommended that you ask for a guide in the village. About 15 km west of San Marcos the road begins its descent from 2500 m to the lowlands. In 53 km to **Malacatán** it drops to 366 m. It is a winding ride with continuous bends, but the scenery is attractive. There is accommodation.

The road to the coastal plain from San Juan Ostuncalco is the most attractive of all the routes down from the highlands, bypassing most of the small towns through quickly changing scenery as you lose height. After San Juan, go south for 1.5 km to **Concepción Chiquirichapa**, with a bright blue and yellow church, which is one of the wealthiest villages in the country. It has a small market early every Thursday morning and a fiesta on 5-9 December. About 6 km beyond is **San Martín Sacatepéquez**, which used to be known as San Martín Chile Verde, and is famous for its hot chillies. This village appears in Miguel Angel Asturias' *Mulata de Tal*. It stands in a windy, cold gash in the mountains. The slopes are superbly steep and farmed, giving fantastic vistas on the climb up and down from Laguna Chicabal (see above). The men wear very striking long red and white striped tunics, beautifully embroidered around the hem. Market day is Sunday. The fiesta runs from 7-12 November (main day 11 November).

Listings Quetzaltenango and around *map p109*

Tourist information

General information can be found at www.xelapages.com and www.xelawho.com, which has good listings.

INGUAT
7 Calle, 11-35, on the park, T7761-4931. Mon-Fri 0900-1600, Sat 0900-1300.
Not recommended. Try the recommended tour operators (see What to do, below) for information instead.

Where to stay

$$ Casa Mañen
9a Av, 4-11, Zona 1, T7765-0786.
Reports are consistently good, serves great breakfasts and friendly staff offer a very warm welcome. Room 2 is a great option with a bed on a mezzanine.

Tip...
At Easter, 12-18 Sep and Christmas, rooms need to be booked well in advance.

Some rooms have microwave, fridge and TV. All are comfortable, and furnished with attractive wooden accessories. There

is a small, pretty courtyard area and secure parking.

$$ Casa San Bartolomé
2 Av, 71-17, T7761-9511, www.casasanbartolome.com.
Located in a historical neighbourhood near the Parque Central, Casa San Bartolomé is a colonial-style B&B with 7 simple and unpretentious rooms, all equipped with Wi-Fi, cable TV, hot water and heating. There's a small garden and mountain views from the shared balcony. Breakfast included.

$$ Hotel Modelo
14 Av A, 2-31, T7761-2529, www.hotelmodelo1892.com.
This comfortable colonial-style option enjoys a convenient central location and a handsome interior furnished with antiques and abundant potted plants. They offer 19 spacious rooms complete with hot water, cable TV, private bath and Wi-Fi.

$$-$ 7 Orejas Hostal
2 Calle, 16-92, T7768-3218, www.7orejas.com.

Set in a handsome colonial building, this hotel is well maintained and professionally managed. They offer simple but attractive rooms with cable TV, private bath, and solid hand-carved furniture, as well as a cheaper option in their 8-bed dorm. Upstairs you can enjoy breakfast (US$4) on their pleasant open-air terrace. There are also furnished apartments for long stays. Recommended.

$$-$ Casa Doña Mercedes
6 Calle y 14 Av, 13-42, T5687-3305,
www.hostalcasadonamercedes.com.gt.
Good value, hospitable and affordable, this modest little guesthouse has a range of tidy, spacious and pleasant rooms with hot water and cable TV. There's also a fully equipped kitchen and cheery communal areas.

$$-$ Villa del Centro
12 Av, 3-61, T7761-1767,
www.hotelvilladelcentro.com.
Quiet, clean and friendly, Villa del Centro has a great central location less than a block from the Parque Central. It offers simple, pleasant, recently renovated rooms with firm beds, Wi-Fi and TV.

$ Black Cat Hostel
13 Av, 3-33, Zona 1, T7761-2091,
www.blackcathostels.net.
A hostel in the old Casa Kaehler. Dorms and private rooms all with shared bathrooms. Breakfast included.

$ Casa Renaissance
9 Calle, 11-26, T3121-6315,
www.casarenaissance.com.
Bright, cosy, and full of character, Casa Renaissance is a colonial-style guesthouse that is over a century old. It boasts lots of homey enclaves including 2 patios with hammocks and a living room with sofas and a TV. Rooms are

simple but comfortable. Additional facilities include Wi-Fi, kitchen, free coffee and tea.

$ Casa Seibel
9 Av, 8-10, T5958-7529,
www.casaseibel.com.
Featuring wooden floors, 2 leafy courtyards and an old piano, this charming hostel and guesthouse has lots of character and history. Accommodation includes simple dorms and spacious rooms and there are dining rooms, communal lounges and an open kitchen. Friendly hostess. Economical and recommended.

$ Casa Xelajú
Callejón 15, Diagonal 13-02, T7761-5954,
www.casaxelaju.com.
Part of a Spanish school but also available to non-students, Casa Xelajú has several nice little 1-bed apartments complete with fully equipped kitchens, Wi-Fi, cable TV, hot water and bath tubs. Very quiet and comfortable, a great deal if you're in town for a while. Weekly or monthly rental. Recommended.

$ Hostel Nim Sut
4 Calle, 9-42, T7761-3083, www.
hostelnim sutquetzaltenango.weebly.
com.
A nice little hostel with a pleasant courtyard and good mountain views from the roof terrace. They have economical private rooms and dorms, with or without private bath. Rates include drinking water, Wi-Fi, use of kitchen, but breakfast is extra.

$ Kiktem-Ja
13 Av, 7-18, Zona 1, T7761-4304.
A central location with 16 colonial-style rooms, nicely furnished, locally made blankets on the beds, wooden floors,

all with bath, hot water, open fires, car parking inside gates.

Zunil

$$$-$$ Las Cumbres Eco-Saunas y Gastronomía
T5399-0029, www.las cumbres.com.gt. Daily 0700-1800.
Beyond Zunil on the left-hand side of the road heading to the coast (Km 210). This is the place for some R&R with saunas emitting natural steam from the geothermal activity nearby. There are 12 rooms with sauna, cheaper without, and separate saunas and jacuzzis for day visitors (US$2.50 per hr) and a restaurant serving good regional food and natural juices. Highly recommended. See Transport, below, for transfers.

$ Turicentro Fuentes Georginas.
6 cold bungalows with 2 double beds and 2 bungalows with 3 single beds. They have cold showers, fireplaces with wood, electricity 1700-2200 and barbecue grills for guests' use near the baths. Guests can use the baths after public closing times. Reasonably priced restaurant with breakfasts, snacks and drinks, 0800-1800.

Restaurants

$$$-$$ Cardinali
14 Av, 3-25, Zona 1.
Owned by Benito, a NY Italian, great Italian food, including large pizzas with 31 varieties: 2 for 1 on Tue and Thu; tasty pastas of 20 varieties, extensive wine list. Recommended. Also does home delivery in 30 mins (T7761-0924).

$$$-$ Las Calas
14 Av "A", 3-21, Zona 1. Mon-Sat.

Breakfasts, salads, soups, paella and pastas served around a courtyard with changing art hanging from walls. The food is tasty with delicious bread to accompany, but small portions are served. The breakfast service is far too slow. Adjoining bar.

$$$-$ Restaurante Royal París
14 Av "A", 3-06, Zona 1.
Delicious food (try the fish in a creamy mushroom sauce), excellent choices, including vegetarian. Also cheap options. Run by Stéphane and Emmanuelle. Recommended. Live music from 2000 on Fri.

$$$-$ Restaurante Tertulianos Villa Lesbia
14 Av, 5-26, Zona 3, T7767-4666.
Gourmet quality, specializing in meat, cheese and chocolate fondues, and scrumptious desserts. Recommended.

$$ El Apaste
5 Calle, 14-48, Zona 3, T7776-6249.
Local Xela cuisine, rich stews and meats, traditionally served in the eponymous *apaste* (terracotta dish).

$$ Sabor de India
15 Avenida, 3-64.
Don't miss this fully authentic Indian restaurant. It serves wholesome, flavourful, good value curries complete with naan bread. Lovely sweet mango lassis, good service and relaxed ambience. Recommended.

$$ Ut'z Hua
Av 12, 3-02, Zona 1.
This prettily decorated restaurant with purple tablecloths does typical food, which is always very good and filling. Ask for the *pollo con mole* or fish. Recommended.

$$-$ Asados Puente
7 Calle, 13-29.
Lots of veggie dishes with tofu and
tempeh. Also ceviche. Popular with
expats. Run by Ken Cielatka and Eva
Melgar. Some profits go towards helping
ill children.

$$-$ Salón Tecún
*Pasaje Enríquez, off the park at 12 Av y 4
Calle, Zona 1.*
Bar, local food, breakfasts also, TV.
Always popular with gringos and locals.

$ El Deli Crepe
14 Av, 3-15, Zona 1.
Good tacos, *almuerzo* with soup, great
milkshakes, savoury and sweet crêpes,
juicy *fajitas* that arrive steaming.

Cafés and bakeries

Bakeshop at 18 Av
1-40, Zona 3. Tue and Fri 0900-1800.
Mennonite bakery that is Xela's answer
to *dulce* heaven. They bake a whole
range of cookies, muffins, breads and
cakes and sells fresh yoghurt and
cheeses. Get there early as the goodies
go really fast.

Blue Angel Café
7 Calle, 15-79, Zona 1.
Great salads, light meals, service a
little slow though, movies shown on a
monthly rotation, useful noticeboard.

Café Baviera
5 Calle, 13-14, Zona 1. Open 0700-2000.
Good cheap meals and excellent pies,
huge cake portions (try the carrot cake)
and coffee in large premises, with walls
lined from ceiling to floor with old
photos and posters. Good for breakfasts,
but a little on the expensive side.
Popular, but lacks warmth.

Café y Chocolate La Luna
8 Av, 4-11, Zona 1.
Delicious hot chocolate with or without
added luxuries, good cheap snacks,
also top chocolates and *pasteles*
(the strawberry and cream pie is
recommended), pleasant atmosphere in
a colonial house decorated with moon
symbols, fairy lights, and old photos; a
good meeting place.

Chocolate Doña Pancha
10a Calle 16-67 Zona 1, T7761-9700.
High-quality chocolate factory, with
great range of drinks, cakes and pastries,
also chocolate products to take away.

La Chatia Artesana
*7 Calle, 15-18,
www.lachatia-artesana.com.*
This wonderful café-restaurant serves
superb gourmet sandwiches, such
as chicken teriyaki and portobello
mushrooms, on a variety of artisanal
breads. There's also delicious cookies,
brownies and other snacks, along with
fresh coffee and juice. Lovely outdoor
courtyard. Recommended.

Bars and clubs

El Duende
14 Av 'A,' 1-42, Zona 1. Open 1800-2330.
Popular café-bar. A favourite among
Guatemalans and gringos.

El Zaguán
*14 Av 'A', A-70, Zona 1. Wed, Thu 1900-
2430, Fri, Sat 2100-2430.*
A disco-bar, US$3.25, drink included;
plays salsa music.

La Taberna de Don Rodrigo
14 Av, Calle C-47, Zona 1.
Cosy bar, reasonable food served in dark
wood atmosphere, draught beer.

Ojalá
15 Av 'A', 3-33.
An entertainment venue, popular with both locals and gringos, which also shows films.

Entertainment

See also Blue Angel Café and Ojalá in Cafés and bakeries and Bars and clubs, above.

Cinemas
Cine Sofía, *7 Calle 15-18. Mon-Fri 1800.*
La Pradera, *in shopping mall in Zona 3, next to bus terminal.* 5 screens, latest releases.

Dance
Trópica Latina, *5 Calle 12-24, Zona 1, T5892-8861, tropicalatina@xelawho.com.* Classes Mon-Sat.

Theatre
Teatro Municipal, *14 Av and 1 Calle.* Main season May-Nov, theatre, opera, etc.

Shopping

Bookshops
Vrisa, *15 Av, 3-64, T7761-3237.* A good range of English-language second-hand books.

Markets
The **main market** is at Templo de Minerva on the western edge of town (take the local bus, US$0.10); at the southeast corner of Parque Centro América is the **Centro Comercial Municipal**, a shopping centre with craft and textile shops on the upper levels, food, clothes, etc below. There is another **market** at 2 Calle y 16 Av, Zona 3, south of Parque Benito Juárez, known as La Democracia. Every first Sun of the month there also is an art and handicrafts market, around Parque Centro América.

Supermarkets
Centro Comercial Mont Blanc, *Paiz, 4 Calle between 18-19 Av, Zona 3.*
Despensa Familiar, *13 Av, 6-94.*
La Pradera, *near the Minerva Terminal.*

North of Quetzaltenango
The smallest bottle of bright yellow *rompope* is sold in various shops around Salcajá, including the **Fábrica de Pénjamo**, *2 Av, 4-03, Zona 1, US$1.55,* and it slips down the throat very nicely!

What to do

When climbing the volcanoes make sure your guides stay with you all the time; it can get dangerous when the cloud rolls down.
Adrenalina Tours, *inside Pasaje Enríquez, T7761-4509, www.adrenalinatours.com.* Numerous tours are on offer including bike, fishing, rafting, horse riding, rock climbing and volcano tours as well as packages to Belize, Honduras and the Petén and trips to Huehue and Todos Santos. Specializes in hikes and treks all over Guatemala. Highly recommended.
Agencia de Viajes SAB, *1 Calle, 12-35, T7761-6402.* Good for cheap flights.
Guatemaya Intercultural Travel Agency, *14 Av "A", 3-06, T7765-0040.* Very helpful.
Mayaexplor, *T7761-5057, www.maya explor.com.* Run by Thierry Roquet, who arranges a variety of trips around Xela and around the country. He can also arrange excursions into Mexico, Belize and Honduras and treks, eg Nebaj–Todos Santos. French-speaking. His website offers useful info for travellers.

A proportion of funds goes towards local development projects. Recommended. **Quetzaltrekkers**, *based inside Casa Argentina at Diagonal 12, 8-37, T7765-5895, www.quetzaltrekkers.com*. This recommended, established, non-profit agency is known for its 3-day hike (Sat morning to Monday afternoon) from Xela across to Lake Atitlán. Proceeds go to the **Escuela de la Calle School** for children at risk, and a dorm for homeless kids. Also offers trek from Nebaj–Todos Santos, 6 days, full-moon hike up Santa María and others. Hiking volunteers are also needed for a 3-month minimum period: hiking experience and reasonable Spanish required.

Language schools

See also box, page 53. Many of Xela's schools can be found at www.xelapages. com/schools.htm. There are many schools offering individual tuition, accommodation with families, extra-curricular activities and excursions. Some also offer Mayan languages. Several schools fund community-development projects, and students are invited to participate with voluntary work. Some schools are non-profit making; enquire carefully. Extra-curricular activities are generally better organized at the larger schools. Prices start from US$130 per week including accommodation, but rise in June-August to US$150 and up.

The following have been recommended:

Centro de Estudios de Español Pop Wuj, *1 Calle, 17-72, T7761-8286, www.pop-wuj.org.*

Guatemalensis, *19 Av, 2-14, Zona 1, T7765-1384, www.geocities.com/spanland/.*

Sol Latino, *Diagonal 12, 6-58, Zona 1, T5613-7222, www.spanishschoollatino.com.*

Instituto Central América (ICA), *19 Av, 1-47 Calle, Zona 1, T7763-1871.*

INEPAS (Instituto de Estudios Español y Participación en Ayuda Social), *15 Av, 4-59, T7765-1308, www.inepas. org.* Keen on social projects and has already founded a primary school in a Maya village, extremely welcoming.

Juan Sisay Spanish School, *15 Av, 8-38, Zona 1, T7761-1586, www.juansisay.com.*

Kie-Balam, *Diagonal 12, 4-46, Zona 1, T7761-1636, kie_balam@hotmail.com.* Offers conversation classes in the afternoon in addition to regular hours.

La Paz, *Diagonal 11, 7-36, T7761-2159, xela.escuela lapaz@gmail.com.*

Minerva Spanish School, *24 Av, 4-39, Zona 3, T7767-4427, www. minervaspanishschool.com.*

Proyecto Lingüístico Quetzalteco de Español, *5 Calle, 2-40, Zona 1, T7765-2140, hermandad@plqe.org.* Recommended.

Proyecto Lingüístico 'Santa María', *14 Av "A", 1-26, T7765-1262.* Volunteer opportunities and free internet access.

Sakribal, *6 C, 7-42, Zona 1, T7763-0717, www.sakribal.com.* Community projects are available.

Ulew Tinimit, *4 C, 15-23, Zona 1, T7761-6242, www.spanish guatemala.org.*

Utatlán, *12 Av, 14-32, Pasaje Enríquez, Zona 1, T7763-0446, utatlan_xela@hotmail. com.* Voluntary work opportunities, one of the cheaper schools.

Tranvia de los Altos, *www.tranviadelos altos.com.* Provides daytime and nighttime walking tours in Xela as well as excursions. Guided city tour is only US$4. Recommended.

Zunil
See **Las Cumbres Eco-Saunas y Gastronomía,** T5399-0029, under Where to stay, above.

Bus
Most visitors arrive by bus, a 30-min (14.5 km) journey southwest of Cuatro Caminos. Buses pull into the Zona 3 Minerva Terminal. To get a bus into the city centre, take a path through the market at its far left or its far right, which brings you out in front of the Minerva Temple. Watch out for very clever pickpockets walking through this market. Buses for the town centre face away (left) from the temple. All Santa Fe services go to Parque Centro América, US$0.15. Alternatively take a taxi.

Local City buses run between 0600 and 1900. Between the town centre and Minerva Terminal, bus No 6, Santa Fe, US$0.20, 15-30 mins, depending on traffic. Catch the bus at the corner of 4 Calle and 13 Av by Pasaje Enríquez. Buses to the Rotonda leave from the corner of 11 Av and 10 Calle, US$0.20, or catch bus No 6, 10 or 13, from Av 12 y 3 Calle as they come down to the park, 15 mins. To catch buses to **San Francisco El Alto, Momostenango,** the **south coast** and **Zunil,** get off the local bus at the Rotonda, then walk a couple of steps away from the road to step into a feeder road where they all line up.

Long distance To **Guatemala City,**

Galgos, Calle Rodolfo Robles, 17-43, Zona 1, T7761-2248, 1st-class buses, at 0400, 1230, 1500, US$5, 4 hrs, will carry bicycles; **Marquensita** several a day (office in the capital 21 Calle, 1-56, Zona 1), leaves from the Minerva Terminal, US$4.60, comfortable, 4 hrs. **Líneas América,** from 7 Av, 3-33, Zona 2, T7761-2063, US$5, 4 hrs, between 0515-2000, 6 daily. **Línea Dorada,** 12 Av and 5 C, Zona 3, T7767-5198, 0400 and 1530, US$9. **Transportes Alamo** from 14 Av, 5-15, Zona 3, T7763-5044, between 0430 and 1430, 7 a day, US$5, 4 hrs.

The following destinations are served by buses leaving from the Minerva Terminal, Zona 3 and the Rotonda. For **Antigua,** change at Chimaltenangoby either taking a chicken bus or Pullman. To **Almolonga,** via **Cantel,** every 30 mins, US$0.50, 10 mins. (Buses to Almolonga and Zunil not via Cantel, leave from the corner of 10 Av and 10 Calle, Zona 1.) To **Chichicastenango** with **Transportes Veloz Quichelense de Hilda Esperanza,** several from 0500 to 1530, US$3.80, 2½ hrs. To **Cuatro Caminos** US$0.50, 30 mins. To **Huehuetenango** with **Transportes Velásquez,** every 30 mins 0500-1730, US$2.50, 2½ hrs. To **La Mesilla** at 0500, 0600, 0700, 0800, 1300, 1400 with **Transportes Unión Fronteriza,** US$3.60, 4 hrs. To **Los Encuentros,** US$2.20. To **Malacatán,** US$3.60, 5 hrs. To **Momostenango,** US$1.20, 1½ hrs. To **Panajachel,** with **Transportes Morales,** at 0500, 0600, 1000, 1200, 1500, US$3.20, 2½-3 hrs. To **Retalhuleu,** US$1.20, 1½ hrs. To **Salcajá,** every 30 mins, US$0.40, 15 mins. To **San Andrés Xecul** every 2 hrs, US$0.60, 30 mins. To **San Cristóbal Totonicapán,** every 30 mins, US$0.40, 20 mins. To **San Francisco El Alto,** US$0.70. **San**

Marcos, every 30 mins, US$1, 1 hr. **San Martín Sacatepéquez/San Martín Chile Verde**, US$0.70, 1 hr. **Santiago Atitlán**, with **Ninfa de Atitlán** at 0800, 1100, 1230, 1630, 4½ hrs. To **Ciudad Tecún Umán** every 30 mins, 0500-1400, US$3.60, 4 hrs. To **Totonicapán**, every 20 mins, US$1.20, 1 hr. To **Zunil**, every 30 mins, US$0.70, 20-30 mins.

Shuttle Adrenalina Tours, see Tour operators, above, runs shuttles. To **Cobán**, US$45, Panajachel, US$20 and Antigua, US$25. Adrenalina also runs a shuttle to and from **San Cristóbal de las Casas**, Mexico, US$35.

Car
Car hire Tabarini Renta Autos, 9 Calle, 9-21, Zona 1, T7763-0418.

Mechanic José Ramiro Muñoz R, 1 Calle, 19-11, Zona 1, T7761-8204. Also **Goodyear Taller** at the Rotonda and for motorbikes **Moto Servicio Rudy**, 2 Av, 3-48, Zona 1, T7765-5433.

Taxi
Found all over town, notably lined up along Parque Centro América. **Taxis Xelaju**, T7761-4456.

North of Quetzaltenango
Bus
All buses heading to Quetzaltenango from Cuatro Caminos pass through **Salcajá**, 10 mins. From Xela to **San Andrés Xecul**, US$0.60, 30 mins. Or take any bus heading to Cuatro Caminos and getting off at the Esso station on the left-hand side, and then almost doubling back on yourself to take the San Andrés road. There are pickups from here.

South of Quetzaltenango
Bus
Cantel is 10-15 mins by bus (11 km), and US$0.24 from Xela on the way to Zunil, but you need to take the bus marked for Cantel Fábrica and Zunil, not Almolonga and Zunil. From **Zunil** to Xela via Almolonga leaves from the bridge. Walk down the left-hand side of the church to the bottom of the hill, take a left and you'll see the buses the other side of the bridge, US$0.60. **Fuentes Georginas** is reached either by walking the 8 km uphill just to the south of Zunil, 2 hrs (300-m ascent; take the right fork after 4 km, but be careful as robbery has occurred here), by pickup truck in 15 mins (US$10 return with a 1-hr wait), or hitch. If you come by bus to Zunil and are walking to the Fuentes, don't go down into town with the bus, but get off on the main road at the Pepsi stand and walk to the entrance road, which is visible 100 m away on the left. See also Shuttles, above, for transfer to the thermal pools.

El Viejo Palmar
Bus
Just before San Felipe, and just before the Puente Samalá III, if you're heading south, is the turn to the right for El Viejo Palmar. Take any bus heading to the south coast, and asked to be dropped off at the entrance and walk. Or, take a pickup from San Felipe park. Ask for Beto or Brígido.

Taxi
From Xela round trip is US$25, or take a tour from town.

Volcán Santa María and Santiaguito
Bus

To reach the volcano take the bus to **Llano del Pinal**, 7 km away, from the Minerva Terminal (every 30 mins, last bus back 1800). Get off at the crossroads and follow the dirt road towards the right side of the volcano until it sweeps up the right (about 40 mins), take the footpath to the left (where it is marked for some distance); bear right at the saddle where another path comes in from the left, but look carefully as it is easily missed.

Laguna Chicabal
Bus/car

The last bus to **Quetzaltenango** leaves at 1900, 1 hr. Parking at the entrance, US$2. It is a 40-min walk from the car park (and you'll need a sturdy vehicle if you attempt the steep first ascent in a car).

West of Quetzaltenango
Bus

Volcán Tajumulco can be reached by getting to the village of **San Sebastián** from San Marcos, which takes about 2 hrs.

Southern
Guatemala

The southern coastal plain of Guatemala supports many plantations of coffee, sugar and tropical fruit trees and its climate is unbearably hot and humid. Amid the fincas some of the most curious archaeological finds have been unearthed, a mixture of monument styles such as Maya and Olmec, including Abaj Takalik, the cane field stones at Santa Lucía Cotzumalguapa and the big 'Buddhas' of Monte Alto.

On the coast are the black-sand beaches and nature reserves of the popular and laid-back Monterrico and Sipacate resorts, where nesting turtles burrow in the sand and masses of birds take to the skies around. Casting a shadow over the coast, the Central Highland volcanoes of Lake Atitlán, and the Antigua trio of Fuego, Acatenango and Agua, look spectacular, looming on the horizon above the lowlands.

Routes to El Salvador

Three routes pass through Southern Guatemala to El Salvador. The main towns are busy but scruffy with little to attract the visitor. See also box, page 214, for more information on crossing into El Salvador.

Route 1 The Pan-American Highway: The first route heads directly south along the paved Pan-American Highway from Guatemala City (CA1) to the border at **San Cristóbal Frontera**. **Cuilapa**, the capital of Santa Rosa Department, is 65 km along the Highway. About 9 km beyond Los Esclavos is the El Molino junction. Further east, just off the Pan-American Highway, is the village of **El Progreso**, dominated by the imposing Volcán Suchitán, at 2042 m, now part of the Parque Regional Volcán Suchitán run by La Fundación de la Naturaleza. There is accommodation. The town fiesta with horse racing is from 10-16 November. From El Progreso, a good paved road goes north 43 km to Jalapa through open, mostly dry country, with volcanoes always in view. There are several crater lakes including **Laguna del Hoyo** near Monjas that are worth visiting. The higher ground is forested. Beyond Jutiapa and El Progreso the Pan-American Highway heads east and then south to Asunción Mita. Here there is a turning left to Lago de Güija. Before reaching the border at **San Cristóbal Frontera**, the Pan-American Highway dips and skirts the shores (right) of **Lago Atescatempa**, with several islands set in heavy forest.

Route 2 Via Jalpatagua: The second, quicker way of getting to San Salvador is to take a highway that cuts off right from the first route at El Molino junction, about 7 km beyond the Esclavos bridge. This cut-off goes through El Oratorio and Jalpatagua to the border at **Valle Nuevo**, continuing then to Ahuachapán and San Salvador.

Route 3 El Salvador (La) via the border at Ciudad Pedro de Alvarado: This coastal route goes from **Escuintla** (see below) to the border bridge over the Río Paz at La Hachadura (El Salvador). It takes two hours from Escuintla to the border. At **Taxisco**, there is a white church with a curious hearts and holly design on the façade. Further east is Guazacapán, which merges into **Chiquimulilla**, 3 km to the north, the most important town of the area, with good-quality leather goods available. There is accommodation available. A side excursion can be made from Chiquimulilla up the winding CA 16 through coffee fincas and farmland. About 20 km along there is a turning to the left down a 2- to 3-km steep, narrow, dirt road that goes to **Laguna de Ixpaco**, an impressive, greenish-yellow lake that is 350 m in diameter. It is boiling in some places, emitting sulphurous fumes and set in dense forest. This trip can also be made by heading south off the Pan-American Highway after Cuilapa (just before Los Esclavos) towards Chiquimulilla on the CA 16, with old trees on either side, some with orchids in them, where you will reach the sign to Ixpaco, after 20 km. Thirty kilometres beyond on the Pacific Highway is **Ciudad Pedro de Alvarado** on the border.

Guatemala City to the Pacific coast

tranquil lake and Pacific ports

Amatitlán

Heading south from the capital on Highway CA19, the town of Amatitlán is perched on the banks of a lake of the same name. Sadly, the lake is too polluted for swimming, but rowing boats ply its waters, US$5 per hour. Less demanding is the **teleférico** ① *Fri-Sun 0900-1700, US$2 return*, climbing from its station on the lakeshore to supply commanding views of the surroundings. The main reason for coming to Amatitlán, however, is the **Day of the Cross** on 3 May, when the Christ figure is removed from the church and floated out of a boat amid candles and decorations. South of Amatitlán, the village of **Palín** has a Sunday market in a plaza under an enormous ceiba tree. The textiles are exceptional, but are increasingly difficult to find. There are great views of Pacaya to the east as you head down to the coast, Volcán Agua to the northwest, and the Pacific lowlands to the west.

Escuintla
Highway CA19 from Guatemala City and Highway 14 from Antigua converge in Escuintla: a large, unattractive provincial centre set in a rich tropical valley. This town acts a major transport hub for the Pacific slope with connections to all the main ports, as well as the international borders with Mexico and El Salvador via Highway CA2, which runs east–west through the region. There are cheap lodgings if you get stuck. For entertainment, you could head 25 km southeast to admire the beasts at the **Autosafari Chapín** ① *Carretera a Taxisco Km 87.5, www. autosafarichapin.com, Tue-Sun, 0900-1730, US$8*. Any bus to Taxisco should be able to drop you at the entrance.

Puerto San José, Chulamar and Iztapa
South of Escuintla, a fast paved highway heads to Puerto San José, which first opened for business (especially the coffee trade) in 1853 and was once upon a time the country's second largest port. The climate is hot, the streets and most of the beaches are dirty, and at weekends the town fills up with people from the capital. There are swimming beaches nearby, but beware of the strong undercurrent. One of the more popular ones is Chulamar, some 5 km to the west. Iztapa, 12 km east of Puerto San José, is world renowned for deep-sea fishing. Sail fish, bill fish, marlin, tuna, dorado, roosterfish, yellowfin and snapper are to be found in large numbers here. The **Chiquimulilla Canal** runs either side of Puerto San José parallel to the coast for close to 100 km.

Listings Guatemala City to the Pacific coast

Where to stay

Puerto San José, Chulamar and Iztapa
There are a number of *comedores* in town.

$$$$ Soleil Pacífico
Chulamar, T7879-4444,
www.hotelessoleilguatemala.com.
Set in rambling landscaped grounds, this large all-inclusive resort is the only accommodation of its type in the area. It boasts luxury rooms, suites and bungalows in addition to all the usual luxuries, including 2 jacuzzis, pools, volleyball courts, football

fields, restaurants and lounges. There have been a few mixed reports and maintenance issues.

$$$ Hotel y Turicentro Eden Pacific
Barrio El Laberinto, Puerto San José,
T7881-1605, www.hoteledenpacific.com.
Overlooking the beach, a family-run hotel with a self-contained chalet for 12 guests and 35 reasonable a/c rooms with TV. Facilities include pool and restaurant. Various packages are available.

$$-$ Hotel Club Sol y Playa Tropical
1 Calle, 5-48, on the canal, Iztapa,
T7881-4365.

Adequate lodgings with restaurant, pool, friendly staff and fair standard rooms with fans.

Transport

Bus

To and from Guatemala City to **Amatitlán** (every 30 mins, US$0.50) from 0700-2045 from 14 Av, between 3 y 4 Calle, Zona 1, Guatemala City. From **Escuintla** (1½ hrs) to the capital from 8 Calle and 2 Av, Zona 1, near the corner of the plaza in Escuintla. Buses that have come along the Pacific Highway and are going on to the capital pull up at the main bus terminal on 4 Av. From the terminal there are buses direct to **Antigua** every 30 mins, 1-1½ hrs, US$1.20. To **Taxisco** from Escuintla, every 30 mins, 0700-1700, 40 mins, for connections onwards (hourly) to **La Avellana**, for boats to **Monterrico**. Frequent buses to **Iztapa** with the last bus departing at 2030.

If you are changing in Escuintla for **Santa Lucía Cotzumalguapa** to the west, you need to take a left out of the bus terminal along the 4 Av up a slight incline towards the police fortress and take a left here on its corner, 9 Calle, through the market. Head for 3 blocks straight, passing the Cinammon Pastelería y Panadería on the right at 9 Calle and 2 Av. At the end here are buses heading to Santa Lucía and further west along the Pacific Highway. It is a 5- to 10-min walk. Buses leave here every 5 mins. To **Santa Lucía Cotzumalguapa** (the bus *ayudantes* shout 'Santa'), 35 mins, US$1.20. On the return, buses pull up at the corner of the 8 Calle and 2 Av, where Guatemala City buses also pass.

Puerto San José, Chulamar and Iztapa

Bus

Regular buses from the capital passing through **Escuintla**, 2-3 hrs. If you are heading further east by road from Iztapa along the coast to **Monterrico** (past loofah plantations), see page 127.

Monterrico

a small black-sand resort backed by languid mangroves

★Monterrico is a beachside village where the sunsets are a rich orange and the waves crash spectacularly on to the shore. The village itself is hot and sleepy during the week, but increasingly popular at the weekends. If you are in the area between September and January, thanks to the efforts of local hatcheries, you can sponsor a baby turtle's waddle to freedom.

Tip...
Due to powerful riptides even strong swimmers can get into trouble here, so take care.

The landing stage is 10 minutes' walk from the ocean front, where you'll find the main restaurants and places to stay. When you step off the dock take the first left, and keep left, which heads directly to the main cluster of beach hotels. This road is known as Calle del Proyecto or Calle del Muelle. Walking straight on from the dock takes you to the main drag in town. When you get to the main drag and want to walk to the main group of hotels, take a left along the beach or take the sandy path to the left one block back from the beach where the sand is a tiny bit easier to walk on.

Although Monterrico's popularity is growing fast, its views are undisturbed by high-rise blocks. All the hotels, mostly rustic and laid-back, are lined up along the beach, and there are a few shops and *comedores* not linked to hotels, in this village of just 1500 people. The village is surrounded by canals carpeted in aquatic plants and mangrove swamps with bird and turtle reserves in their midst. These areas make up the **Biotopo Monterrico-Hawaii** (also known as the **Monterrico Nature Reserve**), which can be explored by *lancha* with the turtle hatchery (see below), around US$10 per person for a one- to two-hour tour. Anteater, armadillo, racoon and weasel live in the area, but it is worth taking the boat trip at sunrise or sunset to see migratory North and South American birds, including flamingo.

However, the real stars in this patch are the olive ridleys *Parlama blanca* and *Parlama negra* turtles, which lay eggs between July and October, and the Baule turtle, which lays between between October and February. There is a turtle hatchery in the village, the **Tortugario Monterrico** ① *daily 0800-1200, 1400-1700, US$6.50*, which offers night tours and volunteer opportunities. Just behind the hatchery there are 300 breeding crocodiles, 150 turtles and iguanas. The turtle liberation event takes place every Saturday night between October and February. Around 8 km east of Monterrico is another hatchery, also offering tours and volunteering. It is run by **Arcas Guatemala** ① *inside Parque Hawaii, T4743-4655, www.arcasguatemala. com; buses from Monterrico every 1-2 hrs, 30 mins, US$0.65.*

Listings Monterrico

Where to stay

Most hotels are fully booked by Sat midday and prices rise at weekends so book beforehand.

$$$$-$$$ Isleta de Gaia
East of Monterrico on a small island near Las Lisas, T7885-0044, www.isleta-de-gaia.com.
Managed by a French-American team, an exclusive boutique hotel located on a private island between the Chiquimulilla Canal and the Pacific ocean. Accommodation is in tasteful, traditional bungalows. A great hideaway and the most interesting lodging for miles, but accessible only by private *lancha*; contact in advance to organize transport. Rustic-chic. Recommended.

$$$ Atelie del Mar
Just off the beach, west of Calle Principal, 5752-5528, www.hotelateliedelmar.com.
This personable boutique hotel has a secluded, colourful, well-tended garden, an art gallery featuring work by the owner, Violeta Marroquín, a restaurant and 2 pools. Accommodation includes 16 rooms of different sizes, all equipped with a/c, TV, and private bath. Rates include breakfast and Wi-Fi. Hospitable and helpful. Good service.

$$$ Dos Mundos
8901 Monterrico Rd, east of Calle Principal, T7823-0820, www.hotelsdosmundos.com.
One of Monterrico's more upmarket options, The resort-style Dos Mundos

boasts 14 well-attired bungalows with a/c and a rather beautiful infinity pool overlooking the ocean. Other amenities include restaurant, bar, and tours. Breakfast included.

$$$-$ Café del Sol
250 m west of Calle Principal, T5810-0821, www.cafe-del-sol.com.
Quiet, simple and comfortable beachside lodgings, including 13 pleasant rooms. The newest ones are the most comfortable (**$$$**); those across the road in an annexe are much more spartan (**$**). There is also a bar area, pool, jacuzzi and restaurant. Part of their profits go to Eternal Spring Foundation, a sustainable development organization. Recommended.

$$ Hotel Pez de Oro
At the end of main strip to the east, T2368-3684, www.pezdeoro.com.
18 spacious bungalows with traditional thatched roofs, terraces, and hammocks, all attractively set around a pool. All rooms have private bathroom, mosquito lamps, hand-woven bedspreads, pretty bedside lights and fan; some have a/c. Secluded and tranquil. Recommended.

$$ Hotel Restaurante Dulce y Salado
Some way away from the main cluster of hotels and a 500-m hard walk east through sand if you are on foot, T4154-0252, www.dulceysaladoguatemala.com.
The sea breezes and uninterrupted view of the highland volcanoes at this secluded hotel are fantastic. Set around a pool, the thatched cabins are nice and clean, with bath, fans and mosquito nets. Run by a friendly Italian couple, Fulvio and Graziella. Breakfast included, good Italian food in the restaurant.

$$-$ Johnny's Place
Main strip, T4369-6900, www.johnnysplacehotel.com.
Very popular with locals and gringos, Johnny's Place is a buzzing social space (especially at weekends) with a wide range of accommodation including bungalows (**$$$**), rooms (**$$**), suites, economy 'backpacker' rooms with shared bath, and for the very thrifty, dorms (**$**). There is internet, table tennis, pools and a beachside restaurant with free coffee fill-ups. A good place for groups. Recommended.

$ El Delfín
On the beachfront, 20 m from Calle Principal, T4661-9255, www.hotel-el-delfin.com.
Lots of good reports about this cheery no-frills option, popular with backpackers and families. Accommodation includes a range of good value bungalows and rooms with deals sometimes available if staying more than 3 nights. The restaurant and bar overlook the beach and serve vegetarian food. Organizes shuttles at any hour. Relaxing and recommended.

Restaurants

Be careful, especially with *ceviche*. There are lots of seafood joints and local *comedores* along Calle Principal, which leads to the beach. The best and most popular of the bunch appears to be:

$$$-$$ Taberna El Pelicano
On the seafront past Johnny's Place. Wed-Sat.
Named after a rescued pelican called Pancho, this relaxed and well-established haunt offers a diverse and creative menu of steaks, pastas, salads and seafood,

all very fresh and prepared according to flavourful Swiss and Italian recipes. Try the catch of the day or the toasted camembert salad. Recommended.

Bars and clubs

For drinking and dancing, try Johnny's Place (see Where to stay, above), thronging with party-loving Guatemaltecos on Fri and Sat nights. Also worth a look is Mañanitas Beach Lounge, overlooking the beach at the end of Calle Principal.

What to do

Tour operators
Those preferring to stay on land can rent horses for a jaunt on the beach. *Lancha* and turtle-searching tours are operated by a couple of agencies in town.

Transport

Bus and boat
There are 3 ways of getting to Monterrico: 2 by public transport and 1 by shuttle.

The **1st route** to Monterrico involves heading direct to the Pacific coast by taking a bus from the capital to **Puerto San José**, 1 hr, and changing for a bus to **Iztapa**. Or take a direct bus from Escuintla to Iztapa. Then cross river by the toll bridge to **Pueblo Viejo** for US$1.60 per vehicle (buses excluded), or US$0.80 per foot passenger, 5 mins. The buses now continue to Monterrico, about 25 km east, 1 hr. Buses run to and from Iztapa between 0600-1500, from

the corner of main street and the road to Pueblo Viejo to the left, 3 blocks north of the beach, just past the Catholic church on the right.

The **2nd route** involves getting to Taxisco first and then La Avellana. There are also direct buses to La Avellana from Guatemala City, see page 36. If you are coming from Antigua, take a bus to **Escuintla** 1-1½ hrs. From there, there are regular departures to **Taxisco**, 40 mins. From Taxisco to La Avellana, buses leave hourly until 1800, US$1, 20 mins. If you take an international bus from Escuintla (45 mins), it will drop you off just past the Taxisco town turn-off, just before a bridge with a slip road. Walk up the road (5 mins) and veer to the right where you'll see the bus stop for **La Avellana**. At La Avellana take the **motor boats** through mangrove swamps, 20-30 mins, US$0.60 for foot passengers, from 0630 and then hourly until 1800. The journey via this route from Antigua to Monterrico takes about 3¼ hrs if your connections are good. Return boats to La Avellana leave at 0330, 0530, 0700, 0800, 0900, 1030, 1200, 1300, 1430, 1600. Buses leave La Avellana for Taxisco hourly until 1800. Buses pull up near the **Banco Nor-Oriente** where numerous buses heading to Guatemala and Escuintla pass.

Shuttles Alternatively, numerous travel agencies in **Antigua** run shuttles, US$10-12 one way. You can book a return shuttle journey in Monterrico by going to the language school on the road that leads to the dock. There are also mini buses operating from Monterrico to **Iztapa** and vice versa.

Amid the sugar-cane fields and fincas of this coastal town lie an extraordinary range of carved stones and images with influences from pre-Maya civilizations, believed mostly to be ancient Mexican cultures, including the Izapa civilization from the Pacific coast area of Mexico near the Guatemalan border.

Four main points of interest entice visitors to the area: **Bilbao**, **El Baúl**, **Finca El Baúl** and the **Museo de Cultura Cotzumalguapa**. The town is just north of the Pacific Highway, where some of the hotels and banks are.

Bilbao, El Baúl, Finca El Baúl and Museo de Cultura Cotzumalguapa

You can visit all the sites on foot. However, you are advised not to go wandering in and out of the cane fields at the Bilbao site as there have been numerous assaults in the past. You can walk along the tarmacked road north to the El Baúl sites (6 km and 8 km respectively from town), but there is no shade, so take lots of water. Ask for directions. There is an occasional 'Río Santiago' bus, which goes as far as Colonia Maya, close to the El Baúl hilltop. Only workers' buses go to Finca El Baúl in the morning, returning at night. Alternatively, take a taxi from town (next to the plaza) and negotiate a trip to all 4 areas. They will charge around US$20. Note Do not believe any taxi driver who tells you that Las Piedras (the stones) have been moved from the cane fields to the museum because of the increasing assaults.

There is considerable confusion about who carved the range of monuments and stelae scattered around the town. It is safe to say that the style of the monuments found in the last 150 years is a blend of a number of pre-Columbian styles. Some believe the prominent influence is Toltec, the ancestors of the Maya K'iche', Kaqchikel, Tz'utujil and Pipiles. It is thought the Tolteca-Pipil had been influenced in turn by the Classic culture from Teotihuacán, a massive urban state northeast of the present Mexico City, which had its zenith in the seventh century AD. However, some experts say that there is no concrete evidence to suggest that the Pipiles migrated as early as AD 400 or that they were influenced by Teotihuacán. All in all, the cultural make-up of this corner of Guatemala may never be known.

The remnants at **Bilbao**, first re-discovered in 1860, are mainly buried beneath the sugar cane but monuments found above ground show pre-Maya influences. It is thought that the city was inhabited 1200 BC-AD 800. There are four large boulders – known as Las Piedras – in sugar-cane fields, which can be reached on foot from the tracks leading from the end of 4 Avenida in town. **El Baúl** is a Late Classic ceremonial centre, 6 km north of Santa Lucía, with two carved stone pieces to see; most of its monuments were built between AD 600 and 900. **Finca El Baúl** has a collection of sculptures and stelae gathered from the large area of the finca grounds.

The **Museo de Cultura Cotzumalguapa** ⓘ *Finca Las Ilusiones, Mon-Fri 0800-1600, Sat 0800-1200, US$1.30, less than 1 km east of town, ask the person in charge for the key,* displays numerous artefacts collected from the finca and a copy of the famous Bilbao Monument 21 from the cane fields. To get to the museum, walk east along the Pacific Highway and take a left turn into the finca site.

Santa Lucía Cotzumalguapa to the Mexican border

Beyond Santa Lucía Cotzumalguapa is **Cocales**, where a good road north leads to Patulul and after 30 km, to Lake Atitlán at San Lucas Tolimán. The Pacific Highway continues through San Antonio Suchitepéquez to **Mazatenango** (where just beyond are the crossroads for Retalhueleu and Champerico) and on to Coatepeque and Ciudad Tecún Umán for the Mexican border; see box, page 210. Mazatenango is the chief town of the Costa Grande zone. While not especially attractive, the Parque Central is very pleasant with many fine trees providing shade. There is a huge fiesta in the last week of February, when hotels are full and double their prices. At that time, beware of children carrying (and throwing) flour.

Retalhuleu and around

Retalhuleu, normally referred to as 'Reu' (pronounced 'Ray-oo') is the capital of the department. The entrance to the town is grand with a string of royal palms lining the route, known as Calzada Las Palmas. It serves a large number of coffee and sugar estates and much of its population is wealthy. The original colonial church of **San Antonio de Padua** is in the central plaza. Bordering the plaza to the east is the neoclassical **Palacio del Gobierno**, with a giant quetzal sculpture on top. The **Museo de Arqueología y Etnología** ⓘ *Tue-Sat 0830-1300, 1400-1800, Sun 0900-1230, US$1.30, next to the palacio*, is small. Downstairs are exhibits of Maya ceramics.

If you fancy cooling off, near Reu are the **Parque Acuático Xocomil** ⓘ *Km 180.5 on the road from Xela to Champerio, T7722-9400, www.irtra.org.gt, Thu-Sun 0900-1700, US$9.60*. Nearby is the enormous theme park with giant pyramids of **Xetulul** ⓘ *T7722-9450, www.irtra.org.gt, Thu-Sun 100-1800, US$26*.

Abaj Takalik

Daily 0700-1700, US$3.25, guides are volunteers so tips are welcomed.

One of the best ancient sites to visit outside El Petén is Abaj Takalik, a ruined city that lies, sweltering, on the southern plain. Its name means 'standing stone' in K'iche'. The site was discovered in 1888 by botanist Doctor Gustav Brühl. It is believed to have flourished in the late pre-Classic period of 300 BC to AD 250 strategically placed to control commerce between the highlands and the Pacific coast. There are some 239 monuments, which include 68 stelae, 32 altars and some 71 buildings, all set in peaceful surroundings. The environment is loved by birds and butterflies, including blue morphos, and by orchids, which flower magnificently between January and March. The main temple buildings are mostly up to 12 m high, suggesting an early date before techniques were available to build Tikal-sized structures.

Towards the Mexican border

The main road runs 21 km east off the Pacific Highway to **Coatepeque**, one of the richest coffee zones in the country. There is a bright, modern church in the leafy Plaza Central. The local fiesta takes place from 11-19 March. There are several hotels, *hospedajes* and restaurants. **Colomba**, an attractive typical village east of Coatepeque in the lowlands, has a basic *hospedaje*.

Listings Santa Lucía Cotzumalguapa and around

Where to stay

Santa Lucía Cotzumalguapa

$$ Santiaguito
Pacific Highway at Km 90.4, T7882-5435, hsantiaguito@yahoo.com.mx.
Located on the highway on the west side of Santa Lucía, probably the best option in town (which isn't saying much). Rooms have a/c, TV and hot and cold water. Nice leafy grounds with a pool and restaurant. Non-guests can use the pool for US$2.60.

$$-$ Hotel El Camino
Diagonally opposite Santiaguito across the highway at Km 90.5, T7882-5316.
Large if fairly simple rooms with bath, TV, tepid water and fan. Some have a/c (more expensive). Restaurant attached.

$ Hospedaje La Reforma
A stone's throw from the park on 4 Av, 4-71, T7882-1731.
Lots of dark box rooms and dark shared showers, ask to see before accepting. Clean, ultra-cheap and basic, would suit budget travellers with modest needs.

Retalhuleu and around

$$ Astor
5 Calle 4-60, T7957-8300, www.hotelastorguatemala.com.
Constructed in the late 19th century and converted to a hotel in 1923 by

the Ruiz Javalois family, this handsome colonial-style lodging offers 27 clean, comfortable rooms set around a pretty courtyard. Amenities include a pool, jacuzzi, parking, bar and restaurant. Non-guests can use the pool (better than the one at **Posada de Don José**) for a fee. A good option, recommended.

$$ La Colonia
1.5 km to the north at Km 180.5, T7772-2048, www.hlacoloniareu.com.
This good value highway lodging boasts a relaxing garden space and patio with leafy tropical plants and pools for adults and children. The lodgings encompass a variety of rooms equipped with a/c and cable TV; ask to see a few. Good food is served in the restaurant.

$$ Posada de Don José
5 Calle, 3-67, T7962-2900, www.posadadonjose.com.
Don Jose's is a well-established colonial-style option with 2 floors of comfortable, spacious well-attired rooms overlooking a central courtyard with a pool; some are newer than others, ask to see a few. The restaurant is possibly the best in town, serving such mouth-watering temptations as lobster sautéed in cognac. Non-guests can use the pool for a small fee.

$$ Siboney
5 km northwest of Reu in San Sebastián, Km 180.5, T7772-2174, www.hotelsiboney.com.
A very reasonable 3-star option on the highway, motel-style with comfortable rooms set around pool. There's a water slide for the kids and a jacuzzi for the adults. Try the *caldo de mariscos* or *paella* in the excellent restaurant. Non-guests can pay to use the pool.

Restaurants

Retalhuleu and around
There are lots of pizzerias and a few fast food joints in town. For a quality dining experience, head to **Hotel Astor** or **Posada de Don José** (see Where to stay, above). Alternatively, for something cheap and low-key, try:

$$ Restaurante La Luna
8a Av and 5a Calle, a block from the main plaza.
Well-established and popular, La Luna is the place for good value, hearty, home-cooked *típico* meals.

Transport

Santa Lucía Cotzumalguapa
Bus
Regular departures to the capital. Buses plying the Pacific Highway also pass through, so if you are coming from Reu in the west or Escuintla in the east you can get off here.

Car
If you are driving, there are a glut of 24-hr **Esso** and **Texaco** gas stations here. See under Guatemala City to the Pacific coast, page 124, for catching transport from **Escuintla**.

Santa Lucía Cotzumalguapa to the Mexican border
Bus
5 a day **Cocales-Panajachel**, between 0600 and 1400, 2½ hrs. Frequent buses to **Mazatenango** from Guatemala City, US$5. To the border at **Ciudad Tecún Umán**, US$2.10, an irregular service with Fortaleza del Sur.

Retalhuleu and around
Bus
Services along the Pacific Highway to Mexico leave from the main bus terminal, which is beyond the city limits at 5 Av 'A'. To **Coatepeque** (0600-1800), **Malacatán**, **Mazatenango** and **Champerico** (0500-1800). Buses also leave from here to **El Asintal**, for Abaj Takalik, 30 mins, every 30 mins from 0600-1830, last bus back to Reu 1800. Or catch them before that from the corner of 5 Av 'A' and the Esso gas station as they turn to head for the village. Leaving from a smaller terminal at 7 Av/10 Calle, there are regular buses to **Ciudad Tecún Umán**, **Talismán** and **Guatemala City** via the Pacific route, and to **Xela** (1¾ hrs, every hour 0500-1800).

Abaj Takalik
Bus
Take a bus to El from **Retalhuleu** and walk the hot 4 km to the site entrance. Or, take any bus heading along the Pacific Highway and get off at the **El Asintal** crossroads. Take a pickup from here to El Asintal; then a pickup from the town square to Abaj Takalik. As there are only fincas along this road, you will probably be on your own, in which case it is US$5 to the site or US$10 round trip, including waiting time. Bargain hard.

Taxi and tour

A taxi from central plaza in Reu to the site and back including waiting time is US$13. Alternatively, take a tour from Xela.

Towards the Mexican border

Bus

From Quetzaltenango to **Coatepeque**, catch any bus heading to Ciudad Tecún Umán from Reu.

Guatemala City
to the Caribbean

From the capital to the Caribbean, the main road passes through the Río Motagua Valley, punctuated by cacti and bordered by the Sierra de Las Minas mountains rising abruptly in the west. Dinosaur remains, the black Christ and the Maya ruins of Quiriguá can be found on or close to the highway. The banana port of Puerto Barrios is a large transport and commercial hub and jumping-off point for the Garífuna town of Lívingston. Trips down the lush gorge of the Río Dulce are a highlight; nearby are some great places to see and stay on its banks, as well as accommodation around Lago de Izabal.

The Carretera al Atlántico, or Atlantic Highway, stretches from Guatemala City all the way to Puerto Barrios on the Caribbean coast in the department of Izabal. Most worthwhile places to visit are off this fast main road, along the Río Motagua valley, where cactus, bramble, willow and acacia grow. There are numerous buses plying the route.

Along the Atlantic Highway

Before Teculután is **El Rancho** at Km 85, the jumping-off point for a trip north to Cobán (see page 156). There are a few places to stay here. Geologists will be interested in the **Motagua fault** near Santa Cruz, between Teculután and Río Hondo. Just before Río Hondo (Km 138), a paved road runs south towards Estanzuela. Shortly before this town you pass a monument on the right commemorating the 1976 earthquake, which activated a fault line that cut across the road. It can still be seen in the fields on either side of the road. The epicentre of this massive earthquake, which measured 7.5 on the Richter scale, and killed 23,000 people, was at **Los Amates**, 65 km further down the valley towards Puerto Barrios.

Estanzuela

Estanzuela is a small town fronting the highway. Its **Museo de Palaeontología, Arqueología y Geología** ⓘ *daily 0800-1700, free*, displays the incredible reconstructed skeletal remains of a 4-m prehistoric giant sloth found in Zone 6, Guatemala City and a giant armadillo, among others. To get there, either take a **Rutas Orientales** bus from Guatemala City to Zacapa (every 30 minutes 0430-1800, 2¾ to three hours), or take a minibus south from Río Hondo and ask to be dropped at the first entrance to the town on the right. Then walk right, into the town, and continue for 600 m to the museum, 10 minutes. When you reach the school, walk to the right and you will see the museum. Moving on to Esquipulas, take the same Rutas Orientales service that continues from Zacapa, US$6, 1½ hours.

Chiquimula, Volcán de Ipala and the Honduran border
volcanic lake and impressive Mayan site

Chiquimula is a stop-off point for travellers who stay here on their way to or from Copán Ruinas, Honduras, if they can't make the connection in one day. The town's fiesta, which includes bullfighting, is from 11-18 August.

An alternative route to Chiquimula and Esquipulas is from the southeast corner of Guatemala City (Zona 10), where the Pan-American Highway heads towards the Salvadorean border. After a few kilometres there is a turning to **San José Pinula** (fiesta: 16-20 March). After San José, an unpaved branch road continues for 203 km through fine scenery to **Mataquescuintla**, **Jalapa** (several *hospedajes*, good bus connections; fiesta: 2-5 May), **San Pedro Pinula**, **San Luis Jilotepeque** and **Ipala** to Chiquimula.

Southwest of Chiquimula, the extinct Volcán de Ipala (1650 m) can be visited. The crater lake is cool and good for swimming. To get here, take an early bus to **Ipala** from Chiquimula; stay on the bus and ask the driver to let you off at Aldea El Chaparroncito (10 minutes after Ipala). From here it's a 1½-hour ascent, following red arrows every now and then. Another ascent goes via Municipio Agua Blanca. Take a minibus to **Agua Blanca** from Ipala and get out at the small village of El Sauce, where the trail starts. The last bus from Ipala to Chiquimula is 1700.

At **Vado Hondo**, 10 km south of Chiquimula on the road to Esquipulas, a smooth dirt road branches east to the Honduran border (48 km) and a further 11 km to the great Maya ruins of Copán. The border is 1 km after the village. For more on crossing to Honduras, see box, page 213.

Esquipulas

Esquipulas is dominated by a large, white basilica, which attracts millions of pilgrims from across Central America to view the image of a Black Christ. The town has pulled out the stops for visitors, who, as well as a religious fill, will lack nothing in the way of food, drink and some of the best kitsch souvenirs on the market. If it's possible, stop at the mirador, 1 km from the town, for a spectacular view on the way in of the basilica, which sits at the end of a 1.5-km main avenue.

The history of the famous *Cristo Negro* records that in 1735 Father Pedro Pardo de Figueroa, suffering from an incurable chronic illness, stood in front of the image to pray, and was cured. A few years later, after becoming Archbishop of Guatemala he ordered a new church to be built to house the sculpture. The **basilica** ① *open until 2000*, was completed in 1758 and the *Cristo Negro* was transferred from the parish church shortly after that. Inside the basilica, the Black Christ is on a gold cross, elaborately engraved with vines and grapes. It was carved by Quirio Cataño in dark balsam wood in 1595. The image attracts over 1,000,000 visitors per year, some crawling on their hands and knees to pay homage. The main pilgrimage periods are 1-15 January (with 15 January being the busiest day), during Lent, Holy Week and 21-27 July.

Quiriguá

Daily 0730-1630, US$4. Take insect repellent. There are toilets, a restaurant, a museum and a jade store and you can store your luggage with the guards. There is no accommodation at the site (yet). The site is reached by a paved road from the Atlantic Highway. The village of Quiriguá is about halfway between Zacapa and Puerto Barrios on the highway, and about 3 km from the entrance road to the ruins.

The remarkable Late Classic ruins of Quiriguá include the tallest stelae found in the Maya world. The UNESCO World Heritage Site is small, with an excavated acropolis to see, but the highlight of a visit is the sight of the ornately carved tall stelae and the zoomorphic altars. The Maya here were very industrious, producing monuments every five years between AD 751 and 806, coinciding with the height of their prosperity and confident rule. The earliest recorded monument dates from AD 480.

It is believed that Quiriguá was an important trading post between Tikal and Copán, inhabited since the second century, but principally it was a ceremonial centre. The Kings of Quiriguá were involved in the rivalries, wars and changing alliances between Tikal, Copán and Calakmul. It rose to prominence in the middle of the eighth century, around the time of Cauac Sky who ascended to the throne in AD 724. Cauac Sky was appointed to the position by 18 Rabbit, powerful ruler of Copán (now in Honduras), and its surrounding settlements. It seems that he was fed up with being a subordinate under the domination of Copán, and during his reign, Quiriguá attacked Copán and captured 18 Rabbit. One of the stelae tells of the beheading of the Copán King in the plaza at Quiriguá as a sacrifice after the AD 738 battle. After this event 18 Rabbit disappears from the official chronicle and a 20-year hiatus follows in the historical record of Copán. Following this victory, Quiriguá became an independent kingdom and gained control of the Motagua Valley, enriching itself in the process. And, from AD 751, a monument was carved and erected every five years for the next 55 years.

The tallest stelae at Quiriguá is **Stelae E**, which is 10.66 m high with another 2.5 m or so buried beneath. It is 1.52 m wide and weighs 65 tonnes. One of its dates corresponds with the enthronement of Cauac Sky, in AD 724, but it's thought to date from AD 771. All of the stelae, in parkland surrounded by ceiba trees and palms, have shelters, which makes photography difficult. Some monuments have been carved in the shape of animals, some mythical, all of symbolic importance to the Maya.

Thirteen kilometres from Quiriguá is the turn-off for **Mariscos** and Lago de Izabal (see page 146). A further 28 km on are the very hot twin towns of Bananera/Morales. From Bananera there are buses to Río Dulce, Puerto Barrios and the Petén.

Puerto Barrios

Puerto Barrios, on the Caribbean coast, is a hot and dusty port town, still a central banana point, but now largely superseded as a port by Santo Tomás. The launch to the Garífuna town of Lívingston leaves from the municipal dock here. While not an unpleasant town, it is not a destination in itself, but rather a launch pad to more beautiful and happening spots in Guatemala. It's also the departure point for the Honduran Caribbean. On the way into town, note the cemetery on the right-hand side, where you will pass a small Indian mausoleum with elephant carvings. During the 19th century, *culi* (coolies) of Hindu origin migrated from Jamaica to Guatemala to work on the plantations. The fiesta is 16-22 July.

Listings Chiquimula, Volcán de Ipala and the Honduran border

Where to stay

Chiquimula

\$\$-\$ Posada Perla del Oriente
2 Calle between 11 and 12 Av, T7942-0014.
Near the bus station, this quiet place has plain but spacious rooms with TV and fan (**\$**); some have a/c (**\$\$**). There is parking, a restaurant and a pool; grounds are verdant and tranquil. A good deal. Recommended.

\$ Hernández
3 Calle, 7-41, T7942-0708.
Enjoying a convenient central location, this reliable cheapie offers basic, spartan rooms with fan or a/c, cheaper with shared bath. A pool adds to its attraction. Family-run (the owner, Henry, speaks fluent English), quiet and friendly.

\$ Hotel Posada Don Adán
8 Av, 4-30, T7942-0549.

A good, cheap option. Don Adán has tidy little rooms with private bath, fan, a/c, TV. Run by a friendly, older couple.

Esquipulas

There are plenty of cheap hotels, *hospedajes* and *comedores* all over town, especially in and around 11 Calle, also known as Doble Vía Quirio Cataño. Prices tend to double before the Jan feast day. They also rise at Easter and at weekends. When quiet, midweek, bargain for lower room prices.

\$\$\$ Hotel El Gran Chortí
On the outskirts of town at Km 222, T6685-9696, www.realgranchorti.com.
Rack rates are on the pricey side, but the grounds are lovely. Rooms are dated, restful and OK. They come complete with cable TV, Wi-Fi, a/c, phone and *frigobar*. There is also a great pool with slides, a restaurant serving meat, pasta and seafood dishes, and a bar.

$$$ Legendario
3 Av and 9 Calle, T7943-1824,
www.hotellegendario.com.
The most expensive place in town,
comfortable enough but not great value.
Rooms are simple, fine, well-equipped
and unremarkable. The real draw is the
leafy garden and the massive pool, but
check it is open before checking in.

$$$ Payaquí
2 Av, 11-26, T7943-1143,
www.hotelpayaqui.com.
The 40 rooms are fair and fine (the suites
are comfortable too, if a bit grandiose),
with *frigobars*, full of beers for the
pilgrims to guzzle, hot-water showers
and free drinking water. Facilities include
a pool, jacuzzi, spa services, business
centre, parking, restaurant and bar.
Credit cards, Honduran lempiras and US
dollars accepted.

$$ Hotel El Peregrino
2 Av, 11-94, T7943-1054,
www.elperegrinoesquipulas.com.
A small, quiet, comfortable hotel,
nothing fancy but quite adequate.
Their unique selling point is the
rooftop terrace with a small pool and
unobstructed views of the basilica. Ask
to see rooms before accepting.

$$ Hotel Real Santa María
2 Av y 10a Calle, 20-1, T7943-0214,
www.hotelrealsantamaria.com.
Situated a block from the basilica with
fine views from its terrace, Real Santa
María boasts sumptuous antiques
and elaborate wood carved panels in
the reception area. Rooms are simple
and pleasant. They feature the usual
conveniences including Wi-Fi, a/c,
and hot water, but avoid those facing

the street. There is also a pool and
parking area.

$ Hotel Real Esquipulas
10a Calle, 3-25, T7943-3293,
www.realesquipulashotel.com.
This uninspired cheapie has plain
windowless rooms with hot water, cable
TV and a/c. Not really royal, but perfectly
adequate for thrifty sorts.

Quiriguá

$$ Hotel Restaurante Santa Mónica
In Los Amates, 2 km south of Quiriguá
village on the highway, T7947-3838.
17 rooms all with private bath, TV and
fan, pool, restaurant. It is opposite a
24-hr Texaco gas station and convenient
if you don't want to walk the 10-15 mins
into Quiriguá village. There are a couple
of shops, banks, and *comedores* here.

$$-$ Posada de Quiriguá
Km 204, Barrio Toltec, Aldea Quiriguá,
Los Amates, T5349-5817, www.geocities.
jp/masaki_quirigua.
Designed and managed by Masaki
Kuwada from Japan, Posada de Quiriguá
is an attractive guesthouse with a
lovely tropical garden and a range of
simple but restful rooms, easily the
best place to stay in the area. The
restaurant serves hearty Guatemalan
breakfasts and authentic sushi for dinner.
Recommended, but tricky to find – ask
around town.

$ Hotel y Restaurante Royal
T7947-3639.
Basic budget lodgings with a restaurant
attached. Rooms have bath, cheaper
without, clean, mosquito netting on
all windows. A good place to meet
other travellers.

Puerto Barrios

There is not much reason to stay and good options are thin on the ground. The following are OK for a night:

$$ El Reformador
16 Calle and 7 Av 159, T7948-5489.
Set around shaded patios, 51 rooms with bathroom, fan and TV, some with a/c, restaurant, laundry service, clean, quiet, accepts credit cards. The same management run the **Oguatour** travel agency across the road. OK.

$$-$ Hotel del Norte
At the end of 7 Calle, T7948-2116.
A rickety, old wooden structure with sloping landings on the seafront side. All rooms have bath, some with a/c. There's a pool and expensive restaurant, but worth it for the English colonial tearoom atmosphere, no credit cards, but will change dollars. Ask to see a few different rooms, some have great views. The newest are the most comfortable, but lack the dilapidated style that makes this hotel an attraction.

$ Hotel Europa 2
3a Av, between 11a and 12a Calle, T7948-1292.
Located in a quiet neighbourhood near the dock, acceptable budget lodgings with clean, simple rooms with brick walls, wandering chickens in the grounds. Recommended chiefly for its friendly and helpful Cuban management.

Restaurants

Chiquimula

$ Magic
Corner of 8 Av and 3 Calle.
A good place from which to watch the world go by, and most of what's on offer is seriously cheap. Sandwiches, *licuados* and burgers.

$ Pastelería Las Violetas
7 Av, 4-80, and another near Hotel Victoria.
An excellent cake shop with a fine spread, good-value sandwiches too, plus great cappuccino, and a/c. Next door is its bakery.

Esquipulas

There are plenty of restaurants, but prices are high for Guatemala.

$$$ La Hacienda
2 Av, 10-20.
Delicious barbecued chicken and steaks. Kids' menu available, breakfasts available. One of the smartest restaurants in town.

$$ Restaurante Payaquí
2 Av, 11-26, inside the hotel of the same name.
Specialities include turkey in *pipián*, also lunches and breakfasts. A poolside restaurant makes a pleasant change.

$ Café Pistachos
Close to Hotel Calle Real.
Clean, cheap snack bar with burgers, hotdogs, etc.

Puerto Barrios

$$$-$$ Restaurante Safari
At the north end of 5 Av and 1 Calle, overlooking the bay with views all around.
Basically serving up oceans of fish, including whole fish, *ceviche* and fishburgers.

$$ La Fonda de Quique
An orange and white wooden building at 5 Av and corner of 12 Calle.
Nicely a/c with hand-made wooden furniture, serving lobster, fish and meats, plus snacks.

Bars and clubs

Puerto Barrios

Mariscos de Izabal
Open until 0100.
One of the most popular spots in Puerto Barrios, this thatched bar is mostly a drinking den but also has tacos, tortillas and burgers served amid beating Latin rhythms.

The Container
Just past the Hotel del Norte overlooking the sea. Open 0700-2300.
An unusual bar constructed from the front half of an old ship equipped with portholes, and a number of banana containers from the massive banana businesses just up the road.

Transport

Chiquimula
Bus
There are 3 terminals in Chiquimula, all within 50 m of each other. To **Guatemala City**, Transportes Guerra and **Rutas Orientales**, hourly, US$4, 3¼-3½ hrs, leave from 11 Av between 1 and 2 Calle, as do buses for **Puerto Barrios**, several companies, every 30 mins, between 0300-1500, 4 hrs, US$6.50. To **Quiriguá**, US$3.20, 1 hr 50 mins. Take any Puerto Barrios-bound bus. On to **Río Dulce** take the Barrios bus and get off at La Ruidosa junction and change, or change at Bananera/Morales. To **Flores** with **Transportes María Elena**, 8 hrs, 0400, 0800, 1300. Buses to **Ipala** and **Jalapa** also leave from here; 4 buses daily to Jalapa between 0500-1230, 4½ hrs, US$5.80; to Ipala, US$2.20. Supplemented by minibuses 0600-1715 to Ipala. To **Zacapa**, 25 mins, from the terminal inside the market at 10 Av between 1 and 2 Calle. Same for those to

Esquipulas, every 10 mins, US$2.70, until 1900. To and from **Cobán** via El Rancho (where a change must be made). Buses to **El Florido** (on the Honduras border) leave with **Transportes Vilma** from inside the market at 1 Calle, between 10 and 11 Av, T7942-2253, between 0530-1630, US$2.70, 1½ hrs. Buses return from the border at 0530, 0630 and then hourly 0700-1700. For more on crossing to Honduras, see box, page 213.

Esquipulas
Bus
Rutas Orientales. Leaving Esquipulas, 1 Av "A" and 11 Calle, T7943-1366, for **Guatemala City** every 30 mins from 0200-1700, 4½ hrs, US$8.50. To **Chiquimula** by minibus, every 30 mins, 0430-1830, US$1.40.

Quiriguá
Bus
Emphasize to the bus driver if you want Quiriguá *pueblo* and not the *ruinas*. Countless travellers have found themselves left at the ruins and having to make a return journey to the village for accommodation.

To get to the **ruins** directly, take any bus heading along the highway towards Puerto Barrios and ask to be let off at the *ruinas*. At this ruins crossroads, take a pickup (very regular), 10 mins, US$0.50, or bus (much slower and less regular) to the ruins 4 km away. The last bus back to the highway is at 1700. You can walk, but take lots of water, as it's hot and dusty with little shade.

To get to the **village** of Quiriguá, 3 km south from the ruins entrance road, it is only a 10-min walk to the **Hotel Royal**. Keep to the paved road, round a left-hand bend, and it's 100 m up on the left. Or take a local bus heading from the highway into the village. The **Hotel Edén** is a further 5 mins on down the hill. There is a frequent daily bus service that runs a circular route between Los Amates, Quiriguá village and then on to the entrance road to the ruins. You can also walk through the banana plantations from Quiriguá village to the ruins as well. From **Hotel Royal** walk past the church towards the old train station and the **Hotel Edén**, and follow the tracks branching to the right, through the plantation to the ruins.

Puerto Barrios
Boat

It's a 10-min walk to the municipal dock at the end of Calle 12, from the **Litegua** bus station. Ferries *(barca)* leave for **Lívingston** at 1030 and 0500 (1½ hrs, US$2.50). *Lanchas* also leave when a minimum of 12 people are ready to go, 30 mins, US$3.80. The only scheduled *lanchas* leave at 0630, 0730, 0900 and 1100, and the last will leave, if there are enough people, at 1800. **Transportes El Chato**, 1 Av, between 10 and 11 Calle, T7948-5525, pichilingo2000@yahoo.com, also does trips from here to **Punta de Manabique**, and other places near and far.

To Belize *Lanchas* leave for **Punta Gorda** at 1000 with **Transportes El Chato**, address above, returning at 1400, 1 hr 20 mins, US$22. Also services with **Requena** to Punta Gorda at 1400, returning at 0900. See also Border crossing box, page 212.

Bus

To **Guatemala City**, with **Litegua**, 6 Av between 9 and 10 Calle, T7948-1002, www.litegua.com. 18 a day, 5 hrs, US$11-7.50. Bus to **El Rancho** (turn-off for Biotopo del Quetzal and Cobán), 4 hrs, take any bus to Guatemala City. To **Quiriguá**, 2 hrs, take any capital-bound bus. To **Chiquimula**, operated by **Carmencita**, 4 hrs. Alternatively, catch a bus to Guatemala City, getting off at Río Hondo, and catch a *colectivo* or any bus heading to Chiquimula. For **Río Dulce**, take any bus heading for Guatemala City and change at **La Ruidosa** (15 mins). For minibuses to **Entre Ríos**, for the El Cinchado border crossing to **Honduras** (**Corinto**), with connections to **Omoa**, **Puerto Cortés** and **La Ceiba**. See also box, page 213, for more information on crossing into Honduras.

★Lívingston, or La Buga, is populated mostly by Garífuna, who bring a colourful flavour to this corner of Guatemala. With its tropical sounds and smells, it is a good place to hang out for a few days, sitting on the dock of the bay, or larging it up with the locals, *punta*-style.

Coco pan and *cocado* (a coconut, sugar and ginger *dulce*) and locally made jewellery are sold in the streets. The town is the centre of fishing and shrimping in the Bay of Amatique and only accessible by boat. It is nearly 23 km by sea from Puerto Barrios and there are regular daily boat runs that take 35 minutes in a fast *lancha*.

The bulk of the town is up a small steep slope leading straight from the dock, which is at the mouth of the Río Dulce estuary. The other part of town is a linear spread along the river estuary, just north of the dock and then first left. The town is small and everything is within walking distance. The Caribbean beach is pretty dirty nearer the river estuary end, but a little further up the coast, it is cleaner, with palm trees and accommodation. Closer to the town are a couple of bars and weekend beach discos. The town's **Centro Cultural Garífuna-Q'eqchi'** is perched on a hillock, and has the best views in the whole of Lívingston. The town's fiestas are 24-31 December, in honour of the Virgen del Rosario, with dancing including the *punta*, and Garífuna Day, 26 November. The small but helpful **tourist office** ⓘ *on the east side of the Parque Municipal, www.livingston.com.gt, daily 0600-1800,* with a café and exhibition space behind.

Around Lívingston

Northwest along the coastline towards the Río Sarstún, on the border with Belize (where manatee can be seen), is the **Río Blanco beach** (45 minutes by *lancha* from Lívingston), followed by **Playa Quehueche** (also spelt Keueche). Beyond Quehueche, about 6 km (1½ hours) from Lívingston, are **Los Siete Altares**, a set of small waterfalls and pools hidden in the greenery. They are at their best during the rainy season when the water cascades down to the sea. In the drier seasons much of the water is channelled down small, eroded grooves on large slabs of grey rock, where you can stretch out and enjoy the sun. Early *Tarzan* movies were filmed here. Don't stroll on the beach after dark and be careful of your belongings at the Siete Altares end. Police occasionally accompany tourists to the falls; check on arrival what the security situation is. Boats can be hired in Lívingston to visit beaches along the coast towards San Juan and the Río Sarstún.

For one of the best trips in Guatemala take a boat up the **Río Dulce** through the sheer-sided canyon towards El Golfete, where the river broadens. Trees and vegetation cling to the canyon walls, their roots plunging into the waters for a long drink below. The scenery here is gorgeous, especially in the mornings, when the waters are unshaken. Tours can be arranged from Lívingston for US$12. You can also paddle up the Río Dulce gorge on *cayucos*, which can be hired from some of the hotels in Lívingston.

The **Biotopo Chocón Machacas** ⓘ *0700-1600, US$2.50 (private hire at US$125 is the only transport option)*, is one place where the elusive manatee (sea cow) hangs out, but you are unlikely to see him munching his way across the lake bottom, as he is very shy and retreats at the sound of a boat motor. The manatee is an aquatic herbivore, which can be up to 4 m long when adult, and weigh more than 450 kg. It eats for six to eight hours daily and can consume more than 10% of its body weight in a 24-hour period. Administered by CECON, the reserve is a mangrove zone, halfway between Río Dulce town and Lívingston, on the northern shore of **El Golfete**, an area where the Río Dulce broadens into a lake 5 km across. Four Q'eqchi' communities of 400 people live on land within the 6245-ha reserve. Within the reserve are carpets of water lilies, dragonflies, blue morpho butterflies, pelicans and cormorants. On land, spot army ants, crabs, mahogany trees and the *labios rojos* ('hot lips') flower.

Proyecto Ak' Tenamit ⓘ *www.aktenamit.org*, meaning 'new village' in Q'eqchi', is 15 minutes upriver from Lívingston. It was set up to help 7000 Q'eqchi' Maya displaced by the civil war. Volunteers are needed for a minimum of a month's work (board and transport are available, and volunteers get weekends off). A working knowledge of Spanish is required. There's also a shop and restaurant, with excursions, run by locally trained volunteer guides. Near here is the **Río Tatín tributary** the wonderfully sited **Finca Tatín** and **Hotelito Perdido**; see Where to stay, below. **Reserva Ecológica Cerro San Gil**, with its natural pools, karstic caves and biostation, can be visited from here, or from Río Dulce. Contact FUNDAECO ⓘ *www.fundaeco.org.gt*.

Punta de Manabique

Punta de Manabique is a fine, finger-shaped peninsula northeast of Puerto Barrios and just visible across the bay from Lívingston, coated in a beach of white sand on its eastern side, and by mangrove on the other. Travelling north to the point of the peninsula, you pass the Bahía de Graciosa, where dolphins frolic and manatees silently graze under the surface. In its virgin tropical forest live howler monkeys, parrots, snakes, pizote, tapirs and peccary and, on its beaches, turtles. There is a visitor centre, scientific station and a hotel. For more information contact the **Fundación Mario Dary** ⓘ *www.guate.net/fundary manabique/fundacion.htm*, which operates conservation, health, education and ecotourism projects.

Listings Lívingston and around

Where to stay

$$$ Hotel Villa Caribe
Up Calle Principal from the dock on the right, T7947-0072, www.villasdeguatemala.com.

Part of an upscale Guatemalan hotel chain, Villa Caribe enjoys a privileged vantage from its hillside perch. All rooms have views of the Río Dulce or the Caribbean, there is also a pool (available to non-guests when the hotel is not busy for US$6.50), bar and a large restaurant. The best in town, popular with tour groups, but needs some maintenance.

$$ Posada El Delfín
T7947-0976, www.posadaeldelfin.com.
Located at the mouth of the Río Dulce on a long pier that juts out into the sea, El Delfín promises tranquil views of the local wildlife and boat traffic. They offer 24 reasonable rooms and suites, chill-out areas with hammocks, and a restaurant. Tours available.

$$ Vecchia Toscana
Barrio Paris, T7947-0884, www.livingston-vecchiatoscana.com.
This Italian-owned lodging on the beach features a leafy garden with a refreshing pool, breezy rooftop terraces, private pier and a decent Italian restaurant with sea views. Accommodation is in a variety of simple, tranquil, comfortable and occasionally brightly painted rooms, most of them equipped with a/c.

$ Casa de la Iguana
Calle Marcos Sánchez Díaz, 5 mins from the dock, T7947-0064, www.casadelaiguana.com.
A very cool party hostel with ultra-cheap dorms, private rooms with shared bath, and economical 'jungle huts' set around well-tended garden, as well as space for tents and hammocks. Hot showers, Wi-Fi, bar, daily happy hour and a pub quiz on Sun; what more could you need?

$ Casa Nostra
Near the river, T7947-0842, www.casanostralivingston.com.
Rooms at this simple little bed and breakfast are clean, cheap and colourful. It is recommended chiefly for its friendly host, Stuart Winand, and for its good food, which includes excellent pizza and fresh seafood prepared with international flavours. Very hospitable, good reports.

$ Casa Rosada
600 m from the dock, T7947-0303, www.hotelcasarosada.com.
This pastel-pink house set on the waterfront offers 10 bungalows furnished with attractive hand-painted furniture. The room upstairs overlooks the bay. Meals are set for the day, ranging from pasta to delicious shrimps bathed in garlic. Good, friendly and chilled out, but reservations advisable.

$ Flowas
Barrio Compoamor, on the beach, T7947-0376, infoflowas@gmail.com.
Rustic beach bungalows for those who like to be up close to the lapping ocean. Each unit has a porch and hammock. Tranquil and secluded with a hippy backpacker vibe.

$ Hotel Ríos Tropicales
T7947-0158, www.mctropic.webs.com.
This place has some nice touches to distinguish it from the majority of other places in town, like terracotta-tiled floors. They offer 11 rooms, with fans, 5 with private bath, book exchange and the **McTropic** restaurant up the road with internet and a tour operator.

Around Lívingston

$$-$ Q'ana Itz'am
Lagunita Salvador, T5992-1853, www.lagunitasalvador.com.
This excellent Q'eqchi community tourism project includes an ecolodge with rustic wooden cabins and a lovely jungle setting. Activities include kayaking, hiking, nature observation and traditional dances. Advance reservation absolutely necessary. Highly recommended.

$ Finca Tatín
Río Tatín tributary, with great dock space to hang out on, T5902-0831, www.fincatatin.centroamerica.com.
This lovely, rustic, wood-built B&B offers a range of Robinson Crusoe lodgings including dorms, private rooms and simple bungalows nestled in the jungle. The Casa Grande (main house) is the focal point for evening gatherings where you can enjoy games, books, table tennis and music. Tours and kayak rental available.

$ Hotel Ecológico Salvador Gaviota
Along the coast, towards Siete Altares, beyond Hotel Ecológico Siete Altares, T7947-0874, www.hotelsalvadorgaviota.com.
The beach here is lovely, hummingbirds flit about and the owner Lisette is friendly. Rooms have shared bath, but the bungalows for 2 or 4 people have private bath. Rooms available for monthly rent, all set in lush surroundings. There is a bar and restaurant (0730-2200), and free *lancha* service; ring beforehand. Tours available. Highly recommended.

$ Hotelito Perdido
On the Río Lampara, can be dropped off on the Livingston–Río Dulce boat service, T5725-1576, www.hotelitoperdido.com.
This quiet, rustic very attractive hideaway is located across the river from the mineral hot springs. Grounds include tropical gardens, winding pathways, bar-restaurant and 5 types of wood-built jungle lodgings. They also rent kayaks and wooden *cayucos*. Ecologically oriented with solar power, recycling and organic vegetable plots. Recommended.

$ The Roundhouse
La Pintada, 20 mins by boat from Livingston, T4294-9730, www.roundhouseguatemala.com.
The Roundhouse is a popular party hostel with a great setting on the riverbank. It has an environmentally aware ethos with solar hot water, a natural feed water system and bio-sand purification. Accommodation is in dorms or private rooms, both very affordable.

Restaurants

Fresh fish is available everywhere; in restaurants ask for *tapado*, a rich soup with various types of seafood, banana and coconut. Women sell *pan de coco* on the streets.

$$ Bahía Azul
Calle Principal.
Serving excellent breakfasts but dreadful coffee, this place specializes in salsas, *camarones* and *langosta*. There You can sit at tables on the street or in the dining room. There is also a tourist service and the **Exotic Travel Agency**.

$$ Buga Mama
An excellent example of an innovative development project and well worth checking out. Local Mayan young people staff this large restaurant located next to the water as part of their training with the Ak'Tenamit project (www.aktenamit.org). The food is OK, the service excellent, and it's in a great spot too.

$$ El Malecón
50 m from the dock on the left.
Serves *chapín* and Western-style breakfasts, seafood and chicken *fajitas*, all in a large, airy wooden dining area.

$$ Happy Fish
Just along from the Hotel Río Dulce.
A popular restaurant with an internet café. Serves a truckload of fish (not quite so happy now) with good coffee. Occasional live music at weekends.

$ McTropic
Opposite the Hotel Río Dulce.
This popular place offers great breakfasts and cocktails at street tables, with good service.

$ Rasta Mesa Restaurant
In Barrio Nevago, just past the cemetery, www.site.rasta mesa.com.
Garífuna cultural centre and restaurant with music, history, and classes in cooking and drumming. A great place to hang out.

$ Tiburón Gato
Far end of Calle Principal.
A simple open-fronted place, serving a good range of fish, seafood and pasta. It's open for breakfasts too.

Bars and clubs

Lugudi Barana
Sun 1500-0100 only.
A disco that's also on the beach and popular with visitors and locals.

Festivals

26 Nov Garífuna Day.
24-31 Dec In honour of the **Virgen del Rosario**, with traditional dancing.

What to do

Tour operators
Captain Eric, *located at the Pitchi Mango snack bar on the main street, T4265-5278.* Will arrange 1- to 2-day boat tours for groups of up to 5 people to the surrounding region.

You can also contract any of the *lancheros* at the dock to take you to Río Dulce, Playa Blanca and Siete Altares.

Transport

Boat
Ferry to **Puerto Barrios** to (22.5 km), 1½ hrs, US$1.60 at 0500 and 1400 Mon-Sat. Private *lanchas* taking 16-25 people also sail this route, 30 mins, US$4. They leave at 0630 and 0730 each day and at 0900 and 1100 Mon-Sat to Puerto Barrios and then when full. Lívingston to **Río Dulce**, with short stops at **Aguas Calientes** and the **Biotopo Chacón Machacas**, US$15.50 1 way. *Lanchas* definitely leave at 0900 and 1430 for **Río Dulce**, but these make no stops. To **Honduras** (Omoa, Puerto Cortés, La Ceiba), *lanchas* can be organized at the dock or through tour operators, see above. See also box, page 213. To **Belize** (Punta Gorda, Placencia, Cayos Zapotillos), check with tour operators, see above, about boats to Belize. Anyone who takes you must have a manifest with passengers' names, stamped and signed at the immigration office. On Tue and Fri fast *lanchas* make the trip to Punta Gorda (US$22). Enquire at the dock and negotiate a fare with the *lanchero* association. See also Border crossings box, page 212, for more information on crossing into Belize. Boats to Placencia and the Zapotilla cayes can also be arranged.

beautiful riverside and lakeside places to stay

★The vast Lago de Izabal, the largest lake in Guatemala at 717 sq km, narrows to form a neck at the town of Fronteras. Better known as Río Dulce, it is famed for its riverside setting. Just south of Río Dulce on the lake is the restored Castillo de San Felipe, while on the northern shore of the lake is the town of El Estor, and on its southern shore the smaller town of Mariscos. Further east, beyond Río Dulce, the river broadens out to El Golfete, where there is the Biotopo Chacón Machacas, see above. It then narrows into one of the finest gorges in the world, and opens out at its estuary, with Lívingston at its head. This area can be wet in the rainy season, but it experiences a lull in July, known as the *canícula*.

Fronteras/Río Dulce and around

Río Dulce is a good place to stop and kick back for a couple of days. Allow yourself to be tempted to laze on a boat for the afternoon, walk in the nearby jungle, or eat and drink at one of several dockside restaurants. Río Dulce, www.mayaparadise.com, is 23 km upstream from Lívingston at the entrance to Lago de Izabal, is easily accessible from Puerto Barrios by road, and is the last major stop before the Petén. It's also a good place to collect information about the area stretching from El Estor to Lívingston.

On the shore of Lago de Izabal is **Casa Guatemala** ① *14 Calle, 10-63, Zona 1, Guatemala City, T2231-9408, www.casa-guatemala.org* (also known as **Hotel Backpacker's**), an orphanage where you can work in exchange for basic accommodation and food. At the entrance to Lago de Izabal, 2 km upstream, is the old Spanish fort of **Castillo de San Felipe** ① *0800-1700, US$3.30*. The fortification was first built in 1643 to defend the coast against attacks from pirates; it has been well preserved and in lovely grounds; great views from the battlements. Between Río Dulce and El Estor is **Finca El Paraíso**, a hot waterfall with waters that plunge into a cool-water pool below.

El Estor and around

Strung along the northwest shore of Lago de Izabal, backed by the Santa Cruz mountain range and facing the Sierra de las Minas, El Estor enjoys one of the most beautiful vistas in Guatemala. It's a great place to relax, swim (down a nearby canyon), go fishing and spot manatee. Some businesses are expecting the new road to bring a surge of tourist visitors. For the next few years though you'll still have the place mostly to yourself. The town dates back to the days when the Europeans living in the Atlantic area got their provisions from a store situated at this spot, now the **Hotel Vista al Lago**. Briton Skinner and Dutchman Klee supplied the region from *el store* 1815-1850. Nickel mining began just outside town in 1978, but was suspended at the **Exmibal plant** after the oil crisis of 1982, because the process depended on cheap sources of energy.

You can hire a boat from Río Dulce to El Estor, passing near the hot waterfall, inland at Finca El Paraíso, which can be reached by a good trail in about 40 minutes. The Río Sauce cuts through the impressive **Cañón El Boquerón**, where you can swim with the current all the way down the canyon, which is brilliant fun. It's a deep canyon with lots of old man's beard hanging down, strange rock formations and otters and troops of howler monkeys whooping about. One of the locals will paddle you upstream for about 800 m (US$1). Exploring the Río Zarco, closer to town, also makes for a good trip, with cold swimming. The **Refugio de Vida Silvestre Bocas del Polochic** (Bocas del Polochic Wildlife Reserve) is a 23,000-ha protected area on the western shores of the lake. Howler monkeys are commonly seen. In addition to over 350 bird species, there are iguanas, turtles and the chance of sighting crocodiles and manatees. The NGO **Defensores de la Naturaleza** ⓘ *2 Calle and 5 Av, El Estor, T2440-8138 in the capital, www.defensores. org.gt*, has a research station at Selempim with bunk beds ($ per person), food, showers and kitchen. It's a two- or three-hour boat ride from El Estor to Ensenada Los Lagartos. Tours are available from town for US$30 for two people. Contact the office in El Estor or ask at a hotel about boat services.

Mariscos is on the southern shore of Lago de Izabal. The best reason to come here is the nearby **Denny's Beach**; see Where to stay, below.

Listings Lago de Izabal

Where to stay

Fronteras/Río Dulce and around
All the establishments below are located out of town on the water. If you need to stay in the less attractive locale of Río Dulce itself, try **Hotel Vista al Río** ($), just past **Bruno's** under the bridge, T7930-5665, www.hotelvistario.com.

$$$-$$ Hacienda Tijax
T7930-5505, www.tijax.com. 2 mins by lancha *from the dock, yacht moorings available.*
There is a beautiful jungle trail with canopy walkway at the tranquil Hacienda Tijax, also a rubber plantation, bird sanctuary, pool with whirlpool and jacuzzi, and natural swimming pools. Activities include horse riding, kayaking, sailing and rowboat hire and a medicine trail.

Accommodation is in well-built wooden cabins with mod cons, including a/c. There is excellent food in the riverside bar and restaurant. Highly recommended.

$$-$ Tortugal Hotel and Marina
T5306-6432, www.tortugal.com.
Beautifully presented bungalows with gorgeous soft rugs on the floor and various other types of accommodation including open-air ranchos and a *casita*. There is plentiful hot water. Also here is a riverside restaurant and bar, pool table in a cool upstairs attic room with books, satellite TV, internet, phone and fax service. Very highly recommended.

$ Hotel Backpacker's
Just out of town by the bridge on the south bank of the river, T7930-5169, www.hotelbackpackers.com.

Profits of Hotel Backpacker's go to the Casa Guatemala Orphanage and guests have the option of working for their lodging as part of a volunteer holiday. There are basic dorms with lockers and simple private rooms with bathroom, as well as a restaurant and bar,and internet and telephone service. Recommended.

$ Hotel Kangaroo
On the Río La Colocha, T5363-6716, www.hotelkangaroo.com.
Perched on the water's edge, this Mexican-Australian owned river lodge has rustic wood-built rooms, dorms and bungalows, all very simple and close to nature. There's a bar-restaurant on the decking serving Aussie and Mexican grub, and an unheated jacuzzi.

El Estor and around

$$$-$$ Denny's Beach
T5398-0908, www.dennysbeach.com.
This remote place offers resort-style lodgings with a gorgeous lakeside location, accessible by *lancha* from Río Dulce (minimum fee US$41), or free from Mariscos if you call ahead. Tours, wake boarding and horse riding can be arranged. Internet service.

$ Hotel Vista al Lago
6 Av, 1-13, T7949-7205.
21 clean rooms with private bath and fan. Ask for the lakeview rooms, where there is a pleasant wooden balcony on which to sit. Friendly owner Oscar Paz will take you fishing, and runs ecological and cultural tours.

$ Villela
6 Av, 2-06, T7949-7214.
With a flower-filled garden with chairs to sit out in, this place has 9 big, clean rooms with bath, although some are quite dark. Recommended.

Restaurants

Fronteras/Río Dulce and around
There are restaurants in the hotels and a couple along the main road.

$$-$ Ranchón Mary
El Relleno, T7930-5103.
Thatch-roofed waterfront deck with tables, serving delicious fish and seafood and ice-cold beer.

$$-$ Rosita's Restaurant
San Felipe de Lara, T5054-3541.
Lovely waterfront location with open deck, overlooking the bridge, 5 mins by *lancha* from Río Dulce. Great seafood, nachos and home-made banana pie.

El Estor and around

$ Dorita
Popular with the locals, this *comedor* serves good seafood meals which are excellent value.

$ Marisabela
8 Av and 1 Calle.
Good and cheap spaghetti, as well as fish and chicken, with lake views.

$ Restaurant del Lago
West side of main square.
This popular restaurant overlooks the main square and offers local dishes.

$ Restaurant Elsita
2 blocks north of the market on 8 Av.
This is a great people-watching place with a large menu and good food.

What to do

Fronteras/Río Dulce
Sailing
Captain John Clark's sailing trips on his 46-ft Polynesian catamaran, *Las Sirenas*, are highly recommended. Food,

taxes, snorkelling and fishing gear, and windsurf boards included. Contact **Aventuras Vacacionales SA**, Antigua, www.sailing-diving-guatemala.com; see page 52.

Coastguard For emergencies, call Guarda Costa on VHF channel 16, T4040-4971.

Tour operators
Atitrans Tours, *on the little road heading to the dockside*. To **Finca Paraíso** for US$20.
Otiturs, *opposite Tijax Express, T5219-4520*. Run by the friendly and helpful Otto Archila. Offers a minibus service as well as tours to local sites, internal flights and boat trips.
Tijax Express, *opposite Atitrans, T7930-5505, info@tijax.com*. Agent for Hacienda Tijax (over the river).
Lancheros offer trips on the river and on Lago de Izabal. They can be contacted at the *muelle principal*, under the bridge. Ask for César Mendez, T5819-7436, or ask at **Atitrans** for collection.

Transport

Fronteras/Río Dulce and around
Boat
Lanchas colectivas leave for **Lívingston** at 0930 and 1300, US$15.50. Private *lanchas* can be arranged at the dock to any of the river or lakeside hotels.

Bus
Local To get to **Castillo de San Felipe**, take a boat from Río Dulce, or *camioneta* from the corner of the main road to Tikal, and the first turning left after the bridge by **Pollandia**, 5 mins, or a 5-km walk. From Río Dulce to **Finca El Paraíso**, take the same road, 45 mins, US$1.70. Buses to Río Dulce pass the finca between 40 and

50 mins past the hour. To **El Estor**, from the same Pollandia turn-off, US$2.50, 1½ hrs on a paved road, 0500-1600, hourly, returning 0500-1600. To **Puerto Barrios**, take any bus to **La Ruidosa** and change, 35 mins to junction then a further 35 mins to Puerto Barrios.

Long-distance To **Guatemala City** and **Flores**: through buses stop at Río Dulce. To **Guatemala City** with Litegua, T7930-5251, www.litegua.com, 7 a day between 0300 and 1515, US$7.54, 6 hrs. **Fuente del Norte**, T5692-1988, 23 services daily, US$6.30. Luxury service 1300, 1700 and 2400, US$13. **Línea Dorada**, at 1300, luxury service, 5 hrs, US$13. To **Flores** from 0630-0300, 25 buses daily, 4½ hrs with **Fuente del Norte**, US$8. Luxury service, 1430, US$13. This bus also stops at **Finca Ixobel** and **Poptún**, US$3.90. **Línea Dorada**, to Flores, 1500, 3 hrs, luxury service with a/c, TV and snacks, US$13, and on to **Melchor de Mencos** for Belize; see also Border crossing box, page 212, for more information on crossing into Belize. **Fuente del Norte**, also to **Melchor de Mencos**, at 1300, 2130 and 2330, 6 hrs, US$12.50. Also to, **Sayaxché** at 2200 and one to **Naranjo** at 2100.

Shuttles Atitrans, T7930-5111, www.atitrans.com, runs shuttles to **Antigua**, **Flores**, **Copán Ruinas** and **Guatemala City**.

El Estor and around
Bus The ferry from Mariscos no longer runs, but a private *lancha* can be contracted.

To **Río Dulce**, 0500-1600, hourly, 1 hr, US$2.20. Direct bus to **Cobán**, at 1300, 7 hrs, US$5.60. Also via either Panzós and Tactic, or Cahabón and Lanquín. For the **Cañón El Boquerón**, take the Río Dulce bus and ask to be dropped at the entrance. Or hire a bike from town (8 km) or a taxi, US$6.50, including waiting time.

To **Cobán**, with **Transportes Valenciana**, 1200, 0200, 0400 and 0800, 8 long and dusty hrs, with no proper stop. To **Guatemala City**, 0100 direct, via Río Dulce, 7 hrs, US$6.30, or go to Río Dulce and catch one. At 2400 and 0300 via Río Polochic Valley. For **Santa Elena, Petén** take a bus to Río Dulce and pick on up from there.

The Verapaces

Propped up on a massive limestone table eroded over thousands of years, the plateau of the Verapaz region is riddled with caves, underground tunnels, stalagtites and stalagmites. Cavernous labyrinths used by the Maya for worship, in their belief that caves are the entrances to the underworld, are also now visited by travellers who marvel at the natural interior design of these subterranean spaces.

Nature has performed its work above ground too. At Semuc Champey, pools of tranquil, turquoise-green water span a monumental limestone bridge; beneath the bridge a river thunders violently through. The quetzal reserve also provides the opportunity to witness a feather flash of red or green of the elusive bird, and dead insects provide curious interest in Rabinal, where their body parts end up on ornamental gourds.

The centre of this region – the imperial city of Cobán – provides respite for the traveller with a clutch of museums honouring the Maya, coffee and orchid, and a fantastic entertainment spectacle at the end of July with a whirlwind of traditional dances and a Maya beauty contest.

Baja Verapaz region is made up of a handful of Achi'-Maya speaking towns, namely Salamá, Rabinal, San Jerónimo and Cubulco. The department is known for the quetzal reserve, the large Dominican finca and aqueduct, and the weird decorative technique of the crafts in Rabinal.

Sierra de las Minas Biosphere Reserve

To visit, get a permit in San Augustín from the office of La Fundación de Defensores de la Naturaleza, Barrio San Sebastián, 1 block before the Municipalidad, T7936-0681, ctot@ defensores.org.gt, www.defensores.org.gt. The contact is César Tot. Alternatively, contact the Fundación offices in Santa Elena, Petén, at 5 Calle, 3 Av "A", Zona 2, T7926-3095, lacandon@ defensores.org.gt, or in the capital at 7 Av, 7-09, Zona 13, T2440-8138.

Just north of El Rancho, in the Department of El Progreso, is **San Agustín Acasaguastlán**, an entrance for the Sierra de las Minas Biosphere Reserve, one of Guatemala's largest conservation areas with peaks topping 3000 m and home to the quetzal, harpy eagle and peregrine falcon, puma, jaguar, spider monkey, howler monkey, tapir and pizote.

Biotopo del Quetzal

Daily 0700-1600, US$2.60, parking, disabled entrance. Run by Centro de Estudios Conservacionistas (CECON), Av Reforma, 0-63, Zona 10, Guatemala City, T2331-0904, cecon@usac.edu.gt.

The Biotopo del Quetzal, or **Biosphere Mario Dary Rivera**, is between Cobán and Guatemala City at Km 160.5, 4 km south of Purulhá and 53 km from Cobán. There are two trails. Increasing numbers of quetzals have been reported in the Biotopo, but they are still very elusive. Ask for advice from the rangers. The area around the Biotopo has been protected as a **Corredor Biológico Bosque Nuboso**, with numerous privately run reserves and restaurants by the roadside offering birdwatching trails, waterfalls, natural swimming holes and caves. For more information, see www.bosquenuboso.com.gt.

Salamá, Rabinal and Cubulco

Just before Salamá is **San Jerónimo**, with a Dominican church and convent, from where friars tended vineyards, exported wine and cultivated sugar. There is an old sugar mill (*trapiche*) on display at the finca and a huge aqueduct of 124 arches to transport water to the sugar cane fields and the town. Salamá sits in a valley with a colonial cathedral, containing carved gilt altarpieces as its centrepiece. The town also has one of a few remaining **Templos de Minerva** in the country, built in 1916. Behind the Calvario church is the hill Cerro de la Santa Cruz, from where a view of the valley can be seen. Market day is Monday and is worth a visit.

BACKGROUND

The Verapaces

Before the Spanish conquest of the region, Las Verapaces had a notorious reputation; it was known as Tezulutlán (land of war) for its aggressive warlike residents, who fought repeated battles with their neighbours and rivals, the K'iche' Maya. These warring locals were not going to be a pushover for the Spanish conquerors and they strongly resisted when their land was invaded. The Spanish eventually retreated and the weapon replaced with the cross. Thus, Carlos V of Spain gave the area the title of Verdadera Paz (true peace) in 1548.

The region's modern history saw it converted into a massive coffee- and cardamom-growing region. German coffee fincas were established from the 1830s until the Second World War, when the Germans were invited over to plough the earth by the Guatemalan government. Many of the fincas were expropriated during the war, but some were saved from this fate by naming a Guatemalan as the owner of the property. The area still produces some of Guatemala's finest coffee – served up with some of the finest cakes. The Germans also introduced cardamom to the Verapaces, when a *finquero* requested some seeds for use in biscuits. Guatemala is now the world's largest producer of cardamom.

The village of **Rabinal** was founded in 1537 by Fray Bartolomé de las Casas. It has a 16th-century church, and a busy Sunday market, where lacquered gourds, beautiful *huipiles* and embroidered napkins are sold. The glossy lacquer of the gourd is made from the body oil of a farmed scaly insect called the *niij*. The male *niij* is boiled in water to release its oil, which is then mixed with soot powder to create the lacquer. The **Museo Rabinal Achí** ⓘ *2 Calle y 4 Av, Zona 3, T5311-1536, museoachi@hotmail.com*, displays historical exhibits and has produced bilingual books about the Achí culture.

West of Rabinal, set amid maize fields and peach trees, Cubulco is known for its tradition of performing the pole dance, *Palo Volador,* which takes place every 20-25 July. Men, attached by rope, have to leap from the top of the pole and spiral down, accompanied by marimba music. There are three basic *hospedajes* in town.

Listings Baja Verapaz

Where to stay

Biotopo del Quetzal

$$ Posada Montaña del Quetzal
At Km 156, T7823-9636,
www.hposadaquetzal.com.

Rustic and remote, this tranquil highland *posada* offers modest bungalows or rooms with spartan furnishings, private bathrooms and hot water; try to get one with a fireplace so you can get good and toasty after dark. There's also café, bar, pool and gardens. Simple, romantic and rugged.

$$ Ram Tzul
Km 158, T5908-4066, www.ramtzul.com.
Set in rambling 100-ha grounds, the
wood-built cabins at Ram Tzul are
very beautiful and creatively rendered,
some of them featuring stained-glass
windows, lovely stonework and superb
views of the forested hills. The restaurant
is equally interesting and serves hearty
comida típica. Dozens of excursions can
be arranged. Recommended.

$ Hospedaje Ranchitos del Quetzal
Km 160.8, T7823-5860.
Conveniently located just 200 m from
the Biotopo entrance, this economical
place has clean and simple rooms in
old and new buildings, with shared
or private bathrooms and hot water.
There's also a *comedor.* It's good for early
morning foray.

Transport

Biotopo del Quetzal
Bus
From **Guatemala City**, take a Cobán
bus with **Escobar-Monja Blanca** and
ask to be let out at the Biotopo, hourly
from 0400-1700, 3½ hrs, US$3.50. From
Cobán, 1 hr, US$0.80, take any capital-
bound bus or a minibus from Campo
2 near football stadium every 20 mins,
US$0.80. From **El Rancho**–Biotopo,
1¼ hrs. Cobán–Purulhá, local buses ply
this route between 0645-2000 returning
until 1730, 1 hr 20 mins.

Salamá, Rabinal and Cubulco
Bus
Salamá–Rabinal, 1-1½ hrs. Rabinal is
reached by travelling west from Salamá
on a paved road. From **Guatemala
City**, 5½ hrs, a beautiful, occasionally
heart-stopping ride, or via El Progreso,
and then Salamá by bus. Buses leave
0330-1600 to Guatemala City via Salamá
from Cubulco. There is a bus between
Rabinal and Cubulco, supplemented by
pickup rides.

Alta Verapaz
mountainous limestone region with caves and a mystical lake

The region of Alta Verapaz is based on a gigantic mountain, Sierra de Chamá.
Dinosaurs roamed the area more than 65 million years ago before it was engulfed
by sea. It later emerged, covered with limestone rock, which over millions of
years has left the area riddled with caves, and dotted with small hills. In the far
northwest of the department are the emerald-green waters of Laguna Lachuá.

Santa Cruz Verapaz and around
Santa Cruz Verapaz has a fine white 16th-century church with a fiesta between
1-4 May when you can see the wonderful Danza de los Guacamayos (scarlet
macaws). This **Poqomchi' Maya** village is 15 km northwest of Tactic, at the junction
with the road to Uspantán. To get there, take the San Cristóbal Verapaz bus, 25
minutes, or take a bus heading to the capital, get off at the junction and walk 200

m into town. The local fiestas are 15, 20 January, 21-26 July with the *Palo Volador*. The devil-burning dance can be seen on 8 December. Six kilometres west towards Uspantán is **San Cristóbal Verapaz**, which has a large, white, colonial church. From the church, a 1-km long, straight, road (Calle del Calvario) slopes down and then curves upwards to a hilltop **Calvario Church**. At Easter, the whole road is carpeted in flowers that rival those on display in Antigua at this time of year. There is **Museo Katinamit** ① *T7950-4039, cecep@intelnet. net.gt, Mon-Fri 0900-1200, 1500-1700, run by the Centro Comunitario Educativo Poqomchi'*, dedicated to the preservation and learning of the Poqomchi' culture.

Listings Alta Verapaz

Where to stay

$$$-$$ Casa Kirvá
Km 204.4, Tontem village, T4693-4800, www.casakirva.com.
Perched on a hill, Casa Kirvá is a reasonably new, beautifully constructed lodge with fine stone and woodwork, wonderful landscaped grounds and a striking architectural design that successfully blends contemporary and colonial styles. Rooms veer toward comfort and simplicity rather than ostentatiousness.

$$$-$$ Hotel Park
Km 196, on the main road south of the junction to the Poqomchi' Maya village, Santa Cruz, T7955-3600, www.parkhotelresort.com.
This Italian-owned resort on the highway has a lavish and immaculately landscaped garden, restaurants, gym, tennis court, heated pool, convention centre, wildlife rescue centre and, should you require it for a dramatic entrance or exit, a helipad. Accommodation includes 158 rooms and *casitas* spread across 7 complexes.

$ Eco Hotel Chi' Ixim
Km 182.5, just beyond Tactic, T7953-9198.
Simple and rustic, Chi' Ixim offers economical rooms and cabins with

private bath, hot water and fireplaces. There is also a restaurant, garden and lots of wandering livestock.

$ Hotel El Portón Real
4 Av, 1-44, Zona 1, Santa Cruz Verapaz, T7950-4604.
This hotel may look dreary from the outside, but inside it's lovely, with lots of wood furnishings and run by a very friendly *señora*. There are rooms with bath, cheaper without, as well as hot water and free drinking water. The hotel closes its doors at 2130.

Transport

Bus
From **Cobán** between 0600-1915 every 15 mins, US$0.700, 40 mins. All capital-bound buses from Cobán run through **Tactic**, or take a local bus between 0645-2000, returning between 0500-1730, 40 mins, US$0.80. Bus from Cobán to **Senahú**, 6 hrs, from opposite INJAV building, from 0600-1400, 4 daily, US$2.90. If you are coming from El Estor, get off at the Senahú turn-off, hitch or wait for the buses from Cobán. Trucks take this road, but there is little traffic, so you have to be at the junction very early to be in luck.

attractive colonial town surrounded by coffee plantations

The cathedral and centre of the Imperial City of Cobán (www.cobanav.net, altitude 1320 m), is perched on a long, thin plateau with exceptionally steep roads climbing down from the plaza. To the south the roads are filled with the odd, well-preserved colonial building and a coffee finca.

There is year-round soft rainfall, known as *chipi-chipi*, which is a godsend to the coffee and cardamom plants growing nearby. Most visitors use the city as a base for visiting sights in the surrounding area, trips to Semuc Champey, Languin and as a stepping-off point for rafting trips on the Río Cahabón. English is spoken at the **city tourist office** ⓘ *Parque Central*, where they have lots of information and can help organize tours. The **INGUAT office** ⓘ *7 Av 1-17, in Los Arcos shopping centre, T7951-0216, Mon-Fri 0800-1600, Sat 0900-1300*, is very helpful with leaflets and maps on the whole Verapaz region. For online information on northern Alta Verapaz and the southern Petén, check www.puertamundomaya.com.

The **cathedral** is on the east side of the Parque Central and dates from the middle of the 16th century. The chapel of **El Calvario**, in the northwest, has its original façade still intact. On the way up to the church are altars used by worshippers who freely blend Maya and Roman Catholic beliefs. It's worth climbing the 142 steps to get a bird's-eye view of Cobán. The **Museo El Príncipe Maya** ⓘ *6 Av, 4-26, Zona 3, Mon-Sat 0900-1300, 1400-1800, US$1.30*, is a private museum of pre-Columbian artefacts. The **Parque Nacional Las Victorias** ⓘ *just west of El Calvario, daily 0700-1800, US$0.80*, has two little lagoons in its 84 ha. There are paths and you can picnic and camp, toilets but no showers, but check with the tourist office about safety before going. The daily market is near the bus terminal.

Starbucks coffee fans can check out where their mug of the old bean comes from, direct from **Finca Santa Margarita** ⓘ *on the edge of town, 3 Calle, 4-12, Zona 2, T7951-3067, Mon-Fri 0800-1230, 1330-1700, Sat 0800-1200, 45-min tour with English/Spanish-speaking guides, US$2.50*. Don't miss a visit to the flower-filled world of **Vivero Verapaz** ⓘ *2.5 km southwest of town, 40-min walk, or taxi ride, 0900-1200, 1400-1700 daily, US$1.30; US$1.30 for guided tour*, an orchid farm with more than 23,000 specimens, mostly flowering from December to February – the best time to go – with the majority flowering in January.

Around Cobán

Southeast of Cobán (8 km) is **San Juan Chamelco** with an old colonial church. A one-hour walk from here is **Aldea Chajaneb** (see Where to stay, below). Along this road are the caves of **Grutas Rey Marcos** ⓘ *US$1.30*, and **Balneario Cecilinda** ⓘ *0800-1700*. **San Pedro Carchá** is 5 km east of Cobán on the main road and used to be famous for its pottery, textiles, wooden masks and silver, but only the pottery and silver are available now. The local food speciality here is *kaq Ik*, a turkey broth.

Where to stay

Accommodation is extremely hard to find on the Fri and Sat of Rabin Ajau (last week of Jul) and in Aug. For Rabin Ajau you need to be in town a few days beforehand to secure a room, or ring and reserve.

$$ Casa Duranta
3 Calle, 4-46, Zona 3, T7951-4188, www.casaduranta.com.
With a convenient central location near the plaza, Casa Duranta has 10 large, simple rooms with hot water, cable TV, Wi-Fi, hardwood furnishings and hand-woven Guatemalan bedspreads. The leafy garden and interior courtyard are popular with hummingbirds, a definite plus. Ask for a quieter room away from reception and the street.

$$ Casa Gaia
9 Av Final, Zona 10, Barrio San Jorge, T7941-7021, www.hotelcasagaia.com.
Surrounded by native pine forests on the edge of the city, 14 blocks from central park (20 mins' walk), Casa Gaia is a lovely secluded lodge set in well-tended 10-ha grounds. Rooms are simple, tasteful and tranquil, and their restaurant overlooks

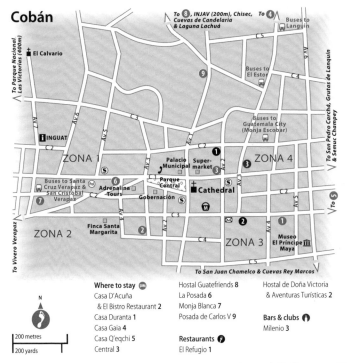

Cobán

To **8**, INJAV (200m), Chisec, To **4**
Cuevas de Candelaria & Laguna Lachuá

Buses to Lanquín

To Parque Nacional Las Victorias (400m)

■ El Calvario

Buses to El Estor

Buses to Guatemala City (Monja Escobar)

INGUAT

ZONA 1

Palacio Municipal Super-market

ZONA 4

Buses to Santa Cruz Verapaz & San Cristóbal Verapaz

Adrenalina Tours

Parque Central

Gobernación

✝ Cathedral

ZONA 2

Finca Santa Margarita

ZONA 3

Museo El Príncipe Maya

To San Juan Chamelco & Cuevas Rey Marcos

To San Pedro Carchá, Grutas de Lanquín

To Semuc Champey

To Vivero Verapaz

N

200 metres
200 yards

the trees with a pleasant open-air veranda.

$$ Casa Q'eqchi
4 Calle, 7-29, Zona 3, T3295-9169, www.hotelencoban.com.
Family-owned and operated, Casa Q'eqchi is a very helpful, friendly and personable boutique B&B. The emphasis is on service and hospitality, and they are also quite knowledgeable about Mayan culture. The rooms are attractive and comfortable, tastefully combining colonial and modern styles. There is a pleasant courtyard too. Recommended.

$$ La Posada
1 Calle, 4-12, Zone 2, T7952-1495, www.laposadacoban.com.gt.
One of Cobán's best, this handsome colonial hotel offers 16 atmospheric rooms decorated with popular and religious art, antique furnishings, tiled bathrooms and fireplaces. The gardens are flourishing and well-kept. Featuring a terrace and fireplace, the restaurant is stylish too; stop by for a drink, if nothing else. Credit cards accepted.

$$-$ Hostal Guatefriends
Carretera Cobán-Guatemala Km 205, T4715-3508.
Located 10 mins out of the city, this very restful and highly appealing B&B is in a beautiful and unusual building reminiscent of an Alpine lodge with its fine stonework, slanted ceilings and cosy wood-panelled enclaves. It's set in verdant grounds, with expansive views of the hills. The owners are lovely and helpful, and it's a great choice for couples and families. There are economical dorms too ($). Recommended.

$$-$ Posada de Carlos V
1 Av, 3-44, Zona 1, T7951 3501, www.hotelcarlosvcoban.com.
This is a calm oasis hidden from the chaos of the market outside. The attractive landscaped grounds include a rocky hillside and walking trail laden with flowers and trees. Accommodation spans 22 rooms with pine furniture, cable TV, Wi-Fi and hot water.

$ Casa D'Acuña
4 Calle, 3-11, Zona 2, T7951-0482, www.casadeacuna.com.
Housed by a fine colonial edifice, Casa D'Acuña is a decent hostel with 4 small dorms and 2 private rooms, shared ultra-clean bathrooms with hot water, laundry service, internet, excellent meals, tempting goodies and coffee in **El Bistro** restaurant, which overlooks a pretty courtyard (see Restaurants, below). The owners also run a tourist office, shop and tours. Recommended.

$ Central
1 Calle, 1-79, T7952-1442.
A stone's throw from the cathedral in a great location, Hotel Central has 15 very clean large rooms with hot shower, all set around a central patio. Rooms with TV cost a little extra. A good budget option.

$ Monja Blanca
2 Calle, 6-30 Zona 2, T7952-1712.
The peaceful, simple, comfortable place is run by a slightly eccentric *señora* and looks shut from the outside. Once inside, all rooms are set around a tranquil leafy courtyard, which is great for chilling out. There is also an old-fashioned dining room serving good value breakfast. Recommended.

Restaurants

$$$-$$ El Bistro
In Casa D'Acuña, see Where to stay, above.
Excellent menu and massive portions. Try the blueberry pancakes. There's also great yogurt, and don't walk through the restaurant without putting your nose into the cake cabinet! Recommended.

$$ El Refugio
2 Av, 2-28, Zona 4, T7952-1338. Open 1030-2300.
Excellent service and substantial portions at good-value prices of steaks, fish, chicken and snacks, as well as set lunch. There are also cocktails, a big screen TV and a bar.

$$ Hostal de Doña Victoria
See Where to stay, above.
Serves breakfast, lunch and supper in a semi-open area with a pleasant, quiet ambience. Good Italian food, including vegetarian options, is the speciality of the house. There is also a mini cellar bar.

Cafés

Café Fantasia
1 Calle, 3-13, western end of the main park.
A handy spot open for breakfast.

Café La Posada
Part of La Posada (see Where to stay). Open afternoons.
Divine brownies and ice cream, sofas with a view of the Parque Central.

Bars and clubs

Milenio
3 Av 1-11, Zona 4.
A popular place with a mature crowd and 5 rooms, a dance floor, live music weekends, beer by the jug, pool table and big screen TV. There's a minimum consumption of US$3 at weekends.

Entertainment

Cinema
Plaza Magdalena, *a few blocks west of town.* Multi-screen cinema usually showing the latest releases.

Festivals

Mar/Apr **Holy Week**.
Last week of Jul **Rabin Ajau**, the election of the Maya Beauty Queen. Around this time the **Paa banc** is also performed, when the chiefs of brotherhoods are elected for the year.
1-6 Aug **Santo Domingo**, the town's fiesta in honour of its patron.

What to do

Adrenalina Tours, *west of the main square.* Reliable tour operator, with a national presence.
Aventuras Turísticas, *3 Calle, 2-38, Zona 3, T7952-2213, www.aventurasturisticas. com.* Also offers tourist information.
Proyecto Ecológico Quetzal, *2 Calle, 14-36, Zona 1, Cobán, T7952-1047, www. ecoquetzal.org.* Contact David Unger. Trips are organized to the multicoloured Río Ikbolay, northwest of Cobán, see page 161, and the mountain community of Chicacnab.

Transport

Bus
The central bus terminal has attempted to group the multitude of bus stations into one place. While many now depart from this bus terminal, there are still a number of departure points scattered

around town. Seek local advice for updates or changes.

To **Guatemala City** with **Transportes Escobar-Monja Blanca**, T7951-3571, every 30 mins from 0200-1600, 4-5 hrs, US$7, from its own offices near the terminal. **El Estor**, 4 daily from Av 5, Calle 4, 1st at 0830, and mostly morning departures, but check in the terminal beforehand, 7 hrs, US$5.60.

To **Fray Bartolomé de las Casas**, 0600-1600 by bus, pickup and trucks, every 30 mins. Route **Raxrujá–Sayaxché–Flores** there are minibuses **Micro buses del Norte** that leave from the terminal del norte near INJAV 0530 and 0630, 5 hrs, US$7.20. In Sayaxché you take a passenger canoe across the river (there is also a car ferry) where minibuses will whisk you to Flores on a tarmacked road in 45 mins. To **Uspantán**, 1000 and 1200, 5 hrs, US$2 from 1 Calle and 7 Av, Zona 2. Cobán can be reached from **Santa Cruz del Quiché** via Sacapulas and Uspantán, and from **Huehuetenango** via Aguacatán, Sacapulas and Uspantán.

Around Cobán
Bus
Every 20 mins from Cobán to **San Juan Chamelco**, US$0.25, 20 mins from Wasen Bridge, Diagonal 15, Zona 7
To **San Pedro Carchá**, every 15 mins, US$0.25, 20 mins from 2 Calle and 4 Av, Zona 4.

Lanquín and Semuc Champey
limestone caves and green-and-blue coloured pools

★Lanquín is surrounded by mountainous scenery reminiscent of an Alpine landscape. It nestles in the bottom of a valley, where a river runs. With this mountain ambience, caves and the clear water pools at Semuc Champey, it is worth kicking back for a few days and inhaling the high-altitude air.

Lanquín is 56 km east of Cobán, 10 km from the Pajal junction. Just before the town are the **Grutas de Lanquín** ⓘ *0800-1600, US$3, 30-min walk from town*. The caves are lit for 200 m and strange stalactite shapes are given names, but it's worth taking a torch. The cave, whose ceiling hangs with thousands of stalactites, is dangerously slippery from guano mud, although handrails will help you out. The sight of the bats flying out at dusk is impressive. Outside the cave you can swim in the river and camp for free.

From Lanquín you can visit the natural bridge of **Semuc Champey** ⓘ *0600-1800, US$6, parking available*, a liquid paradise stretching 60 m across the Cahabón Gorge. The limestone bridge is covered in stepped, glowing blue and green water pools which span the length and breadth of it. Upstream you can see the water being channelled under the bridge. As it thunders through, it is spectacular. At its voluminous exit you can climb down from the bridge and see it cascading. You can swim in all the pools and little hot flows pour into some of them. Tours of Semuc Champey from Cobán cost around US$31.

ON THE ROAD

Nature tourism

The majority of tour operators listed in this guide will offer nature-oriented tours. There are several national parks, biotopes and protected areas in Guatemala, each with their highlights. CECON (Centro de Estudios Conservacionistas) and INGUAT have set up conservation areas for the protection of Guatemalan wildlife (the quetzal, manatee, jaguar, etc) and their habitats. Several other national parks (some including Maya archaeological sites) and forest reserves have been set up or are planned. For wildlife volunteering opportunities, see page 227.

CONAP (Consejo Nacional de Areas Protegidas), T2238-0000, http://conap. online.fr, is the national parks and protected areas authority.

Proyecto Ecológico Quetzal, T7952-1047, www.ecoquetzal.org, a non-profit-making project, is another useful organization. It offers eco-tourism stays with indigenous families in remote areas.

Parque Nacional Laguna Lachuá
T5704 1509 to hire a guide for the day, US$4, main entrance, US$5.20, Mon-Sat 0900-1700.

Near **Playa Grande**, northwest of Cobán, is Parque Nacional Laguna Lachuá. The deep velvet-green lake, formed by a meteor impact, is 5 sq km and 220 m deep in places. It is surrounded by virtually unspoilt dense jungle, and the chances of seeing wildlife at dawn and dusk are high. There is a guided nature trail and camping and a basic guesthouse. In this area is the **Río Ikbolay**, a green river that runs underground through caves. When it emerges the other side it is blue. The river has changed its course over time leaving some of its run-through caves empty, making it possible to walk through them. The **Proyecto Ecológico Quetzal**, see page 159, runs jungle hikes in this area.

Listings Lanquín and Semuc Champey

Where to stay

Semuc Champey

$$-$ Greengo's
400 m from Semuc Champey, T3020-8016, www.greengoshotel.com.
A good Israeli-run hostel in a natural setting and a convenient location near the pools. There are simple dorms,

rooms and brightly painted wooden cabins with slanted roofs. The interiors are very rustic, but feature comfy enough beds and an electrical socket. Facilities include a volleyball court, table football, Wi-Fi, backgammon and a shared kitchen.

$$-$ Utopia
By the river, 11 km from Lanquín and 3 km from Semuc Champey, T3135-8329, www.utopiaecohotel.com.
In great natural surrroundings a 30- to 60-min hike to the pools, this relaxed, rustic eco-hotel has a friendly and sociable atmosphere. It offers a wide range of accommodation including riverside *cabañas* with stone walls and floors ($$), simple wood-built cabins ($), semi-private 'nooks' in the dormitory loft, bunk beds and hammocks. There is also a restaurant-bar and Spanish school.

$ El Muro
Calle Principal, Lanquín, T5413-6442, www.elmurolanquin.com.
Although not exactly a party hostel, this place has a bar, and sometimes can get lively. Accommodation includes simple rooms, dorms, and for the ultra-thrifty, open-air hammocks. There is an attractive porch overlooking the jungle foliage. It's conveniently located for early morning or late night transport connections in Lanquín, or any other amenities you might need in town.

$ El Portal de Champey
At the entrance to Semuc Champey, T4091-7878, www.elportaldechampey.com.
Built from local materials on the banks of the Río Cahabón, this is the closest accommodation to Semuc Champey itself and located at the end of the road. Accommodation include very simple and rustic cabins and dorms. Like many other places in the area, electricity is limited. There's no hot water and you'll need insect repellent.

$ El Retiro
5 mins from Lanquín on the road to Cahabón, T3225 9251, www.elretirolanquin.com.
Campsite, *cabañas*, rooms, dorms and restaurant, all in a gorgeous riverside location. There's an open fire for cooking, hammocks to chill out in, a sauna for detoxing, and inner tubes for floating on the river. A fun, relaxing, sociable place which is very popular, with a summer camp feel. To get there don't get off in town, continue for 5 mins and ask to be dropped off. Recommended.

$ Hostal Oasis
Just outside Lanquín by the river, a 5-min tuk-tuk ride, T5870-9739, www. carlosmeza2.wix.com/hostaloasis.
Recommended as one of the few locally owned lodgings in the area and a friendly, low-key alternative to the party places. Like most other hostels around Lanquín, it has rustic dorms and *cabañas*, and offers filling fare at its restaurant, along with very occasional evening shindigs. The guys running the place are great and stand out for their helpfulness. Located steps from the river, you can go inner tubing too.

Transport

Lanquín and Semuc Champey
Bus
From **Cobán** there are minibuses that leave from the 3 Av, 5-6 Calle, 9 a day 0730-1745, US$3.80. From Lanquín to Semuc Champey hire a pickup, see below. From Lanquín to **Flores**, take a Cobán-bound bus to **Pajal**, 1 hr, then any passing bus or vehicle to **Sebol**, 2-2½ hrs (there are Las Casas–Cobán buses passing hourly in the morning

only) and then pickup, hitch or bus to Sayaxché and then Flores.

Semuc Champey is a 10-km walk to the south from Lanquín, 3 hrs' walking along the road, which is quite tough for the first hour as the road climbs very steeply out of Lanquín. If planning to return to Lanquín the same day, start very early to avoid the midday heat. To get there in a pickup start early (0630), US$0.85, or ask around for a private lift (US$13 return). Transport is very irregular so it's best to start walking and keep your fingers crossed. By 1200-1300 there are usually people returning to town to hitch a lift with. If you are on your own and out of season, it would be wise to arrange a lift back.

Car
There is a petrol station in Lanquín near the church.

Car hire Inque Renta Autos, T7952-1431, **Tabarini**, T7952-1504.

Parque Nacional Laguna Lachuá
Heading for **Playa Grande** from Cobán, also known as **Ixcán Grande**, ask the bus driver to let you off before Playa Grande at 'la entrada del parque', from where it's a 4.2-km (1-hr) walk to the park entrance. Minibuses leave Cobán every 30 mins via Chisec, 4 hrs, US$8 opposite INJAV.

North of Cobán and southern Petén crossroads

rugged karst landscapes and subterranean marvels

About 100 km northeast of Cobán is Sebol, reached via Chisec and unappealing Raxrujá. From here roads go north to Sayaxché and east to Modesto Méndez via Fray Bartolomé de las Casas.

West of Raxrujá are the **Grutas de Candelaria** ① *US$5.35 including a guided tour*, an extensive cavern system with stalagmites. Tubing is available. Take the road to Raxrujá and look for the Candelaria Camposanto village at Km 310 between Chisec and Raxrujá or look for a sign saying 'Escuela de Autogestión Muqbilbe' and enter here to get to the caves and eco-hotel. Camping is possible. Both points of access offer activities for visitors. North of Raxrujá is the Maya site of **Cancuén** ① *www.puertamundomaya.com, ask in Cobán about tours*, reached by *lancha* in 30 minutes (US$40 for one to 12 people), from the village of La Unión (camping and meals are available at the site). Ten kilometres east of Sebol, and 15 minutes by bus, is **Fray Bartolomé de las Casas**, a town that is just a stop-off for travellers on the long run between Poptún and Cobán or Sayaxché. A road (that is nearly all tarmacked) links Fray Bartolomé de las Casas, Sebol and Sayaxché via Raxrujá. The scenery is beautiful with luscious palms, solitary sheer-sided hills and thatched-roofed homes.

Where to stay

$$$-$$ Complejo Cultural y Ecoturístico Cuevas de Candelaria
T7861-2203, www.cuevasdecandelaria. com.
Set in 40 ha of grounds, including pleasant walking paths where you can admire the tropical flora and fauna, accommodation in La Candelaria includes very comfortable thatched *cabañas* and private rooms. There's a good restaurant and café on site. Full board is available.

$ Las Diamelas
Fray Bartolomé de las Casas, just off park, T5810-1785.
This place offers the cleanest rooms in town. The restaurant food is OK and cheap.

$ Rancho Ríos Escondidos
Near Grutas de Candelaria, on the main road.
Camping is possible at this farmhouse. Ask for Doña América.

Transport

Bus
Local transport in the form of minibuses and pickups connects most of the towns in this section before nightfall.

Bus to **Poptún** from Fray Bartolomé de las Casas leaves at 0300 from the central park, 5¾ hrs, US$5.10. This road is extremely rough and the journey is a bone-bashing, coccyx-crushing one. Buses to **Cobán** at 0400 until 1100 on the hour. However, do not be surprised if one does not turn up and you have to wait for the next one. To **Flores** via Sebol, Raxrujá and Sayaxché at 0700 (3½ hrs) a further 30 mins to 1 hr to Flores. The road from **Raxrujá** via Chisec to Cobán is very steep and rocky. **Chisec** to Cobán, 1½ hrs. The Sayaxché–Cobán bus arrives at Fray Bartolomé de las Casas for breakfast and continues between 0800 and 0900. You can also go from here to Sebol to Modesto Méndez to join the highway to **Flores**, but it is a very slow, a killer of a journey. Buses leave from Cobán for Chisec from Campo 2 at 0500, 0800, 0900.

El Petén

Deep in the lush lowland jungles of the Petén lie the lost worlds of Maya cities, pyramids and ceremonial centres, where layers of ancient dust speak ancient tales. At Tikal, where battles and burials are recorded in intricately carved stone, temples push through the tree canopy, wrapped in a mystical shroud.

Although all human life has vanished from these once-powerful centres, the forest is humming with the latter-day lords of the jungle: the howler monkeys that roar day and night. There are also toucans, hummingbirds, spider monkeys, wild pig and coatimundi. Jaguar, god of the underworld in Maya religion, stalks the jungle but remains elusive, as does the puma and tapir.

Further into the undergrowth away from Tikal, the adventurous traveller can visit El Mirador, the largest Maya stronghold, as well as El Zotz, El Perú, El Ceibal and Uaxactún by river, on foot and on horseback.

Essential El Petén

When to go

The dry season and wet season offer different advantages and disadvantages. In the months of November through to early May, access to all sites is possible as tracks are bone-dry. There are also less mosquitoes and if you are a bird lover, the mating season falls in this period. In the rainy winter months, from May to November, tracks become muddy quagmires making many of them impassable, also bringing greater humidity and mosquitoes. Take plenty of repellent, and reapply frequently. It's also fiercely hot and humid at all times in these parts so lots of sun screen and drinking water are essential.

Safety

Roadside robbery used to be a problem on the road to Tikal and to Yaxhá. Get independent, up-to-date advice before visiting these places and leave all valuables at your hotel. Asistur, see Safety, page 223, can assist and have a base at Tikal.

Best places to stay

Finca Ixobel, Poptún, see Where to stay in the right-hand column
Flores Hotel Boutique, Flores, page 170
Hostal Los Amigos, Flores, page 171
La Lancha, Lake Petén Itzá, page 171
Posada del Cerro, near El Remate, page 172

Poptún

a rural backdoor to the Petén

Poptún is best known for its association with Finca Ixobel; see Where to stay, below. Otherwise, it is just a staging-post between Río Dulce and Flores, or a stop-off to switch buses for the ride west to Cobán.

Listings Poptún

Where to stay

$$-$ Finca Ixobel
T5410-4307, www.fincaixobel.com.
A working farm owned by Carole Devine, widowed after the assassination of her husband in 1990. This highly acclaimed 'paradise' has become the victim of its own reputation and is frequently crowded especially at weekends. However, you can still camp peacefully and there are great treehouses, dorm beds, private rooms and bungalows. One of the highlights is the food. The finca offers a range of trips that could keep you there for days. Recommended.

Transport

Bus
Take any **Fuente del Norte** bus or any bus heading to the capital from **Flores**, 2 hrs. To Flores catch any Flores-bound bus from the capital. To **Río Dulce**, 2 hrs. Buses will drop you at the driveway to **Finca Ixobel** if that's your destination, just ask. From there it's a 15-min walk. Or, get off at the main bus stop and arrange a taxi there or through **Finca Ixobel**. To **Guatemala City** there are plenty daily, 7-8 hrs, US$10-13. The only bus that continues to **Fray Bartolomé de las Casas** (Las Casas on the bus sign) leaves at 1030, 5¾ hrs, US$8.

BACKGROUND

El Petén

Predominantly covered in jungle, the Petén is the largest department of Guatemala although it has the smallest number of inhabitants. This jungle region was settled by the Maya Itzá Kanek in about AD 600, with their seat then known as La Isla de Tah Itzá (Tayasal in Spanish), now modern-day Flores. The northern area was so impenetrable that the Itzás were untouched by Spanish inroads into Guatemala until the Mexican conquistador Hernán Cortés and Spanish chronicler Bernal Díaz del Castillo dropped by in 1525 on their way from Mexico to Honduras. In 1697 Martín Urzua y Arismendi, the governor of the Yucatán, fought the first battle of the Itzás, crossing Lake Petén Itzá in a galley killing 100 indigenous people in the ensuing battle, and capturing King Canek. He and his men destroyed the temples and palaces of Tayasal and so finished off the last independent Maya state.

In 1990, 21,487 sq km of the north of the Petén was declared a Reserva de la Biósfera Maya (Maya Biosphere Reserve), by CONAP, the National Council for Protected Areas. It became the largest protected tropical forest area in Central America. Inside the boundaries of the biosphere are the Parque Nacional Tikal, Parque Nacional Mirador–Río Azul and Parque Nacional Laguna del Tigre.

Flores and Santa Elena

a colourful island town and its less elegant mainland counterpart

Flores is perched on a tiny island in Lake Petén Itzá. Red roofs and palm trees jostle for position as they spread up the small hill, which is topped by the white twin-towered cathedral. Some of the streets of the town are lined with houses and restaurants that have been given lashings of colourful paint, giving Flores a Caribbean flavour. A pleasant new lakeshore *malecón* has been built around the island, with benches, street lamps and jetties for swimming. *Lanchas*, drifting among the lilies and dragonflies, are pinned to the lake edges.

Santa Elena is the dustier and noisier twin town on the mainland where the cheapest hotels, banking services and bus terminal can be found.

Sights

The **cathedral**, Nuestra Señora de los Remedios y San Pablo del Itzá, is plain inside, and houses a Cristo Negro, part of a chain of Black Christs that stretches across Central America, with the focus of worship at Esquipulas. **Paraíso Escondido** is home to the **zoo** ① *US$2.70*. A dugout to the island costs US$16 round trip. Near the zoo is **ARCAS (Asociación de Rescate y Conservación de Vida Silvestre)** ① *T5208-0968, www.arcasguatemala.com, US$2*, where they care for rescued animals and release them back into the wild. Volunteers are welcome. There is a centre and interactive trails at the site. Boat tours of the lake depart from the end of the causeway in Flores, around US$20 for one hour, but it's worth bargaining. There is also a longer tour that costs around U$50 for three to four hours, calling at the zoo and **El Mirador** on the Maya ruin of **Tayasal** ⓘ *US$2.70*.

Actún Kan caves ⓘ *0800-1700, US$2.70*, are a fascinating labyrinth of tunnels where, legend has it, a large serpent lived. They are 3 km south of Santa Elena and a 30- to 45-minute walk. To get there take the 6 Avenida out of Santa Elena to its end, turn left at a small hill, then take the first road to the right where it is well marked. South of Santa Elena at Km 468 is **Parque Natural Ixpanpajul** ⓘ *T2336-0576, www.ixpanpajul.com*, where forest canopy Tarzan tours, zip-wire, night safari, birdwatching and horse riding and more are on offer. Local fiestas include 12-15 January, the Petén *feria*, and 11-12 December in honour of the Virgen de Guadalupe.

Flores

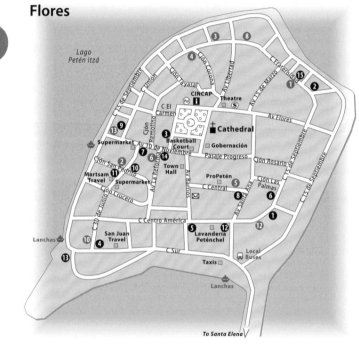

N

50 metres
50 yards

Where to stay 🛏
Casa Amelia 13
Casazul 3
Flores Hotel Boutique 1
Hospedaje Doña Goya 4
Hostal Los Amigos 5
Isla de Flores 6
La Casona de la Isla 2
Sabana 8
Santana 10
Villa del Lago 12

Restaurants 🍴
Café Arqueológico Yax-há 1
Café Uka 12
Capitán Tortuga 11
Cool Beans 2
El Mirador 3
Hacienda del Rey 4
La Albahaca 10
La Canoa 5

La Galería del Zotz 6
La Luna 7
Las Puertas Café Bar 8
La Villa del Chef 9
Mayan Princess Restaurant
 Café Bar & Cinema 14
Raíces 13
Suica 15

Around Lake Petén Itzá

San Andrés, 16 km by road from Santa Elena, enjoys sweeping views of Lake Petén Itzá, and its houses climb steeply down to the lakeshore. There is a language school, **Eco-Escuela Español** ① *T5940-1235, www.ecoescuelaespanol.org*, which offers 20 hours of classes, homestay and extra-curricular activities for a week, US$150. Adonis, a villager, takes good-value tours to El Zotz and El Mirador and has been recommended. Ask around for him; his house is close to the shoreline. You can also volunteer in the village with **Volunteer Petén** ① *Parque Nueva Juventud, T5711-0040, www.volunteerpeten.com*, a conservation and community project.

The attractive village of **San José**, a traditional Maya Itzá village, where efforts are being made to preserve the Itzá language and revive old traditions, is 2 km further northeast on the lake from San Andrés. Its painted and thatched homes huddling steeply on the lakeshore make it a much better day trip than San Andrés. It also has a Spanish school, the **Escuela Bio-Itzá** ① *www.ecobioitza. org*, which offers classes, homestay and camping for US$150 a week. Some 4 km beyond the village a signed track leads to the Classic period site of **Motul**, with 33 plazas, tall pyramids and some stelae depicting Maya kings. It takes 20 minutes to walk between the two villages. On 1 November San José hosts the **Holy Skull Procession**.

At the eastern side of Lake Petén Itzá is **El Remate**. The sunsets are superb and the lake is flecked with turquoise blue in the mornings. You can swim in the lake in certain places away from the local women washing their clothes and the horses taking a bath. There are many lovely places to stay, as it is also a handy stop-off point en route to Tikal. West of El Remate is the 700-ha **Biotopo Cerro Cahuí** ① *daily 0800-1600, US$2.70, administered by CECON*. It is a lowland jungle area where three species of monkey, deer, jaguar, peccary, ocellated wild turkey and some 450 species of bird can be seen. If you don't want to walk alone, you can hire a guide. Ask at your *posada*.

Listings Flores and Santa Elena *map p168*

Tourist information

If you wish to make trips independently to remote Maya sites, check with ProPetén to see if they have vehicles making the journey.

CINCAP (Centro de Información sobre la Naturaleza Cultura y Artesanía de Petén
On the plaza, T7926-0718, housed in the same building is the Alianza Verde. Closed Mon.

An organization promoting sustainable ecotourism. Free maps of Tikal, and other local information.

INGUAT
In the airport, T7956-0533. Daily 0700-1200 and 1500-1800.

ProPetén
Calle Central, T7867-5155, www. propeten.org.
Associated with Conservation International.

Where to stay

There are hotels in Santa Elena and Flores across the causeway (10 to 15 mins from Santa Elena).

Flores

$$$$ Flores Hotel Boutique
Calle Fraternidad, T7867-7568,
www.floreshotelboutique.com.
The chic modern suites at Flores Hotel Boutique are impeccably attired with classy furnishings and all mod cons including LCD satellite TVs, high-speed internet and fully equipped kitchens. Spa services are also available, including massage and shiatsu, along with tours, transport and room service. Attentive and hospitable: the best luxury option on the island.

$$$ Isla de Flores
Av La Reforma, T7867-5176,
www.hotelisladeflores.com.
Bright, young and stylish, Hotel Isla de Flores partly occupies a traditional island townhouse, recently renovated with several extensions and tasteful modern decor. Amenities include wooden sun deck and jacuzzi overlooking the lake and a restaurant downstairs. Rooms are comfortable, airy and tranquil.

$$ Hotel Casa Amelia
Calle La Unión, T7867-5430,
www.hotelcasamelia.com.
Cheerful and friendly hotel with 15 comfortable, a/c rooms, 6 of which have lake views. There's also a terrace and a pool table.

$$ Hotel Casazul
Calle Fraternindad, T7867-5451,
www.hotelesdepeten.com.
The 9 rooms are all blue and most have a lakeside view. All come with cable TV, a/c and fan.

$$ Hotel Santana
Calle 30 de Junio, T7867-5123,
www.santanapeten.com.
Clean rooms, all with their own terrace a/c, and TV. There's also a lakeside restaurant and a pool.

$$ La Casona de la Isla
Callejón San Pedrito, on the lake,
T7867-5163, www.hotelesdepeten.com.
This friendly place has elegant, clean rooms with fans and TV. Good restaurant, nice breakfasts, bar, garden and pool.

$$ Sabana
Calle La Unión, T7867-5100,
www.hotelsabana.com.
Huge, airy rooms, good service, clean, pleasant, with funky green wavy paintwork in lobby. Good views, lakeside pool and restaurant. Caters for European package tours.

$$ Villa del Lago
Calle 15 de Septiembre, T7867-5181,
www.hotelvilladelago.com.gt.
Very clean rooms with a/c and fan, cheaper with shared bath, some rooms have a lake view and balcony. Breakfast is served on a terrace overlooking the lake, but the service is excruciatingly slow. Breakfast is open to non-guests, but avoid it in high season unless you don't mind a long wait.

$ Chal Tun Ha Hostel
San Miguel peninsula, 3 mins
by boat from Flores, T4219-0851,
www.chaltunhahostel.com.
This family-owned hostel offers cheap dorm beds and a variety of basic wooden *cabañas* on stilts, each with screens and

and 2 rooms have a private bathroom. Humberto runs a daily service to Tikal, as well as other trips.

Restaurants

Flores

$$$-$$ Raíces
T5521-1843,
raicesrestaurante@gmail.com.
Excellent waterfront restaurant beside the *lanchas* near the far west end of Calle Sur. Specialities include *parillas* and kebabs. Great seafood.

$$ La Villa Del Chef
T4366-3822, lavilladelchefguatemala@
yahoo.com.
Friendly German-owned restaurant at the south end of Calle Unión that specializes in *pescado blanco*. It has a happy hour and also rents canoes for lake tours. Recommended.

$$ Mayan Princess Restaurant Café Bar and Cinema
Reforma and 10 de Noviembre.
Closed Sun.
Has the most adventurous menu on the island including daily specials, many with an Asian flavour, relaxed atmosphere, with bright coloured textile cloths on the tables. Internet and free films.

$$-$ Café Arqueológico Yax-há
Calle 15 de Septiembre, T5830-2060,
www.cafeyaxha.com.
Cheap daily soups, Maya specialities, such as chicken in tamarind sauce, great smoothies, and home-made nachos. German owner Dieter (who speaks English too) offers tours to little-known Maya sites and works with local communities to protect them.

$$-$ Capitán Tortuga
Calle 30 de junio.

Pizzas, pasta and bar snacks, with dayglo painted walls and lakeside terrace.

$$-$ Hacienda del Rey
Calle Sur.
Expensive Argentine steaks are on the menu, but the breakfasts are seriously cheap.

$$-$ La Albahaca
Calle 30 de Junio.
First-class home-made pasta and chocolate cake.

$$-$ La Galería del Zotz
15 de Septiembre.
A wide range of food, delicious pizzas, good service and presentation, popular with locals.

$$-$ La Luna
Av 10 de Noviembre. Closed Sun.
Refreshing natural lemonade, range of fish, meat and vegetarian dishes. The restaurant has a beautiful courtyard with blue paintwork set under lush pink bougainvillea. Recommended.

$$-$ Las Puertas Café Bar
Av Santa Ana and Calle Central, T7867-5242. Closes at 2300 for food and 2400 completely. Closed Sun.
Cheap breakfasts, huge menu, good, large pasta portions. It's popular at night with locals and travellers and is in an airy building, chilled atmosphere, games available.

$ Café Uka
Calle Centro América. Open from 0600.
Filling breakfasts and meals.

$ Cool Beans
Calle Fraternidad, T5571-9240,
coolbeans@itelgua.com.
Cheap food with home-made bread and pastries.

$ El Mirador
Overlooking the lake but view obscured by restaurant wall.
Seriously cheap food and snacks but service is slow.

$ La Canoa
Calle Centro América.
Good breakfasts (try the pancakes), dinners start at US$1.50, with good *comida típica*, very friendly owners.

$ Suica
Calle Fraternidad. Mon-Sat 1200-1900.
Small place serving an unusual mix of sushi, tempura and curries.

Santa Elena

$$ El Rodeo
1 Calle.
Excellent restaurant serving reasonably priced food. Plays classical music and sometimes there's impromptu singing performances.

$ El Petenchel
Calle 2.
Vegetarian food served here as well as conventional meats and meals. Excellent breakfasts and a good-value *menú del día*. Music played, prompt service.

$ Restaurante Mijaro
Calle 2 and Av 8.
Great filling breakfasts and a bargain *menú del día* at US$1.70, all in a thatched-roofed roadside location.

What to do

Tour operators
Beware 'helpful' touts, especially those on buses, and don't be pressured into buying tours, transport or accommodation; there's plenty to choose from in Flores.

Martsam Travel, *Calle 30 de Junio, Flores, T7867-5377, www.martsam.com.* Guided tours to Tikal, El Zotz, El Mirador, El Perú, Yaxhá, Nakum, Aguateca, Ceibal and Uaxactún. Guides with wildlife and ornithological knowledge in addition to archaeological knowledge. Highly recommended.
Mayan Adventure, *Calle 15 de Septiembre, Flores, T5830-2060, www.the-mayan-adventure.com.* Led by German archaeologist Dieter Richter, this company offers insightful expeditions and tours to a range of sites under excavation. An insider look at the scientific work of archaeology.
San Juan Travel Agency, *T7926-0042.* Offers transport (US$7.50 return) to Tikal and excursions to Ceibal, Uaxactún, and Yaxhá (US$80). Mixed reports, not a first choice.
Tikal Connection, *international airport, T7926-1537, www.tikalcnx.com.* Runs tours to El Perú, El Mirador, Nakbé, El Zotz, Yaxhá, Dos Aguadas, Uaxactún. It also sells bus tickets.

Transport

Air
Flores is 2 km from the international airport on the outskirts of Santa Elena. A taxi from the airport into Santa Elena or Flores costs US$1.30 and takes 5 mins, but bargain hard.

Be early for flights, as overbooking is common. The airport departures hall has an internet place. Tour operator and hotel representatives are based in the arrival halls. The cost of a return flight is between US$180-220, shop around.
Grupo Taca, *T2470-8222, www.taca. com,* leaves **Guatemala City** daily at 0645, 0955, 1725, 1 hr, returns 0820, 1605 and 1850. **Tag**, *T2360-3038, www.*

tag.com.gt, flies at 0630 returning 1630. To **Cancún**, Grupo Taca. To **Belize City**, **Tropic Air**, www.tropicair.com.

Boat

Lanchas moor along Calle Sur, Flores; behind the **Hotel Santana**; from the dock behind **Hotel Casona de Isla**; and beside the arch on the causeway.

Bus

If you arrive by long-distance bus from Guatemala City, Mexico or Belize, the terminal is 10 blocks south of the causeway, which links Flores and Santa Elena. Chicken buses run between the two, US$0.35. Tuk-tuks charge US$0.90 for journeys between them.

Local Local buses (chicken buses), US$0.26, Flores to Santa Elena, leave from the end of the causeway in Flores.

Long distance All long-distance buses leave from the relocated bus terminal, 6 blocks south of the Calle Principal in Santa Elena. It has a snack bar, toilets, seating and ATM. Opposite are restaurants, *comedores*, and a bakery. Banrural is down the side. To **Guatemala City**, **Línea Dorada**, daily office hours 0500-2200, www.tikalmayan world. com, leaves 1000, 2100, 1st class, US$30; 2200, US$16, 8 hrs. **Autobuses del Norte (ADN)**, T7924-8131, www.adnauto busesdelnorte.com, luxury service, 1000, 2100, 2300, US$23. **Fuente del Norte**, T7926-0666, office open 24 hrs, buses every 45 mins-1 hr, 0330-2230, US$12, 9 hrs. At 1000, 1400, 2l00, 2200, US$20, 7-8 hrs. 2nd-class buses, **Rosita**, T7926-5178 and **Rápidos del Sur**, T7924-8072, also go to the capital, US$13. If you are going only to **Poptún**, 2 hrs, or **Río Dulce**, 3½-4 hrs, make sure you do not pay the full fare to Guatemala City. To **Sayaxché** with **Pinita**, T9926-0726, at 1100, returns next day at 0600, US$2.50. With **Fuente del Norte** at 0600, US$1.70, returning 0600. *Colectivos* also leave every 15 mins 0530-1700, US$2.40. Buses run around the lake to **San Andrés**, with one at 1200 with **Pinita** continuing to **Cruce dos Aguadas,** US$2.90 and **Carmelita**, US$3.30 for access to El Mirador. Returning from Carmelita at 0500 the next day. Minibuses also run to San Andrés. To **Chiquimula**, take **Transportes María Elena**, T5550-4190, at 0400, 0800, 1300, US$3. The **María Elena** bus continues onto **Esquipulas**, 9 hrs, US$12. **Fuente del Norte** to **Cobán**, 0530, 0630, 1230, 1330, 5 hrs, US$8. Or take a minibus to Sayaxché and change. Shuttle transfers may also be possible. To **Jutiapa**, 0500, 0530, 7 hrs, returning 0900, US$10-12.

International To **Melchor de Mencos** at the Belize border, 0500, 0600, 1630, 2300, 1½ hrs, US$3.30. Returning 0200, 0500, 0600, 1630, 2300. See also Border crossing box, page 212, for more information on crossing into Belize. Also with **Línea Dorada** and on to **Chetumal**, **Mexico.** See also Border crossing box, page 210.

To **Copán Ruinas**, **Honduras**, take **Transportes María Elena**, T5550-4190, to Chiquimula at 0400, 0800, 1300, US$13 then from Chiquimula to El Florido and finally on to Copán Ruinas. Alternatively, take any bus to the capital and change at Río Hondo. See also box, page 213, for more on crossing to Honduras. To **San Salvador**, 0600, 8 hrs, US$26.70; see also box, page 214, for crossing into El Salvador.

Car

There are plenty of agencies at the airport, mostly Suzuki jeeps, which cost about US$65-80 per day. **Hertz**, at the airport, T7926-0332. **Garrido** at Sac-Nicte Hotel, Calle 1, Santa Elena, T7926-1732.

Petrol Available in Santa Elena at the 24-hr Texaco garage on the way to the airport.

Around Lake Petén Itzá
Boat

Public *lanchas* from San Benito have virtually come to a stop. Visitors can still charter a *lancha* from Flores for about US$10.

Bus

There's a bus ticket and internet office opposite the turning to El Remate. Any bus/shuttle heading for Tikal can stop at El Remate, US$2.50, last bus around 1600; taxi around US$10. Returning to **Flores**, pick up any shuttle heading south (this is a lot easier after 1300 when tourists are returning). There is a bus service heading to **Flores** from El Remate at 0600, 0700, 0830, 0930, 1300 and 1400. Shuttles leave every 30 mins for San Andrés, US$0.70, 30 mins and go on to San José.

Parque Nacional Tikal

Mayan skyscrapers pushing up through the jungle canopy

★Tikal will have you transfixed. Its steep-sided temples for the mighty dead, stelae commemorating the powerful rulers, inscriptions recording the noble deeds and the passing of time, and burials that were stuffed with jade and bone funerary offerings, make up the greatest Mayan city in this tropical pocket of Guatemala.

The ruins *Numbers in brackets refer to the map, page 178.*

The **Great Plaza (3)** is a four-layered plaza with its earliest foundations laid around 150 BC and its latest around AD 700. It is dwarfed by its two principal temples – Temples I and II. On the north side of the plaza between these two temples are two rows of monuments. It includes Stela 29, erected in AD 292, which depicts Tikal's emblem glyph – the symbol of a Mayan city – and the third century AD ruler Scroll Ahau Jaguar, who is bearing a two-headed ceremonial bar.

ON THE ROAD
Wildlife

Tikal is a fantastic place for seeing animal and bird life of the jungle. Wildlife includes spider monkeys, howler monkeys, three species of toucan (most prominent being the keel-billed toucan), deer, foxes and many other birds and insects. Pumas have been seen on quieter paths and coatimundis (pizotes), in large family groups, are often seen rummaging through the bins. The ocellated turkeys with their sky-blue heads with orange baubles attached are seen in abundance at the entrance, and at El Mundo Perdido.

Essential Parque Nacional Tikal

Getting there

From Flores, it's possible to visit Tikal in a day. San Juan Travel Agency minibuses leave hourly between 0500 and 1000, one at 1400 and return at 1230 and hourly between 1400 and 1700 (though on the way back from Tikal, buses are likely to leave 10-15 minutes before scheduled), one hour, US$7.50 return. Several other companies also run trips such as Línea Dorada at 0500, 0830, 1530, returning 1400 and 1700. If you have not bought a return ticket you can often get a discounted seat on a returning bus if it's not full. Minibuses also meet Guatemala City–Flores flights. A taxi to Tikal costs US$60 one way. You can also visit Tikal with a one-day or two-day package tour from Guatemala City or Antigua.

Opening times and entry fee

Daily 0600-1800, US$20 per day, payable at the national park entrance, 18 km from the ruins (park administration, T7920-0025).

Time required

An overall impression of the ruins may be gained in five hours, but you need at least two days to see them properly. If you enter after 1600 your ticket is valid for the following day. To enter the site before or after closing time costs US$13 and you must be accompanied by a guide. If you stay the night in the park hotels, you can enter at 0500 once the police have scoured the grounds. This gives you at least a two-hour head start on visitors coming in from Flores.

Tourist information

A guide is highly recommended as outlying structures can otherwise be missed. The official Tourist Guide Association offers various tours in different languages, US$40 for four people plus US$5 for each additional person, just turn up at the visitor centre. A private guide can be hired for US$60 or you can join up with a group for US$15 per person. Tours are available in Spanish, English, Italian, German and French. The guidebook *Tikal*, by WR Coe, in several languages, has an excellent map; or you can buy a reasonable leaflet/map at the entrance, US$2.50. Free transport around the site is available for elderly and disabled visitors, in an adapted pickup truck, with wheelchair access.

Facilities

At the park's visitor centre there is a post office, which stores luggage, a tourist guide service (see under Tourist information), exchange facilities, toilets, a restaurant and a few shops that sell relevant guidebooks.

When to go

Try to visit the ruins after 1400, or before 0900, as there are fewer visitors. From April to December it rains every day for a while; it is busiest November to January, during the Easter and summer holidays and most weekends. The best time for birdwatching tours is December to April, with November to February being the mating season. Mosquitoes can be a real problem even during the day if straying away from open spaces.

What to take

Bring a hat, mosquito repellent, water and snacks with you as it's extremely hot, drinks at the site aren't cheap and there's a lot of legwork involved.

Temple I (Temple of the Great Jaguar) (1), on the east side of the Great Plaza, rises to 44 m in height with nine stepped terraces. It was ordered to be built by the ruler Ah Cacao, who ruled between AD 682 to around AD 720-724, who probably planned it for use as his shrine. His tomb, the magnificent Burial 116, was discovered beneath Temple I in 1962 with a wealth of burial goods on and around his skeleton. The display is reconstructed in the Museo Cerámico/Tikal.

Temple II (Temple of the Masks) (2) faces Temple I on the Great Plaza and rises to 38 m, although with its roof comb it would have been higher. It's thought Ah

Tikal

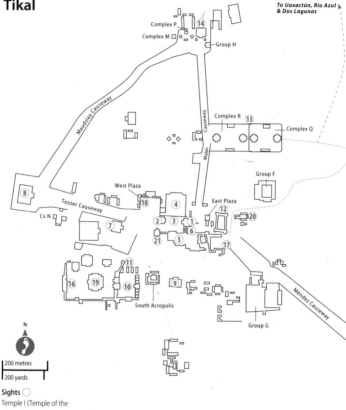

Sights ○

Temple I (Temple of the
  Great Jaguar) **1**
Temple II (Temple of the
  Masks) **2**
Great Plaza **3**
North Acropolis **4**
Central Acropolis **5**

Ball Court **6**
Temple III (Temple of the
  Jaguar Priest) **7**
Temple IV (Temple of the
  Double-Headed Serpent) **8**
Temple V **9**

Plaza of the Seven
  Temples **10**
Triple Ball Court **11**
Market **12**
Twin Pyramid Complexes
  Q & R **13**

North Group **14**
Temple VI (Temple of
  Inscriptions) **15**
El Mundo Perdido (Lost
  World) **16**

Cacao ordered its construction as well. The lintel on the doorway here depicted a woman wearing a cape, and experts have suggested that this could be his wife.

The **North Acropolis (4)** contains some 100 buildings piled on top of earlier structures in a 1-ha area and is the burial ground of all of Tikal's rulers until the break with royal practice made by Ah Cacao. In 1960, the prized Stelae 31, now in the Museo Cerámico/Tikal, see below, was found under the Acropolis. It was dedicated in AD 445. Its base was deliberately burnt by the Maya and buried under Acropolis buildings in the eighth century. This burning was thought to be like a 'killing', where the burning ritual would 'kill' the power of the ruler depicted on the monument, say, after death. It's thought to depict the ruler Siyah Chan K'awil (Stormy Sky), who died sometime around AD 457 having succeeded to the throne in AD 411. Yax Moch Xok (Great Scaffold Shark) is thought to be entombed in the first century AD grave, Burial 85. Surrounding the headless male body were burial objects and a mask bearing the royal head band. Under a building directly in the centre of this acropolis Burial 22 – that of ruler Great Jaguar Paw, who reigned in the fourth century, and died around AD 379 – was discovered. Also found here was Burial 10, thought to be the tomb of Nun Yax Ayin I (Curl Nose), who succeeded to the throne in AD 379 after Great Jaguar Paw. Inside were the remains of nine sacrificed servants as well as turtles and crocodile remains and a plethora of pottery pieces. The pottery laid out in this tomb had Teotihuacán artistic influences, demonstrating Tikal's links to the powers of Teotihuacán and Teotihuacán-influenced Kaminal Juyú. Burial 48 is thought to be the tomb of Curl Nose's son, Siyah Chan K'awil (Stormy Sky).

Central Acropolis (5) is made up of a complex of courts connected by passages and stairways, which have expanded over the centuries to cover 1.6 ha. Most of the building work

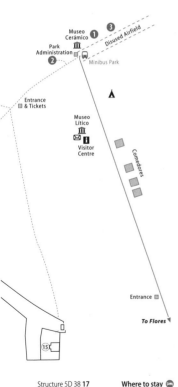

Museo Cerámico **1**
3
Disued Airfield

Park Administration
2
Minibus Park

Entrance & Tickets

Museo Lítico

Visitor Centre

Comedores

Entrance

To Flores

Structure 5D 38 **17**
Structure 5D II **18**
Great Pyramid **19**
Sweat House **20**
Structure 5D 73 **21**

Where to stay
Jaguar Inn **1**
Jungle Lodge **2**
Tikal Inn **3**

BACKGROUND
Tikal

At its height, the total 'urban' area of Tikal was more than 100 sq km, with the population somewhere between 50,000 and 100,000. The low-lying hill site of Tikal was first occupied around 600 BC during the pre-Classic era, but its buildings date from 300 BC. It became an important Maya centre from AD 300 onwards, which coincided with the decline of the mega power to the north, El Mirador. It was governed by a powerful dynasty of 30-plus rulers between about the first century AD until about AD 869, with the last known named ruler being Hasaw Chan K'awill II.

Tikal's main structures, which cover 2.5 sq km, were constructed from AD 550 to 900 during the late-Classic period. These include the towering mega structures of temples – shrines to the glorious dead – whose roof combs were once decorated with coloured stucco figures of Tikal lords. Doorways on the temple rooms were intricately carved – using the termite-resistant wood of the sapodilla tree – with figures and symbols, known as lintels.

Tikal's stelae tell of kings and accessions and war and death. Its oldest stela dates from AD 292. Many Central Mexican influences have been found on the stelae imagery, in burial sites at Tikal and in decorative architectural technique, which led archaeologists to conclude that the city was heavily influenced from the west by forces from the great enclave of Teotihuacán, now just outside Mexico City. This war-like state bred a cult of war and sacrifice and seemed intent on spreading its culture. After the collapse of Teotihuacán in AD 600, a renaissance at Tikal was achieved by the ruler Ah Cacao (Lord Cocoa, Ruler A, Moon Double Comb, Hasaw Chan K'awil I, Sky Rain) who succeeded to the throne in AD 682 and died sometime in the 720s.

However, in the latter part of the eighth century the fortunes of Tikal declined. The last date recorded on a stela is AD 889. The site was finally abandoned in the 10th century. Most archaeologists now agree the collapse was due to warfare with neighbouring states, overpopulation, which resulted in environmental destruction, and drought. Tikal's existence was first reported by Spanish monk Andrés de Avendaño, but its official discovery is attributed to Modesto Méndez, commissioner of the Petén, and Ambrosio Tut, governor of the Petén, in 1848. They were both accompanied by the artist Eusebio Lara.

carried out took place between AD 550-900 in the late-Classic era. The **East Plaza** behind Temple I is the centre of the highway junctions of the Maler Causeway in the north, and the Méndez Causeway heading southeast.

On the western side of the **West Plaza** is structure 5D II under which Burial 77 was brought to light. The skeleton was adorned with a jade pendant, which was stolen from the site museum in the 1980s.

Temple III (Temple of the Jaguar Priest) (7) is so called because of the scene of a figure in a glamorous jaguar pelt on a lintel found on the temple. Some experts believe this figure is Ah Chitam (Nun Yax Ayin II, Ruler C), son of Yax Kin, and grandson of the great Ah Cacao, and so propose that this is his shrine, although there has been no confirmation of this. Temple III was constructed around AD 810 and is 55 m tall.

Temple IV (Temple of the Double-Headed Serpent) (8) is the highest building in Tikal at 70 m. It was built in the late-Classic period around AD 741, as proven by hieroglyphic inscriptions and carbon dating. It's thought it was built to honour Yax Kin, the son of Ah Cacao, who became ruler in AD 734. A date on the lintel is AD 741, the same year that Temple I was dedicated.

Temple V (9), constructed between AD 700-750 during the reign of Yax Kin, is 58 m high. It is the mortuary temple of an unknown ruler.

El Mundo Perdido (The Lost World) (16). The **Great Pyramid** is at the centre of this lost world. At 30 m high, it is the largest pyramid at Tikal. It is flat topped and its stairways are flanked by masks. From the top a great view over the canopy to the tops of other temples can be enjoyed. Together with other buildings to the west, it forms part of an astronomical complex. The Lost World pyramid is a pre-Classic structure, but was improved upon in the Early Classic. East of El Mundo Perdido is the **Plaza of the Seven Temples (10)**, constructed during the Late Classic period (AD 600-800). There is a triple ball court lying at its northern edge.

Temple VI (Temple of the Inscriptions) (15) was discovered in 1951. The 12-m-high roof comb is covered on both sides in hieroglyphic text and is the longest hieroglyphic recording to date. It was carved in AD 766, but the temple was built under the rule of Yax Kin some years before. Altar 9 is at the base of the temple as is Stela 21, said to depict the sculptured foot of the ruler Yax Kin to mark his accession as ruler in AD 734. Unfortunately because of the location of this temple away from the rest of the main structures it has become a hideout for robbers and worse. Some guides no longer take people there. Take advice before going, if at all.

The North Group has several twin pyramid complexes, including Complexes Q and R, marking the passing of the *katun* – a Maya 20-year period.

The **Museo Cerámico (Museo Tikal)** ⓘ *near the Jungle Lodge, Mon-Fri 0900-1700, Sat and Sun, 0900-1600, US$1.30*, has a collection of Maya ceramics, but its prize exhibits are Stela 31 with its still clear carvings, and the reconstruction of the tomb of Tikal's great ruler, Ah Cacao. In the **Museo Lítico** ⓘ *inside the visitor centre, Mon-Fri 0900-1700, Sat and Sun, 0900-1600*, there are stelae and great photographs of the temples as they were originally found, and of their reconstruction, including the 1968 rebuild of the Temple II steps. **Note** Photography is no longer permitted in either of these museums.

Where to stay

You are advised to book when you arrive; in high season, book in advance. Take a torch: 24-hr electricity is not normally available.

$$$-$$ Jungle Lodge
T5361-4098,
www.quik.guate.com/jltikal/index.html.
These spacious, comfortable bungalows have bath, 24-hr hot water and a fan (electricity 0700-2100); it's cheaper without bath. There's also a pool and they can cash TCs. Full board is available (although we've had consistent reports of unsatisfactory food, slow service and small portions). Jungle Lodge's Tikal tours have been recommended.

$$$-$$ Tikal Inn
T7926-1917.
This place has bungalows and rooms, hot water 1800-1900, electricity 0900-1600 and 1800-2200, and helpful staff. The beautiful pool is for guest use only. Natural history tours at 0930 for US$10 for a minimum 2 people.

$$ Jaguar Inn
T7926-0002, www.jaguar tikal.com.
Full board is available, less without food. There is also a dorm with 6 beds, hammocks with mosquito nets, and lockers. Electricity is available 1800-2200 and there's hot water in the morning or on request Mar-Oct and Nov-Feb, 0600-2100. They will provide a picnic lunch and can store luggage.

Camping

$ Camping Tikal
Run by the Restaurante del Parque, reservations T2370-8140, or at the Petén Espléndido, T7926-0880.
If you have your own tent or hammock it's US$5; if you need to rent the gear it's US$8. There are also *cabañas* with mattresses and mosquito nets for US$7 per person. It also does deals that include breakfast, lunch and dinner ranging from US$15-30 for a double. Communal showers available. Take your own water as the supply is very variable.

There are literally hundreds of Mayan sites in the Petén. Below is a handful of sites, whose ruins have been explored, and of whose histories something is known.

Uaxactún

In the village of Uaxactún (pronounced Waash-ak-tún) are ruins, famous for the oldest complete Maya astronomical complex found, and a stuccoed temple with serpent and jaguar head decoration. The village itself is little more than a row of houses either side of a disused airstrip. The site is 24 km north of Tikal on an unpaved road. It is in fairly good condition taking less than one hour in any vehicle.

Uaxactún is one of the longest-occupied Mayan sites. Its origins lie in the middle pre-Classic (1000-300 BC) and its decline came by the early post-Classic (AD 925-1200) like many of its neighbouring powers. Its final stelae, dated AD 889, is one of the last to be found in the region. The site is named after a stela, which corresponds to Baktun 8 (8 x 400 Maya years), carved in AD 889; *uaxac* means 8, *tun* means stone.

South of the remains of a ball court, in **Group B**, a turtle carving can be seen, and Stela 5, which marks the takeover of the city, launched from Tikal. Next door to this stela under Temple B-VIII were found the remains of two adults, including a pregnant woman, a girl of about 15 and a baby. It is believed this may have been the governor and his family who were sacrificed in AD 378. From Group B, take the causeway to **Group A**. In Group A, Structure A-V had 90 rooms and there were many tombs to be seen. The highest structure in the complex is Palace A-XVIII, where red paint can still be seen on the walls. In **Group E** the oldest observatory (E-VII-sub) ever found faces structures in which the equinoxes and solstices were observed. When the pyramid (E-VII) covering this sub-structure was removed, fairly well preserved stucco masks of jaguar and serpent heads were found flanking the stairways of the sub-structure.

The ruins lie either side of the village, the main groups (**Group A** and **Group B**) are to the northwest (take a left just before **Hotel El Chiclero** and follow the road round on a continuous left to reach this group). A smaller group (**Group E**) with the observatory is to the southwest (take any track, right off the airstrip, and ask. This group is 400 m away.

El Zotz

El Zotz, meaning bat in Q'eqchi', is so called because of the nightly flight from a nearby cave of thousands of bats. There is an alternative hiking route as well (see below). Incredibly, from Temple IV, the highest in the complex at 75 m, it is possible to see in the distance, some 30 km away, Temple IV at Tikal. The wooden lintel from Temple I (dated AD 500-550) is to be found in the Museo Nacional de Arqueología y Etnología in the capital. Each evening at about 1850 the sky is darkened for 10 minutes by the fantastic spectacle of tens of thousands of bats flying out of a cave near the camp. The 200-m-high cave pock-marked with holes is a 30-minute walk from the camp. If you are at the cave you'll see the flight above you and get doused in falling excrement. If you remain at the campsite you will see them streaking the dark blue sky with black in straight columns. It's also accessible via Uaxactún. There is some basic infrastructure for the guards, and you can camp.

One of the best trips you can do in the Petén is a three-day hike to El Zotz and on through the jungle to Tikal. The journey, although long, is not arduous, and is accompanied by birds, blue morpho butterflies and spider monkeys chucking branches at you all the way.

El Perú and the Estación Biológica Guacamayo

A visit to El Perú is included in the **Scarlet Macaw Trail**, a two- to five-day trip into the **Parque Nacional Laguna del Tigre**, through the main breeding area of the scarlet macaw. There is little to see at the Mayan site, but the journey to it is worthwhile. In 2004 the 1200-year-old tomb and skeleton of a Maya queen were found. A more direct trip involves getting to the isolated Q'eqchi'-speaking community of **Paso Caballos** (1¾ hours). Here, the **Comité de Turismo** can organize transport by *lancha* along the Río San Pedro. From Paso Caballos it is one hour by *lancha* to the El Perú campsite and path.

It's possible to stop off at the **Estación Biológica Guacamayo** ⓘ *US$1.30, volunteers may be needed, contact Propeten, www.propeten.org*, where there is an ongoing programme to study the wild scarlet macaws (*ara macao*). The chances of seeing endangered scarlet macaws during March, April and May in this area is high because that's when they are reproducing.

A couple of minutes upriver is the landing stage, from where it's a 30-minute walk to the campsite of El Perú: howler monkeys, hummingbirds, oropendola birds and fireflies abound. From there, it is a two-hour walk to the El Perú ruins. Small coral snakes slither about, howler monkeys roar, spider monkeys chuck branches down on the path. White-lipped peccaries, nesting white turtles, eagles, fox and kingfishers have also been seen. The trip may be impossible between June and August because of rising rivers during the rainy season and because the unpaved road to Paso Caballos may not be passable. Doing it on your own is possible, although you may have to wait for connections and you will need a guide, about US$20 per day.

El Mirador, El Tintal and Nakbé

El Mirador is the largest Mayan site in the country. It dates from the late pre-Classic period (300 BC-AD 250) and is thought to have sustained a population of tens of thousands. It takes five days to get to El Mirador. From Flores it is 2½ to three hours to the village of Carmelita by bus or truck, from where it is seven hours walking, or part horse riding to El Mirador. It can be done in four days – two days to get there and two days to return. The route is difficult and the mosquitoes and ticks and the relentless heat can make it a trying trip. Organized tours are arranged by travel agents in Flores; get reassurance that your guides have enough food and water.

If you opt to go to El Mirador independently, ask in Carmelita for the **Comité de Turismo**, which will arrange mules and guides. Take water, food, tents and torches.

It is about 25 km to El Tintal, a camp where you can sling a hammock, or another 10 km to El Arroyo, where there is a little river for a swim near a *chiclero* camp. It takes another day to El Mirador, or longer, if you detour via Nakbé. You will pass *chiclero* camps on the way, which are very hospitable, but very poor. In May, June and July there is no mud, but there is little chance of seeing wildlife or flora. In July to December, when the rains come, the chances of glimpsing wildlife is much greater and there are lots of flowers. It is a lot fresher, but there can be tonnes of mud, sometimes making the route impassable. The mosquitos are also in a frenzy during the rainy season. Think carefully about going on the trip (one reader called it "purgatory").

The site, which is part of the Parque Nacional Mirador-Río Azul, is divided into two parts with the **El Tigre Pyramid** and complex in the western part, and the **La Danta** complex, the largest in the Maya world, in the east, 2 km away. The larger of two huge pyramids – La Danta – is 70 m high; stucco masks of jaguars and birds flank the stairways of the temple complex. The other, El Tigre, is 55 m in height and is a wonderful place to be on top of at night, with a view of endless jungle and other sites, including Calakmul, in Mexico. In **Carmelita** ask around for space to sling your hammock or camp. There is a basic *comedor*. **El Tintal**, a day's hike from El Mirador, is said to be the second largest site in Petén, connected by a causeway to El Mirador, with great views from the top of the pyramids. **Nakbé**, 10 km southeast of El Mirador, is the earliest known lowland Maya site (1000-400 BC), with the earliest examples of carved monuments.

Río Azul and Kinal

From Uaxactún a dirt road leads north to the *campamento* of **Dos Lagunas**. It's a lovely place to camp, with few mosquitoes, but swimming will certainly attract crocodiles. The guards' camp at **Ixcán Río**, on the far bank of the Río Azul, can be reached in one long day's walk, crossing by canoe if the water is high. If low enough to cross by vehicle you can drive to the Río Azul site, a further 6 km on a wide, shady track. It is also possible to continue into Mexico if your paperwork is OK. A barely passable side track to the east from the camp leads to the ruins of Kinal. The big attraction at Río Azul are the famous black and red painted tombs, technically off limits to visitors without special permission, but visits have been known.

Yaxhá, Topoxte, Nakum and Melchor de Mencos
T7861-0250, www.conap.com.gt. Yaxhá is open 0800-1700. Entry to each site US$9.

This group of sites has been designated as a national park. About 65 km from Flores, on the Belize road ending at Melchor de Mencos, is a turning left, a dry weather road, which brings you in 8.5 km to Laguna Yaxhá. On the northern shore is the site of Yaxhá (meaning Green Water), the third largest known Classic Maya site in the country, accessible by causeway. This untouristy site is good for birdwatching and the views from the temples of the milky green lake are outstanding. The tallest structure, **Templo de las Manos Rojas**, is 30 m high. In the lake is the unusual Late post-Classic site (AD120-1530) of Topoxte. (The island is accessible by boat from Yaxhá, 15 minutes.) About 20 km further north of Yaxhá lies Nakum, which is thought to have been both a trading and ceremonial centre. You will need a guide and your own transport if you have not come on a tour.

Northwest Petén and the Mexican border
An unpaved road runs 151 km west from Flores to **El Naranjo** on the Río San Pedro, near the Mexican border. Close by is **La Joyanca**, a site where the chance of wildlife spotting is high. You can camp at the *cruce* with the guards.

Parque Nacional Laguna del Tigre and Biotopo
The park and biotope is a vast area of jungle and wetlands north of El Naranjo. The best place to stay is the CECON camp, across the river below the ferry. This is where the guards live and they will let you stay in the bunk house and use their kitchen. Getting into the reserve is not easy and you will need to be fully equipped, but a few people go up the Río Escondido. The lagoons abound in wildlife, including enormous crocodiles and spectacular bird life. Contact CECON ⓘ *Centro de Estudios Conservacionistas (CECON), Av Reforma, 0-63, Zona 10, Guatemala City, T2331-0904, cecon@usac.edu.gt,* for more information.

Sayaxché
Sayaxché, south of Flores on the road to Cobán, has a frontier town feel to it as its focus is on a bend on the Río de la Pasión. It is a good base for visiting the southern Petén including a number of archaeological sites, namely El Ceibal. You can change US dollar bills and traveller's cheques at **Banoro**.

El Ceibal
This major ceremonial site is reached by a 45-minute *lancha* ride up the Río de la Pasión from Sayaxché. It is about 1.5 km from the left bank of Río de la Pasión hidden in vegetation and extending for 1.5 sq km. The height of activity at the site was from 800 BC to the first century AD. Archaeologists agree that it appears to have been abandoned in between about AD 500 and AD 690 and then repopulated at a later stage when there was an era of stelae production between AD 771 and 889. It later declined during the early decades of the 10th century and was abandoned. You can sling a hammock at El Ceibal and use the guard's fire for making coffee if you ask politely – a mosquito net is advisable, and take repellent for walking in the jungle surroundings. Tours can be arranged in Flores for a day trip to Sayaxché and El Ceibal (around US$65) but there is limited time to see the site. From Sayaxché the ruins of the **Altar de los Sacrificios** at the confluence of the Ríos de la Pasión and Usumacinta can also be reached. It was one of the earliest sites in the Péten, with a founding date earlier than that of Tikal. Most of its monuments are not in good condition. Also within reach of Sayaxché is **Itzán**, discovered in 1968.

Piedras Negras

Still further down the Río Usumacinta in the west of Petén is Piedras Negras, a huge Classic period site. In the 1930s Tatiana Proskouriakoff first recognized the periods of time inscribed on stelae here coincided with human life spans or reigns, and so began the task of deciphering the meaning of Maya glyphs. Advance arrangements are necessary with a rafting company to reach Piedras Negras. **Maya Expeditions** (see page 34) run expeditions, taking in Piedras Negras, Bonampak, Yaxchilán and Palenque. This trip is a real adventure. The riverbanks are covered in the best remaining tropical forest in Guatemala, inhabited by elusive wildlife and hiding more ruins. Once you've rafted down to Piedras Negras, you have to raft out. Though most of the river is fairly placid, there are the 30-m **Busilhá Falls**, where a crystal-clear tributary cascades over limestone terraces and two deep canyons, with impressive rapids to negotiate, before reaching the take-out two days later.

Petexbatún

From Sayaxché, the Río de la Pasión is a good route to visit other Maya ruins. From **Laguna Petexbatún** (16 km), a fisherman's paradise can be reached by outboard canoe from Sayaxché. Excursions can be made from here to unexcavated ruins that are generally grouped together under the title Petexbatún. These include **Arroyo de la Piedra**, Dos Pilas and Aguateca. **Dos Pilas** has many well-preserved stelae, and an important tomb of a king was found here in 1991 – that of its Ruler 2, who died in AD 726. Dos Pilas flourished in the Classic period when as many as 10,000 lived in the city. There are many carved monuments and hieroglyphic stairways at the site, which record the important events of city life. **Aguateca**, where the ruins are so far little excavated, gives a feeling of authenticity. The city was abandoned in the early ninth century for unknown reasons. Again, a tour is advisable. It's a boat trip and a short walk away. The site was found with numerous walls (it's known the city was attacked in AD 790) and a chasm actually splits the site in two. The natural limestone bridge connects a large plaza with platforms and buildings in the west with an area of a series of smaller plazas in the east. These places are off the beaten track and an adventure to get to.

Listings Other Maya ruins

Uaxactún

$ Aldana's Lodge
T5801-2588, edeniaa@yahoo.com.
Run by a friendly family, Aldana's Lodge has small, white, clean *casitas*, as well as tent and hammock space behind **El Chiclero**. Just before El Chiclero take a left on the road to the ruins and then take the 1st right until you see a whitewashed *casita* on the right (2 mins).

$ El Chiclero
T7926-1095.
Neat and clean, hammocks and rooms in a garden, also good food by arrangement.

Sayaxché

$ Guayacán
Close to ferry, T7928-6111.
Owner Julio Godoy is a good source of information.

$ Hotel Posada Segura
Turn right from the dock area and then 1st left, T7928-6162.
One of the best options in town, clean, and some rooms have a bath and TV.

Petexbatún

$$$ Chiminos Island Lodge
T2335-3506, www.chiminosisland.com.
Remote, small ecolodge close to a Maya site on a peninsula on the river, in a great for exploring local sites, fishing and wildlife spotting. Rates includes all food.

$$$ Posada Caribe
T7928-6117.
Comfortable *cabañas* with bathroom and shower. They offer trips to **Aguateca** by launch and a guide for excursions. Rates include 3 meals.

Camping
Camping is possible at Escobado, on the lakeside.

Restaurants

Uaxactún

$ Comedor Imperial
At the village entrance.
Bargain *comida típica* for US$1.30.

Sayaxché

$$$ El Botanero Café Restaurante and Bar
Straight up from the dock and 2nd left.
A funky wooden bar with logs and seats carved from tree trunks.

$ Restaurant La Montaña
Near dock.
Cheap food, local information given.

$ Yakín
Near dock.
Cheap, good food; try the *licuados*.

What to do

Uaxactún
For guided walks around the ruins ask for one of the trained guides, US$10. For expeditions further afield, contact Elfido Aldana at **Posada Aldana**. Neria Baldizón at **El Chiclero** has high-clearance pickups and plenty of experience in organizing both vehicle and mule trips to any site. She charges US$200 per person to go to Río Azul.

Sayaxché
Viajes Don Pedro, *on the river front near the dock, T7928-6109.* Runs launches to El Ceibal (US$35 for up to 3), Petexbatún and Aguateca (US$60 for up to 5), Dos Pilas (US$50 for small group). Trip possible by jeep in the dry season, Altar de los Sacrificios (US$100 minimum 2 people) and round trips to Yaxchilán for 3 days (US$400). Mon-Sat 0700-1800, Sun 0700-1200.

Transport

Uaxactún
Bus
To Uaxactún from **Santa Elena** at 1200 arriving between 1600-1700, US$2.60, returning 0500 with **Transportes Pinita**. Foreigners have to pay US$2 to pass through Parque Nacional Tikal on their way to Uaxactún, payable at the main entrance to Tikal.

El Mirador, El Tintal and Nakbé
Bus

1 bus daily with **Transportes Pinita** to **Carmelita**. See Flores for information.

Northwest Petén and the Mexican border
Boat and bus

To **El Naranjo** at 0500 and 1000, returning at 0500, 1100 and 1300, US$4. Or hire a *lancha* from Paso Caballos.

Sayaxché
Bus

There are buses to **Flores**, 0600, 0700, 1-2 hrs, and microbuses every 30 mins. To **Raxrujá** and on to **Cobán** via **Chisec** at 0400, US$.80, 6½ hrs direct to Cobán. There are pickups after that hourly and some further buses direct and not via Chisec. For **Lanquín** take the bus to Raxrujá, then a pickup to Sebol, and then a pickup to Lanquín, or the Lanquín *cruce* at Pajal, and wait for onward transport. If you are heading to **Guatemala City** from here it could be quicker to head north to Flores rather than take the long road down to Cobán. However, this road has now been entirely tarmacked.

Petaxbatún
Boat

It is 30-40 mins in *lancha* from Sayaxché to the stop for **Dos Pilas** to hire horses. It's 50 mins-1 hr to **Chiminos** lodge and 1 hr 20 mins to the **Aguateca** site. To Dos Pilas and Aguateca from Chiminos, US$27 return to each site.

Background
Guatemala

Regional history

Arrival of the American people

While controversy continues to surround the precise date humans arrived in the Americas, the current prevailing view suggests the first wave of emigrants travelled between Siberia and Alaska across the Bering Strait ice bridge created in the last Ice Age, approximately 15,000 years ago. Small hunter-gatherer groups quickly moved through the region, and in fertile lands they developed agriculture and settled. By 1500 BC sedentary villages were widespread in many parts of the Americas, including Central America, where stone-built cities and complex civilizations also began to emerge.

Pre-Columbian civilizations

Despite the wide variety of climates and terrains that fall within Central America's boundaries, the so-called Mesoamerican civilizations were interdependent, sharing the same agriculture based on maize, beans and squash, as well as many sociological traits. These included an enormous pantheon of gods, pyramid-building, a trade in valuable objects, hieroglyphic writing, astronomy, mathematics and a complex calendar system. Historians divide Mesoamerican civilizations into three broad periods, the pre-Classic, which lasted until about AD 300, the Classic, until AD 900, and the post-Classic, from AD 900 until the Spanish conquest.

Olmecs
Who precisely the Olmecs were, where they came from and why they disappeared is a matter of debate. It is known that they flourished from about 1400-400 BC, lived in the Mexican Gulf coast region between Veracruz and Tabasco, and that all later civilizations have their roots in Olmec culture. They are particularly renowned for their carved colossal heads, jade figures and altar. They gave great importance to the jaguar and the serpent in their imagery and built large ceremonial centres such as San Lorenzo and La Venta. The progression from the Olmec to the Maya civilization seems to have taken place at Izapa on the Pacific border of present-day Mexico and Guatemala.

Maya
The best known of the pre-Conquest civilizations were the Maya, thought to have evolved in a formative period in the Pacific highlands of Guatemala and El Salvador between 1500 BC and about AD 100. After 200 years of growth it entered what is known today as its Classic period, when the civilization flourished in Guatemala, El Salvador, Belize, Honduras and southern Mexico. The height of the Classic period lasted until AD 900, after which the Maya resettled in the Yucatán,

possibly after a devastating famine, drought or peasant uprising. They then came under the influence of the central Mexican Toltecs, who were highly militaristic, until the Spanish conquest in the 16th century.

Throughout its evolution, Mayan civilization was based on independent city states that were governed by a theocratic elite of priests, nobles and warriors. Recent research has revealed that these cities, far from being the peaceful ceremonial centres once imagined, were **warring adversaries** striving to capture victims for sacrifice. This change in perception of the Maya was largely due to a greater understanding of Mayan **hieroglyphic writing**, which appears both on paper codices and on stone monuments. Aside from a gory preoccupation with sacrifice, Mayan culture was rich in **ceremony, art, science, folklore** and **dance**. Their cities were all meticulously designed according to strict and highly symbolic geometric rules: columns, figures, faces, animals, friezes, stairways and temples often expressed a date, a time or a specific astronomical relationship. Impressively, the Mayan calendar was so advanced that it was a nearer approximation to sidereal time than either the Julian or the Gregorian calendars of Europe; it was only .000069 of a day out of true in a year. The Maya also formulated the concept of 'zero' centuries in advance of the Old World, plotted the movements of the sun, moon, Venus and other planets, and conceived a time cycle of more than 1800 million days.

Conquest

It was only during his fourth voyage, in 1502, that **Columbus** reached the mainland of Central America. He landed in **Costa Rica** and Panama, which he called **Veragua**, and founded the town of Santa María de Belén. In 1508 Alonso de Ojeda received a grant of land on the Pearl coast east of Panama, and in 1509 he founded the town of San Sebastián, later moved to a new site called Santa María la Antigua del Darién (now in Colombia). In 1513 the governor of the colony at Darién was **Vasco Núñez de Balboa**. Taking 190 men he crossed the isthmus in 18 days and caught the first glimpse of the Pacific; he claimed it and all neighbouring lands in the name of the King of Spain. But from the following year, when **Pedrarias de Avila** replaced him as Governor, Núñez de Balboa fell on evil days, and he was executed by Pedrarias in 1519. That same year Pedrarias crossed the isthmus and founded the town of Panamá on the Pacific side. It was in April 1519, too, that **Cortés** began his conquest of Mexico. Central America was explored from these two nodal points of Panama and Mexico.

Settlement

The groups of Spanish settlers were few and widely scattered, a fundamental point in explaining the **political fragmentation** of Central America today. Panama was ruled from Bogotá, but the rest of Central America was subordinate to the Viceroyalty at Mexico City, with Antigua, Guatemala, as an Audiencia for the area until 1773, and thereafter Guatemala City. Panama was of paramount importance for colonial Spanish America for its strategic position, and for the trade passing across the isthmus to and from the southern colonies. The other provinces were of comparatively little value.

The small number of **Spaniards intermarried** freely with the locals, accounting for the predominance of mestizos in present-day Central America. But the picture has regional variations. In Guatemala, where there was the highest native population density, intermarriage affected fewer of the natives, and over half the population today is still purely *indígena* (**indigenous**). On the Meseta Central of Costa Rica, the natives were all but wiped out by disease and, as a consequence of this great disaster, there is a community of over two million whites, with little *indígena* admixture. **Blacks** predominate along the Caribbean coast of Central America. Most were brought in as cheap labour to work as railway builders and banana planters in the 19th century and canal cutters in the 20th. The **Garífuna** people, living between southern Belize and Nicaragua, arrived in the area as free people after African slaves and indigenous Caribbean people intermingled following a shipwreck off St Vincent.

Independence and after

On 5 November 1811, **José Matías Delgado**, a priest and jurist born in San Salvador, organized a revolt with another priest, Manuel José Arce. They proclaimed the Independence of El Salvador, but the Audiencia at Guatemala City suppressed the revolt and took Delgado prisoner. Eleven years later, in 1820, the revolution of Spain itself precipitated the Independence of Central America. On 24 February 1821, the Mexican **General Agustín de Iturbide** announced his **Plan de Iguala** for an independent Mexico. Several months later, the Central American *criollos* followed his example and announced their own **Declaration of Independence** in Guatemala City on 15 September 1821. Iturbide invited the provinces of Central America to join with him and, on 5 January 1822, Central America was annexed to Mexico. Delgado, however, refused to accept this decree and Iturbide, who had now assumed the title of **Emperor Agustín I**, sent an army south under Vicente Filísola to enforce it. Filísola had completed his task when he heard of Iturbide's abdication, and at once convened a general congress of the Central American provinces. It met on 24 June 1823, and thereafter established the **Provincias Unidas del Centro de América**. The Mexican Republic acknowledged their Independence on 1 August 1824, and Filísola's soldiers were withdrawn.

The United Provinces of Central America

In 1824, the first congress, presided over by Delgado, appointed a provisional governing *junta* which promulgated a constitution modelled on that of the United States. The Province of Chiapas was not included in the Federation, as it had already adhered to Mexico in 1821. Guatemala City, by force of tradition, soon became the seat of government.

The first president under the new constitution was **Manuel José Arce**, a liberal. One of his first acts was to **abolish slavery**. El Salvador, protesting that he had exceeded his powers, rose in December 1826. Honduras, Nicaragua and Costa Rica joined the revolt, and in 1828 **General Francisco Morazán**, in charge of the army of Honduras, defeated the federal forces, entered San Salvador and marched against Guatemala City. He captured the city on 13 April 1829, and established that contradiction in terms: a liberal dictatorship. Many conservative leaders were expelled and church and monastic properties confiscated. Morazán himself became President of the Federation in 1830. He was a man of considerable ability; he ruled with a strong hand, encouraged education, fostered trade and industry, opened the country to immigrants, and reorganized the administration. In 1835 the capital was moved to San Salvador.

These reforms antagonized the conservatives and there were several uprisings. The most serious revolt was among the *indígenas* of Guatemala, led by Rafael Carrera, an illiterate mestizo conservative and a born leader. Years of continuous warfare followed, during the course of which the Federation withered away. As a result, the federal congress passed an act which allowed each province to assume the government it chose, but the idea of a federation was not quite dead. Morazán became President of El Salvador. Carrera, who was by then in control of Guatemala, defeated Morazán in battle and forced him to leave the country. But in 1842, Morazán overthrew Braulio Carrillo, then dictator of Costa Rica, and became president himself. At once he set about rebuilding the Federation, but a popular uprising soon led to his capture. He was shot on 15 September 1842 and with him perished any practical hope of Central American political union.

The separate states

The history of **Guatemala**, **El Salvador**, **Honduras** and **Nicaragua** since the breakdown of federation has been tempestuous in the extreme (**Costa Rica**, with its mainly white population and limited economic value at the time, is a country apart, and **Panama** was Colombian territory until 1903). In each, the ruling class was divided into pro-clerical conservatives and anti-clerical liberals, with constant changes of power. Each was weak, and tried repeatedly to buttress its weakness by alliances with others, which invariably broke up because one of the allies sought a position of mastery. The wars were mainly ideological wars between conservatives and liberals, or wars motivated by inflamed nationalism. Nicaragua was riven internally by the mutual hatreds of the Conservatives of Granada and the Liberals of León, and there were repeated conflicts between the Caribbean and interior parts of Honduras. Despite the permutations and combinations of external and civil war there has been a recurrent desire to re-establish some form of **La Gran Patria Centroamericana**. Throughout the 19th century, and far into the 20th, there have been ambitious projects for political federation, usually involving El Salvador, Honduras and Nicaragua; none of them lasted more than a few years.

Regional integration

Poverty, the fate of the great majority, has brought about closer economic cooperation between the five republics, and in 1960 they established the **Central American Common Market** (CACM). Surprisingly, the Common Market appeared to be a great success until 1968, when integration fostered national antagonisms, and there was a growing conviction in Honduras and Nicaragua, which were doing least well out of integration, that they were being exploited by the others. In 1969 the Football War broke out between El Salvador and Honduras, basically because of a dispute about illicit emigration by Salvadoreans into Honduras, and relations between the two were not normalized until 1980. Hopes for improvement were revived in 1987 when the Central American Peace Plan, drawn up by President Oscar Arias Sánchez of Costa Rica, was signed by the presidents of Guatemala, El Salvador, Honduras, Nicaragua and Costa Rica. The plan proposed formulae to end the civil strife in individual countries, achieving this aim first in Nicaragua (1989), then in El Salvador (1991). In Guatemala, a ceasefire after 36 years of war led to the signing of a peace accord at the end of 1996. With the signing of peace accords, emphasis has shifted to regional, economic and environmental integration.

In October 1993, the presidents of Guatemala, El Salvador, Honduras, Nicaragua and Costa Rica signed a new **Central American Integration Treaty Protocol** to replace that of 1960 and set up new mechanisms for regional integration. The Treaty was the culmination of a series of annual presidential summits held since 1986 which, besides aiming for peace and economic integration, established a Central American Parliament and a Central American Court of Justice. Attempts at further economic and regional integration continue. Plans to create a **Free Trade Area of the Americas** (FTAA) appear to have failed, but the 2003 **Dominican Republic-Central American Free Trade Agreement** (DR-CAFTA) has now been signed by several nations including the Dominican Republic, Guatemala, El Salvador, Honduras, Nicaragua and Costa Rica.

The DR-CAFTA closely compliments the 2001 **Plan Puebla-Panama** (the PPP, also known as the Mesoamerican Integration and Development Project) an economic corridor stretching from Puebla, west of Mexico City, as far as Panama. Supporters of the plan see it as a means for economic development. Critics see it as a way of draining cheap labour and natural resources with little concern for the environment or long-term progress. Today, the PPP simmers on the back burner, but the desire for Central American nations to strengthen ties is regularly voiced. This is most apparent in the creation of Central America 4 (CA-4), a 2006 border control agreement between Guatemala, El Salvador, Honduras and Nicaragua, that opens up travel between the four nations. Regional meetings occur periodically to promote and encourage trust and cooperation, and while the final destination of such cooperation is far from clear, the Central America of today is far more productive and safer than it was in the 1980s and early 1990s.

Guatemala

Conservative governments restored Spanish institutions in a hark back to the colonial era. This trend was maintained by fiercely pro-church Rafael Carrera, who became president in 1844. He set about restoring church power and invited the Jesuits back into the country (they had been expelled in 1767). He went into exile in 1848 before returning to power in 1851 where he remained until 1865.

The 1871 Liberal Revolution

On Carrera's death, Conservative General Vicente Cerna ruled Guatemala until 1871, when General Justo Rufino Barrios successfully overthrew his regime and introduced a wave of Liberal leadership. Miguel García Granados (1871-1873) reigned briefly, expelling leading clerics and overturning Carrera's invitation to the Jesuits. Thereafter, Justo Rufino Barrios (1873-1885) himself was elected president. He too was vehemently anticlerical. He expropriated church property, using the proceeds to found a national bank, secularized education and marriage. New ports and railways were constructed and coffee production was reformed, transforming Guatemala into a major producer. This was largely accomplished through the confiscation of indigenous lands. Barrios also tried to restore the federation and when the idea foundered he resorted to dictatorial methods. He invaded El Salvador when they refused to cooperate and died in a battle at Chalachuapa. Manuel Lisandro Barillas (1885-1892) followed in his footsteps and again tried unsuccessfully to re-establish Central American union. The Liberal trend continued with General José María Reina Barrios (1892-1898), who confiscated his enemies' property and spent much time quashing internal rebellion. During his term the price of coffee crashed on the world market, but public works using public money continued to be built, causing widespread outrage and revolts. He was assassinated.

Dictatorship and the rise of the United Fruit Company

When Manuel Estrada Cabrera (1898-1920) came to power, his was the longest one-man rule in Central American history. Cabrera encouraged foreign investment, expansion of the railways and the United Fruit Company's foray into Guatemala, granting it some 800,000 ha for the planting of bananas. The company's privileges included a monopoly on transport and a free rein over their own affairs. American interests in Guatemala grew to the point where 40% of all exports were US controlled. Cabrera was eventually toppled amid widespread discontent. Carlos Herrera followed but was overthrown in a bloodless military coup, bringing José María Orellana to power. Orellana negotiated more concessions for United Fruit and the railway company. However, organized protests over plantation workers' rights grew and periodically met with government crackdowns. Orellana, unlike some of his predecessors, died a natural death in 1926.

Jorge Ubico

Jorge Ubico was an efficient but brutal dictator who came to power in 1931. He tightened political control, introduced a secret police, clamped down on workers' discontent and Communist movements, persecuted writers and intellectuals, promoted forced labour and fixed low wage rates. He also extended privileges to the United Fruit Company. These, and other issues, and the fact that he sought constant re-election, provoked widespread demonstrations calling for his resignation. In June 1944, following the death of a teacher in a protest demanding university autonomy, Ubico resigned and a triumvirate of generals assumed power.

October Revolution

On 20 October 1944 there was an armed uprising of La Guardia de Honor, backed by popular support. The military leaders drew up a democratic constitution, abolished forced labour, and upheld the autonomy of the university. Teacher Juan José Arévalo of the Frente Popular Libertador party was then elected president and drew up a plan of social reform. He separated the powers of state, introduced *comedores* for children of poor workers, set up the Department for Social Security, and accepted the existence of the Communist Party. He survived more than 20 military coups and finished his term of five years (1945-1950).

1954 US-backed military coup

Jacobo Arbenz Guzmán, a member of the 1944 military triumvirate, became the elected president in 1950. His 1952 Agrarian Reform Law saw the expropriation of large, underused estates without adequate compensation awarded to their owners – mainly the United Fruit Company, which for years had been under-declaring the value of its land for tax reasons. According to the company, of its 550,000 acres around the Caribbean, 85% of it was not farmed. It was offered a measly US$2.99 an acre for land (440,000 acres) which it said was worth US$75. The company's connections with high-powered players within the US Government and the CIA, and its constant allegation that Communism was percolating through the Guatemalan corridors of power, eventually persuaded the US to sponsor an overthrow of the Arbenz government. Military strikes were launched on the country in June 1954. At the end of the month Arbenz, under pressure from Guatemalan military and the US ambassador John Peurifoy, resigned.

Military rule

In June 1954 Colonel Carlos Castillo Armas took over the presidency. He persecuted and outlawed Communists. He was assassinated in 1957, which provoked a wave of violence and instability and for the next three decades the army and its right-wing supporters suppressed left-wing efforts, both constitutional and violent, to restore the gains made under Arévalo and Arbenz. Many thousands of people, mostly leftists but also many Maya without political orientation, were killed during this period.

The rise of the guerrilla movement

On 13 November 1960, a military group, inspired by revolution in Cuba, carried out an uprising against the government. It was suppressed but spawned the Movimiento 13 de Noviembre, which then joined forces with the Guatemalan Workers' Party. In 1962, student demonstrations ended in bloodshed, which resulted in the creation of the Movimiento 12 de Abril. These movements then merged to form Fuerzas Armadas Rebeldes (FAR) in 1962.

During this period, Arévalo made a move to re-enter the political fold. A coup d'état followed. Guerrilla and right-wing violence began to increase in the late 1960s. In the early 1970s the guerrillas re-focused. The FAR divided into FAR and the EGP (Ejército Guerrillero de los Pobres, Guerrilla Army of the Poor), which operated in the north of the country. In 1972 the Organización Revolucionaria del Pueblo en Armas (ORPA) was formed. The EGP was led by Rolando Morán, a supporter of the Cuban Revolution. The group's first action took place in the Ixil Triangle in 1975. The ORPA was led by Commandante Gaspar Ilom, also known as Rodrigo Asturias, son of Nobel Prize for Literature winner Miguel Angel Asturias.

The worst of the conflict

Throughout the 1970s and early 1980s the worst atrocities of the war were committed. General Kjell Eugenio Laugerud García's presidency was characterized by escalating violence, which led the US to withdraw its support for the Guatemalan government in 1974. In 1976, a devastating earthquake struck Guatemala killing 23,000 people. This prompted widespread social movements in the country to improve the lives of the poor. At the same time, guerrilla activity surged. Meanwhile, the US, believing the human rights situation had improved, resumed military sales to Guatemala. But in 1981 the military unleashed a huge offensive against the guerrillas who united to confront it with the formation of the Unidad Revolucionaria Nacional Guatemalteca (URNG). The situation worsened when Ríos Montt came to power in 1982 following a coup d'état. He presided over the bloodiest period of violence with the introduction of the scorched-earth policy, massacring whole villages in an attempt to root out bands of guerrillas. Ríos Montt was ousted by his defence minister, General Oscar Mejías Victores, in a coup in August 1983.

Return of democracy

Mejía Victores permitted a Constituent Assembly to be elected in 1984, which drew up a new constitution and worked out a timetable for a return to democracy. He also created numerous 'model villages' to rehouse the displaced and persecuted Maya, who had fled in their thousands to the forests, the capital, Mexico and the US. Presidential elections in December 1985 were won by civilian Vinicio Cerezo Arévalo of the Christian Democrats (DC), who took office in January 1986. He was the first democratically elected president of Guatemala since 1966. In the 1990 elections Jorge Serrano Elías of the Solidarity Action Movement made Guatemalan history by being the first civilian to succeed a previous civilian president in a change of government.

Civil unrest

By 1993, however, the country was in disarray. The social policies pursued by the government had alienated nearly everybody and violence erupted on the streets. Amid growing civil unrest, President Serrano suspended the constitution, dissolved Congress and the Supreme Court, and imposed press censorship. International and domestic condemnation of his actions was immediate. After only a few days, Serrano was ousted by a combination of military, business and opposition leaders and a return to constitutional rule was promised. Congress approved a successor, Ramiro de León Carpio, previously the human rights ombudsman. He soon proved as capable as his predecessors, however, and the public's distaste of corrupt congressional deputies and ineffectual government did not diminish. The reform of election procedures and political parties had been called for by a referendum in 1994, which obliged Congressional elections to be called. The result gave a majority of seats to the Guatemalan Republican Front (FRG), led by ex-president Ríos Montt, who was elected to the presidency of Congress for 1994-1996. Ríos Montt's candidate in the 1995 presidential election, Alfonso Portillo, lost by a slim margin to Alvaro Arzú of the National Advancement Party. Arzú proposed to increase social spending, curtail tax evasion, combat crime and bring a speedy conclusion to peace negotiations with the URNG guerrillas.

Towards peace

One of the earliest moves made by President Serrano was to speed up the process of talks between the government and the URNG, which began in March 1990. The sides met in Mexico City in April 1991 to discuss such topics as democratization and human rights, a reduced role for the military, the rights of indigenous people, the resettlement of refugees and agrarian reform. Progress, however, was slow. In August 1995 an accord was drawn up with the aid of the UN's Guatemala mission (MINUGUA) and the Norwegian government. The timetable proved over-ambitious, but, on taking office in January 1996, President Arzú committed himself to signing a peace accord. In February 1996 he met the URNG leadership, who called a ceasefire in March. On 29 December 1996 a peace treaty was signed ending 36 years of armed conflict. An amnesty was agreed which would limit the scope of the Commission for Historical Clarification and prevent it naming names in its investigations of human rights abuses.

Peacetime elections and the Portillo Government

The 1999 elections went to a second round with self-confessed killer Alfonso Portillo of the FRG winning 62% of the vote against his rival Oscar Berger, the candidate of President Arzú's ruling PAN. Portillo subsequently promised to reform the armed forces, solve the killing of Bishop Gerardi and disband the elite presidential guard, so implicated in the human rights abuses. Common crime, as well as more sinister crimes such as lynchings, plagued Portillo's term and seemed to increase.

The new millennium generally brought mixed results for justice. The former interior minister Byron Barrientos resigned in December 2001 and faced accusations of misappropriating US$6 million in state funds. In June 2002, ex-president Jorge

Serrano was ordered to be arrested on charges which included embezzlement of state funds. He remains exiled in Panama. In October 2002, a former colonel in the Guatemalan army, Colonel Juan Valencia Osorio, was found guilty of ordering the murder of anthropologist Myrna Mack and sentenced to 30 years' imprisonment. However, the appeal court overturned his conviction in 2003.

Also in October 2002, the four men imprisoned for their role in the 1998 murder of Guatemalan Bishop Gerardi had their convictions overturned. A retrial was ordered. In 2003 Ríos Montt mounted a legal challenge to a rule which prohibits former coup leaders running for president. The constitutional court ruled he could stand in the autumn parliamentary elections. The UN High Commission for Human Rights announced it would open an office in Guatemala City. More details can be found at www.ghrc-usa.org.

Oscar Berger

A new era in Guatemalan politics began with the election of Oscar Berger as president in December 2003. After coming second to Portillo in the 1999 elections as candidate for PAN, Berger led the newly formed Gran Alianza Nacional (GANA) to electoral victory with 54% of the vote over his centre-left rival Alvaro Colom. Berger assumed the presidency promising to improve access to clean water, education and health care for all citizens. He also persuaded indigenous leader and Nobel Prize winner Rigoberta Menchú to join his government to work towards a more just country. Berger's presidency provided slight economic growth and attempts to strengthen the country's institutions, despite low tax revenues, organized crime, discrimination and poverty.

Alvaro Colom

Elections in November 2007 were also a close affair, with second round run-off providing Alvaro Colom with a narrow victory for the Unidad Nacional de la Esperanza (National Unity of Hope) and 53% of the vote. Colom took office vowing to fight poverty with a government that would have a Mayan face, while promising to reduce organized crime. During his tenure, Los Zetas drug gang, former wing of the Mexican Gulf Cartel, moved into Guatemala, with smuggling concentrated in northern regions, particularly Petén. Dozens of murders have since been linked with the ruthless gang, which is thought to include former members of the Kaibiles – the elite Guatemalan army squad, notorious for its brutalities during Guatemala's 1960-1996 civil war.

Otto Pérez Molina

In January 2012, Otto Pérez Molina was elected to office. A controversial figure, he graduated from the School of the Americas to become Guatemala's Director of military intelligence. He was also once a member of Guatemala's notorious Kaibiles, and after becoming president, he was accused of participating in scorched earth policies, torture and genocide, which he denied. Despite his authoritarian background, Pérez Molina took the somewhat liberal stance of proposing the full legalization of drugs during a UN visit. In fact, Guatemala continues to receive considerable military aid for the war on drugs, which critics say is being used to beef up security and crush public dissent against mining, hydroelectric and other foreign-owned projects; indigenous activists and trade unionists continue to be assassinated. In 2013, Efraín Ríos Montt was found guilty of genocide and crimes against humanity. Outrageously, the ruling was subsequently overturned by the constitutional court on a technicality. As of January 2015, his re-trail had been suspended.

Culture

The word *ladino* applies to any person with a 'Latin' culture, speaking Spanish and wearing Western clothes, though they may be pure Amerindian by descent. The opposite of ladino is *indígena*; the definition is cultural, not racial. Guatemala's population in 2013 was estimated to be 15.47 million. The indigenous people of Guatemala are mainly of Maya descent. The largest of the 22 indigenous Maya groups are K'iche', Q'eqchi' and Mam. When the Spaniards arrived from Mexico in 1524 those who stayed settled in the southern highlands around Antigua and Guatemala City and intermarried with the groups of native subsistence farmers living there. This was the basis of the present *mestizo* population living in the cities and towns as well as in all parts of the southern highlands and in the flatlands along the Pacific coast; the indigenous population is still at its most dense in the western highlands and Alta Verapaz. They form two distinct cultures: the almost self-supporting indigenous system in the highlands, and the *ladino* commercial economy in the lowlands. *Mestizo* are mixed Amerindian-Spanish or assimilated Amerindian. About half the total population are classed as Amerindian (Maya) – estimates vary from 40-65%.

Costume and dress
Indigenous dress is particularly attractive, little changed from the time the Spaniards arrived: the colourful head-dresses, *huipiles* (tunics) and skirts of the women, the often richly patterned sashes and kerchiefs, the hatbands and tassels of the men vary greatly, often from village to village. Unfortunately a new outfit is costly, the indigenous people are poor, and jeans are cheap. While men are adopting Western dress in many villages, women have been slower to change.

Land and environment

A lowland ribbon, nowhere more than 50 km wide, runs the whole length of the Pacific shore. Cotton, sugar, bananas and maize are the chief crops of this strip. There is some stock raising as well. Summer rain is heavy and the lowland carries scrub forest. From this plain the highlands rise sharply to heights of between 2500 and 4000 m and stretch some 240 km to the north before sinking into the northern lowlands.

A string of volcanoes juts boldly above the southern highlands along the Pacific. There are intermont basins at from 1500 to 2500 m in this volcanic area.

Most of the people of Guatemala live in these basins, which are drained by short rivers into the Pacific and by longer ones into the Atlantic. One basin west of the capital, ringed by volcanoes and with no apparent outlet, is Lago de Atitlán.

The southern highlands are covered with lush vegetation over a volcanic subsoil. This clears away in the central highlands, exposing the crystalline rock of the east–west running ranges. This area is lower but more rugged, with sharp-faced ridges and deep ravines modifying into gentle slopes and occasional valley lowlands as it loses height and approaches the Caribbean coastal levels and the flatlands of El Petén. The lower slopes of these highlands, from about 600 to 1500 m, are planted with coffee. Above 1500 m is given over to wheat and the main subsistence crops of maize and beans. Deforestation is becoming a serious problem. Where rainfall is low there are savannas; water for irrigation is now drawn from wells and these areas are being reclaimed for pasture and fruit growing.

Two large rivers flow down to the Caribbean Gulf of Honduras from the highlands: one is the Río Motagua, 400 km long, rising among the southern volcanoes; the other, further north, is the Río Polochic, 298 km long, which drains into Lago de Izabal and the Bahía de Amatique. There are large areas of lowland in the lower reaches of both rivers, which are navigable for considerable distances; this was the great banana zone.

To the northwest, bordering on Belize and Mexico's Yucatán Peninsula, lies the low, undulating tableland of El Petén almost one-third of the nation's territory. In some parts there is natural grassland, with woods and streams, suitable for cattle, but large areas are covered with dense hardwood forest. Since the 1970s large-scale tree felling has reduced this tropical rainforest by some 40%, especially in the south and east. However, in the north, which now forms Guatemala's share of the Maya Biosphere Reserve, the forest is protected, but illegal logging still takes place.

Ecosystems

Central America is the meeting place of two of the world's major biological regions: the Nearctic to the north and the Neotropical to the south. It has a remarkable geological and climatic complexity and consequently an enormous range of habitats: rainforests, dry forests, cloudforests, mangroves and stretches of wetlands.

Lowland rainforests

The region's lowland rainforests are home to an extraordinary cornucopia of biological life. They are densely vegetated and largely inhospitable places, characterized by high temperatures, humidity and rainfall. Life is sustained by an intricate web of relationships, invariably driven by the struggle for survival. Predation, particularly of nests, is intensive and widespread, as is competition for food and light; anyone unfortunate enough to find themselves stranded in a rainforest may find little to sustain them. Symbiotic relationships are very common, with plants often having creative and specialized methods of pollination and seed dispersal. Parasitic relationships are also prolific and often quite gruesome, such as wasps that inject their eggs inside the living bodies of ants. Rainforests incorporate several distinct layers commencing with the forest floor, which is usually clear of vegetation and quite dark due to the multiple canopies above it. The exception is the site of a recent tree fall, which is always worth scrutinizing for its new growth and activity.

Despite the rainforest's profusion of plants, its topsoil is very thin and nutrient-poor, causing many trees to have sprawling, buttressed roots near the surface. When a plant or animal dies, it is rapidly broken down by bacteria and insects, and its nutrients taken up by living vegetation via a network of mycorrhizal fungi; brush away some topsoil to see it. Between the canopy and the forest floor, the understorey is home to numerous small animals. It is still a relatively dark place and most of its plants – typically shrubs and palms – need large leaves to maximize photosynthesis. Rodents are a fairly common sight, as are amphibians. Rivers, streams, ponds and other bodies of water tend to draw larger mammals, but most are nocturnal and rarely seen by humans. The canopy itself is teeming with plant life as vines, orchids and epiphytes compete for every available ray of light. The rainforest's highest canopy – the emergent layer – contains just a few tall trees, the giants of the forest, home to rare bird species.

Tropical dry forests
Low-lying tropical dry forests receive far less precipitation than rainforests. They are home to numerous deciduous trees that must shed their leaves in the dry season in order to conserve water. The loss of leaves opens many gaps in the forest canopy, encouraging the growth of prolific underbrush. Many plants and trees have found strategies to cope with the dry conditions, including some that have evolved chlorophyll in their bark and others with swollen roots and stems that act as reservoirs. Resident animal species are broadly comparable to those of the rainforests, but ultimately less numerous and biodiverse. Some of them, including a few amphibians and reptiles, practise estivation – a state of dormancy where they burrow deep into the mud and sleep out the summer. The coming of the rains is a fascinating time in the tropical dry forest, when numerous creatures emerge, flowers start blooming and the vegetation turns green virtually overnight.

Cloudforests
Highland cloudforests are characterized by persistent mist and cloud cover. They are considerably cooler than rainforests with daytime temperatures of around 10-20°C. Due to the almost constant blanket of fog, sunlight is greatly reduced, but there is an immense amount of precipitation and cloudforests play a crucial role in maintaining highland drainage and watersheds. They are extremely lush places, home to scores of green mosses, lichens, ferns, fungi, orchids and bromeliads. Trees are generally short with dense, compact crowns that cause wind-driven clouds to condense. Cloudforests also boast reasonably high biodiversity and high rates of endemism thanks to their numerous valleys and ridges, which many animals find impassable.

Wetlands and mangrove forests

Wetlands can be found on all three coastlines and are endowed with an abundance of water in different forms: fresh, salty, flowing and stagnant. Wetlands offer a diversity of ecological niches including sedge marshes, swamps, bogs, flood plains, coastal lagoons and mangrove forests. Proliferating in intertidal or estuarine areas, mangroves include a broad family of halophytic (salt-tolerant) trees. They serve a vital function by trapping sediment, protecting the shore from erosion and building land. The forests have a low canopy and a low diversity of trees, usually dominated by red mangroves, which can be recognized by their dark stilted roots that hold them above the surface of the water. Mangroves are important nurseries for fish, birds, amphibians and crustaceans.

Beaches and shores

The shorelines can be rocky, sandy or muddy. Low tide often reveals rock pools filled with clams and mussels, or teeming mud flats strewn with crabs and shrimps, all drawing waders and hungry seabirds. Larger avian species, including pelicans and pterodactyl-like frigate birds, are a common sight on any shore. Some of the region's beaches see impressive migrations of endangered sea turtles, including leatherback, hawksbill, loggerhead and olive ridley.

Wildlife

Around three million years ago, the merging of North and South America into a single landmass sparked a mass migration of animals between both continents. Known as the Great American Faunal Interchange, it was a significant moment in the earth's natural history, heralding bold new patterns of species settlement, adaptation, predation and, in some cases, extinction. The event was accompanied by the Great American Schism, which separated the Pacific and Atlantic oceans and set marine species on their own unique evolutionary paths.

Today, Guatemala represent the range limit for numerous North and South American animal species, as well as a land bridge for dozens of types of migratory birds. The majority of tour operators listed in this guide will offer nature-oriented tours and there are several national parks, biotopes or protected areas throughout the region, each with its own highlights.

Mammals

Primates are among the most easily sighted mammals in the region. Howler monkeys are noticeable for the huge row they make, especially around dawn or dusk. The spider monkey is more agile and slender and uses its prehensile tail to swing around the canopy. The smaller, white-throated capuchins are also commonly seen, moving around in noisy groups. The most frequently spotted carnivore is the white-nosed coati, a member of the racoon family, with a long snout and ringed tail. Members of the cat family are rarely seen; those in the area include the jaguar, puma, ocelot and margay. The largest land mammal in the region is Baird's tapir, weighing up to 300 kg, but it is a forest species and very secretive. More likely to be seen are peccaries, medium-sized pig-like animals that are active both day and night. The white-tailed deer can often be spotted at dawn or dusk in drier, woodland patches. The smaller red brocket is a rainforest deer and more elusive. Rodent species you might see include the forest-dwelling agouti, which looks rather like a long-legged guinea pig. Considerably larger is the nocturnal paca, another forest species. Many species of bat are found throughout the region.

Birds
Toucans and the smaller toucanets are widespread throughout the tropical areas of the region and easy to spot. Other popular sightings include the hummingbird, frequently drawn to sugar-feeders, and the scarlet macaw. The resplendent quetzal, the national symbol of Guatemala, is brilliant emerald green, with males having a bright scarlet breast and belly and long green tail streamers. The harpy eagle is extremely rare with sightings a possibility in rainforest region of northern Guatemala. Other rare birds include the threatened horned guam, found only in high cloudforests. Along the coasts are masses of different seabirds, including pelicans, boobies and the magnificent frigate bird.

Reptiles and amphibians
Snakes are rarely sighted, but if you are lucky you could see a boa constrictor curled up digesting its latest meal. In contrast, lizards are everywhere, from small geckos walking up walls in your hotel room to the large iguanas sunbathing in the tree tops. The American crocodile and spectacled caiman are both found, with the latter being seen quite frequently. Morlet's crocodile is found only in Mexico, Belize and Guatemala. You'll certainly hear frogs and toads, even if you do not see them. However, the brightly coloured poison-dart frogs and some of the tree frogs are well worth searching out. Look for them in damp places, under logs and moist leaf litter, in rock crevices and by ponds and streams; many will be more active at night. Turtles have been nesting in the region for thousands of years. The eggs will hatch simultaneously and the young turtles will inundate the sea in an evolutionary mechanism believed to give them the best chances of survival.

Insects and spiders
There are uncounted different species of insect in the area. Probably most desirable to see are the butterflies, though some of the beetles, such as the jewel scarabs, are also pretty spectacular. If you are fascinated by spiders, look out for tarantulas, there are many different species.

Marine wildlife
Marine mammals that can be sighted include whales, dolphins and manatees.

Practicalities
Guatemala

Getting there

All countries in Latin America (in fact across the world) officially require travellers entering their territory to have an onward or return ticket and may at times ask to see that ticket. Although rarely enforced at airports, this regulation can create problems at border crossings. In lieu of an onward ticket out of the country you are entering, any ticket out of another Latin American country may sometimes suffice, or proof that you have sufficient funds to buy a ticket (a credit card will do).

Air

Fares from Europe and North America to Latin American destinations vary. Peak periods and higher prices correspond to holiday season in the northern hemisphere. The very busy seasons are as follows: 7 December to 15 January and July to mid-September. If you intend travelling during those times, book as far ahead as possible. Check with an agency for the best deal for when you wish to travel. There is a wide range of offers to choose from in a highly competitive environment. International air tickets are expensive if purchased in Latin America.

Fares fall into three groups, and are all on scheduled services: **Excursion** (return) fares: these have restricted validity either seven to 90 days, or seven to 180 days, depending on the airline. They are fixed-date tickets where the dates of travel cannot be changed after issue without incurring a penalty. **Yearly fares**: these may be bought on a one-way or return basis, and usually the returns can be issued with the return date left open. You must, however, fix the route. **Student** (or Under-26) fares: one way and returns available, or 'open jaws' for people intending to travel a linear route and return from a different point from that which they entered.

Flights from Europe

There are few direct flights to Guatemala, except with Iberia via Madrid, with connecting flights via other European cities. You will usually have to travel via the US.

Flights from the US and Canada

From the US to Guatemala, you can fly with American Airlines, Delta, Spirit Air and United.

Flights from Central America

Connections are available throughout Central America, in most cases travelling through the capital city. There are exceptions with connections to Belize from Flores.

Road

Travelling under your own steam is very popular. Driving your own vehicle – car, camper van, motorbike and bicycle – offers wonderful freedom and may not be as expensive or as bureaucratic as you think. From the emails we receive, the ever-greater cooperation between the nations of Central America is producing

Border cooperation

In June 2006, Guatemala, El Salvador, Honduras, and Nicaragua entered into a 'Central America-4 (CA-4) Border Control Agreement'. Under the terms of the agreement, citizens of the four countries may travel freely across land borders from one of the countries to any of the others without completing entry and exit formalities at immigration checkpoints. US citizens and other eligible foreign nationals, who legally enter any of the four countries, may similarly travel among the four without obtaining additional visas or tourist entry permits for the other three countries. Immigration officials at the first port of entry determine the length of stay, up to a maximum period of 90 days.

dramatic benefits at border crossings for those who decide to go it alone. Indeed, since 2006, when Guatemala, El Salvador, Honduras and Nicaragua signed the **Central America-4**, it's been even easier (see box, above).

There are good road crossings with all of Guatemala's neighbouring countries. There are several crossing points to **southern Mexico** from western Guatemala with additional routes through the jungle from Palenque (see box, page 210). From **Belize** it is possible to cross from Benque Viejo del Carmen (see box, page 212). Links with **Honduras** are possible on the Caribbean near Corinto, and for the ruins at Copán the best crossing is El Florido (see box, page 213). There are four road routes into **El Salvador** (see box, page 214).

Sea

Crossing the Usumacinta river between Guatemala and Mexico is a well-established (if remote) option that connects Chiapas with the Petén. There are also ferry connections between Punta Gorda in Belize and Lívingston in Guatemala.

Getting around

Bus travel is the most popular style of transport for independent travellers. An excellent network criss-crosses Guatemala varying in quality from intercity coaches with air conditioning, videos and fully reclining seats, to beaten-up US-style school buses or 'chicken buses' with busted suspension and holes in the floor.

Even though Guatemala is a relatively small country, don't shun the opportunity to take a short flight. While you'll need to enquire about precise costs, the view from above provides a different perspective and the difference in cost may not be as great as you think. Getting around in Guatemala is rarely a problem whether travelling by bus, car, bike, in fact almost any mode of transport.

There is just one caveat that stands good across all situations: be patient when asking directions. Often Latin Americans will give you the wrong answer rather than admit they do not know. Distances are notoriously inaccurate so ask a few people.

Air

Choices of domestic flights are limited and prices can be steep due to a lack of competition, but it is definitely worth considering an aerial 'hop' if it covers a lot of difficult terrain and you get the bonus of a good view. From Guatemala City, flights operate daily to Flores/Santa Elena for Tikal, taking around 45 minutes. Airlines selling flights on this route are **TAG** and **TACA**. Remote destinations are invariably served by small charter flights with stringent weight restrictions and extra charges for large items such as surf boards; check with the airlines before setting out.

Boat

Keeping all options open, water transport has to be a consideration – although not a very realistic one – in terms of reaching a distant destination. Most water transport consists of small boats with outboard motors. They travel relatively short distances in localized areas, usually along tropical rivers such as the Río Dulce or across bodies of water like Lago Atitlán, where road transport is otherwise lacking. Due to the high cost of fuel, they are frequently crowded and somewhat expensive compared to buses. If hiring a boat privately, it is best to share costs with other travellers. Overcharging is very possible and when calculating costs you need to consider the weight of cargo (including passengers), distance covered, engine horse power, fee for the driver, port taxes (if any) and, most importantly, the quantity of fuel used.

Road

Bus and colectivo

There is an extensive road system with frequent bus services throughout Guatemala. Costs, quality and levels of comfort vary enormously. As a general rule, in mountainous country (and after long journeys), do not expect buses to get to their destination anywhere near on time. Avoid turning up for a bus at the

BORDER CROSSING

Guatemala–Mexico

El Carmen/Ciudad Tecún–Tapachula

The principal border town is Tapachula, with a crossing via the international Talismán Bridge or at Ciudad Hidalgo.

The Talismán–El Carmen route rarely sees much heavy traffic. It's better to change money in Tapachula than with money-changers at the border. Both Mexican and Guatemalan immigration (200 m apart) are open 24 hours. Talismán is 16 km from Tapachula, from where ADO buses depart to major destinations in Chiapas and Oaxaca. This crossing also offers easy access to the Soconusco region along the Mexican Pacific coast. Once in Guatemala, there are connections to Malacatán and onwards to Quetzaltenango.

The main Pan-American Highway crossing, which also connects with Tapachula, is Ciudad Hidalgo–Tecún Umán. Both immigration offices are open 24 hours. Tapachula is 40 km from Ciudad Hidalgo, 30 minutes, with connections to the Soconuso and beyond. Once in Guatemala, there are connections to Coatepeque, Mazatenango and Retalhuleu. There are also a few express buses daily to Guatemala, five hours.

La Mesilla–Ciudad Cuauhtémoc

The fastest, easiest and most scenic route between Chiapas and western Guatemala is via Ciudad Cuauhtémoc. Currency exchange rates are not generally favourable at the border. ATMs are in La Mesilla on the Guatemala side. Immigration offices on both sides are open 0600-2100. On the Mexican

last minute; if it is full it may depart early. Try to sit near the front; going round bends and over bumps has less impact on your body near the front axle, making the journey more comfortable and reducing the likelihood of motion sickness (on some long journeys it also means you are further from the progressively smelly toilets, if available, at the back of the bus). Tall travellers are advised to take aisle seats on long journeys as this allows more leg room.

When the journey takes more than three or four hours, meal stops at country inns or bars, good and bad, are the rule. Often no announcement is made on the duration of the stop; ask the driver and follow him, if he eats, eat. See what the locals are eating – and buy likewise, or make sure you're stocked up on food and drink at the start. For drinks, stick to bottled water, soft drinks or coffee (black). The food sold by vendors at bus stops may be all right; watch if locals are buying. Do not leave valuable items on the bus during stops. Importantly, make sure you have a sweater or blanket to hand for long bus journeys, especially at night; even if it's warm outside, the air conditioning is often set to blizzard.

There is an extensive network of bus routes throughout the country. Like Belize, the chicken buses (former US school buses) are mostly in a poor state of repair and overloaded. Faster and more reliable Pullman services operate on some routes.

side, there is a cheap hotel, a restaurant and ADO bus station, from where infrequent ADO buses operate to major destinations. Frequent *colectivo* shuttles go to Comitán (with onward connections to San Cristóbal de las Casas). The Guatemalan border is a few kilometres from Ciudad Cuautémoc, but cannot be walked; take a taxi/*colectivo* instead. In Guatemala, buses go to Huehuetenango (two hours) and on to Quetzaltenango (four hours).

El Ceibo–Tenosique

An interesting route is southeast from Palenque via Tenosique and El Ceibo, offering access to the Petén in Guatemala. Try to bring the currency you need, although local shops or restaurants may exchange. Both immigration offices are open 0700-1800. *Colectivos* and taxis travel from El Ceibo to the market at Tenosique and there are onward connections to Palenque (two hours). In Guatemala, there are several daily buses to Flores/Santa Elena (four to five hours).

Bethel/La Técnica–Frontera Corozal

Alternatively, you can cross at Bethel/La Técnica– Frontera Corozal for Santa Elena/Flores, a relatively easy crossing on the Río Usumacinta. From Corozal the boat journey to Bethel is 40 minutes, US$30-60 per boat. The journey to La Técnica is five minutes, US$3.50 per person, from where you must take a bus to Bethel for formalities. Immigration on both sides is open 0900-1800. Note robberies have been reported on the road to La Técnica; check the security situation before setting out. In Guatemala there are just a handful of daily buses to Flores/Santa Elena, so arrive early. It is four hours by bus to Palenque from Frontera Corozal, so set out early.

Correct fares should be posted. We receive regular complaints that bus drivers charge tourists more than locals, a practice that is becoming more widespread. One way to avoid being overcharged is to watch for what the locals pay or ask a local, then tender the exact fare on the bus. Many long-distance buses leave very early in the morning. Make sure you can get out of your hotel/*pension*. For international bus journeys make sure you have small denomination local currency or US dollar bills for border taxes. At Easter there are few buses on Good Friday or the Saturday and buses are packed with long queues for tickets for the few days before Good Friday. Many names on bus destination boards are abbreviated; for example, Guate – Guatemala City; Chichi – Chichicastenango; Xela/Xelajú – Quetzaltenango, and so on.

Colectivos (shuttles and taxis) In Guatemala, a *colectivo* can refer to an economical shuttle van, or to a shared taxi, where the fare is divided between four or five passengers, or where the driver picks up and drops off passengers between destinations. The distances covered are comparatively short with most journey times under four hours. The advantage of *colectivos* is that they often travel backdoor routes and supply a speedy alternative to conventional buses. For safety and security, it is best to avoid using *colectivo* taxis in Guatemala City.

BORDER CROSSING
Guatemala–Belize

Menchor de Mencos– Benque Viejo

The most commonly used crossing is between Melchor de Mencos and Benque Viejo del Carmen, popular with those travelling between Tikal and Belize. Taxi rip-offs are common; bargain hard. For currency exchange, there are good rates on the street; or try Banrural at the border (0700-2000). Both immigration offices are open 0600-2000. There are several buses a day from Melchor de Mencos to Santa Elena (Flores), two to three hours; *colectivo* 1½ hours. In Belize, there are regular buses to Belize City. If you leave Santa Elena, Guatemala, at 0500, you can be in Belize City by 1200. Also direct buses operate from Flores to Chetumal (Mexico) with Línea Dorada.

Puerto Barrios/Lívingston–Punta Gorda

Another crossing is by sea between Puerto Barrios and Punta Gorda. Boat services go from Puerto Barrios and Lívingston in Guatemala to Punta Gorda in Belize. They include **Requena Water Taxi**, 12 Front Street, Punta Gorda, T722-2070, departing from the dock opposite immigration. Schedules change and are irregular; arrive as early as possible or better yet, arrange in advance. It's best to buy quetzals in Guatemala. At Belizean immigration, obtain stamps from the customs house near the pier on Front Street and allow up to two hours for processing. If you arrive in Guatemala by boat, check into immigration immediately. Offices are in Puerto Barrios and Lívingston; both open 24 hours. There are highway connections from Puerto Barrios to Guatemala City and Flores and in Belize, there are connections with southern Belize.

On many popular routes throughout the region there are tourist shuttle vans that can be booked through hotels and travel agencies. These are pricier than regular *colectivos* but they travel longer distances and can take a lot of the hassle out of journeys that involve several changes or border crossings (for example, San Cristóbal de las Casas to Antigua). They will also pick you up from your hotel.

International buses These link the region's capital cities providing an effective way of quickly covering a lot of ground. There are several companies but the main operator is **Ticabus** with headquarters in Costa Rica, www.ticabus.com. However, bear in mind that Panama–Guatemala with **Ticabus** takes almost three days and costs over US$100, plus accommodation in Managua and San Salvador. You may want to consider flying if you need to get through more than one country quickly

Crossing borders

Travellers who are eligible for tourist cards or their equivalent (including most European, Australian and North American visitors) find that crossing borders in Central America a relatively straightforward process. Those travellers who

BORDER CROSSING
Guatemala–Honduras

Links with Honduras are possible on the Caribbean near Corinto (see page 140); for the ruins at Copán the best crossing is El Florido (see page 175). The crossing at Agua Caliente is another option.

El Florido
A popular and busy crossing, but straightforward for pedestrians. If entering Honduras just to visit Copán ruins, you can get a temporary 72-hour exit pass, but you must return on time. There are numerous money-changers, but you'll find better rates in Copán. Immigration offices are open 0700-1900. Minibuses run all day until 1700 to Copán ruins and, on the Guatemalan side, there are numerous minibus services to Guatemala City and Antigua.

Entre Ríos–Corinto
This is a Caribbean coast crossing. A road connects Puerto Barrios (Guatemala) and Puerto Cortés (Honduras) with a bridge over the Motagua river. Get your exit stamp in Puerto Barrios or Lívingston if you are leaving by boat to Honduras. If you arrive by boat, go straight to either of these offices. Honduran immigration is at Corinto if crossing from Puerto Barrios in Guatemala. In Honduras, there are connections to the northern coast. Buses leave Corinto for Omoa and Puerto Cortés every hour or so. In Guatemala there is access to Guatemala City and Santa Elena/Flores.

Agua Caliente
A busy crossing, but quicker, cheaper and more efficient than the one at El Florido. There are banks, a tourist office, *comedor* and *hospedaje* on the Honduran side. If leaving Honduras, keep some lempiras for the ride from Agua Caliente to Esquipulas. Immigration on both sides is open 0700-1800. In Honduras there are several buses daily from Agua Caliente to San Pedro Sula, six to seven hours, and frequent services to Nueva Ocotepeque. In Guatemala minibuses go to Esquipulas with connections to Guatemala City, Chiquimula and the highway to Flores.

require visas, however, may not always find them available; approach the relevant consulate (offices in the capital or big cities) before setting out for the border. Some crossings levy exit and entrance taxes, along with occasional *alcaldía* fees; the amounts vary. 'Unofficial' taxes are not uncommon and sometimes it can be easier to pay a few extra dollars than enter into drawn-out dispute. Asking for a *'factura'* (receipt) can help. Many immigration officers will ask for evidence of onward travel – either a return flight or a bus ticket – along with funds. If you use international buses, expect long queues and tedious custom searches. If you're light on luggage, it is usually quicker to use local buses and cross the border on your own. Some drivers may be subjected to bureaucratic delays. Preparation is

BORDER CROSSING
Guatemala–El Salvador

El Salvador and Guatemala are covered under the CA-4 border control agreement (see box, page 208) but you must still submit to immigration formalities before proceeding.

Frontera–San Cristóbal
The main Pan-American highway crossing, used by international buses and heavy traffic. Immigration on both sides is open 0600-2200, but it's usually possible to cross outside these hours with extra charges. In El Salvador, there are regular buses to Santa Ana, No 201, with connections to San Salvador, 1½ hours. In Guatemala, there are buses to Guatemala City, two to three hours.

Valle Nuevo–Las Chinamas
The fastest road link from San Salvador to Guatemala City, but it's busy. It's a straightforward crossing though with quick service if your papers are ready. Change currency with the women in front of the ex-ITSU office; there's a good quetzal-dollar rate. Immigration offices on both sides are open 0800-1800. In El Salvador there are frequent buses to Ahuachapán, No 265, 25 minutes, with connecting services to San Salvador, No 202. Alternatively, try to negotiate a seat with an international Pullman bus; most pass between 0800 and 1400. Onwards to Guatemala there are connections to Guatemala City, two hours.

Ciudad Pedro Alvarado–La Hachadura
This border is at the bridge over the Río Paz, with a filling station and a few shops nearby. It's increasingly popular, thanks to improved roads. Private vehicles require a lot of paperwork and can take two hours to process. It gives access to El Salvador's Pacific Coast, and there are services to San Salvador's Terminal Occidente, No 498, three hours, and to Ahuachapán, No 503, one hour. The last bus to Sonsonate is at 1800. In Guatemala, there is access to the Pacific coast and Guatemala City.

Anguiatú
Normally a quiet border crossing, except when there are special events at Esquipulas in Guatemala. Immigration offices are open 0600-1900. Once in El Salvador there are buses to Santa Ana, No 235A, two hours, and to Metapán, 40 minutes, from where a rough but very scenic road runs to El Poy. In Guatemala, there's good access north to Tikal. Head for the Padre Miguel junction, 19 km from the border, from where you can make connections to Chiquimula and Esquipulas.

the best guarantee of a speedy crossing; check in advance which documents you will require and make several copies before setting out (see car documents below for more on procedures). The busiest borders are often frequented by unpleasant characters. Changing money is OK, but check the rate and carefully count what

you're given; rip-offs can occur. For essential information on border crossing
pages 208, 210, 212, 213 and 214.

Car

Think carefully before driving a vehicle in Guatemala as it can be hazardous. Of the
14,000 km of roads, the 45% that are paved have improved greatly in recent years
and are now of a high standard, making road travel faster and safer. Even cycle tracks
(*ciclovías*) are beginning to appear on new roads. However, a new driving hazard in
the highlands is the deep gully (for rainwater or falling stones) alongside the road.
High clearance is essential on many roads in remoter areas and a 4WD vehicle is useful.

An international driving licence is useful, although not always essential.

Petrol/diese 'Normal' costs US$1.07, 'premium' US$1.09, and diesel is US$1.09
per litre, though prices are in flux due to changing oil prices. Unleaded (*sin plomo*)
is available in major cities, at Melchor de Mencos and along the Pan-American
Highway, but not in the countryside, although it is gradually being introduced
across the country.

Security Avoid driving at night. Spare no ingenuity in making your car secure.
Avoid leaving the car unattended except in a locked garage or guarded parking
space. Remove all belongings and leave the empty glove compartment open
when the car is unattended. Also lock the clutch or accelerator to the steering
wheel with a heavy, obvious chain or lock. Street children will generally protect
your car in exchange for a tip. Note down key numbers and carry spares of the
most important ones, but don't keep all spares inside the vehicle.

Car hire

The main international car hire companies operate in all countries, but tend to be
expensive. Hotels and tourist agencies will tell you where to find cheaper rates,
but you will need to check that you have such basics as a spare wheel, toolkit,
functioning lights, etc. If you plan to do a lot of driving and will have time at the end
to dispose of it, investigate the possibility of buying a second-hand car locally; since
hiring is so expensive it may work out cheaper and will probably do you just as well.
Average rates are US$35-100 per day. Credit cards or cash are accepted for rental.

Cars may not always be taken into neighbouring countries (none are allowed
into Mexico or Belize); rental companies that do allow their vehicles to cross
borders charge for permits and paperwork. If you wish to drive to Copán, you must
check this is permissible and you need a letter authorizing you to take the vehicle
in to Honduras. **Tabarini** and **Hertz** allow their cars to cross the border.

Car hire insurance Check exactly what the hirer's insurance policy covers. In
many cases it will only protect you against minor bumps and scrapes, not major
accidents, or 'natural' damage (for example flooding). Ask if extra cover is available.
Also find out, if using a credit card, whether the card automatically includes
insurance. Beware of being billed for scratches that were on the vehicle before

you hired it. When you return the vehicle make sure you check it with someone at the office and get signed evidence that it is returned in good condition and that you will not be charged.

Cycles and motorbikes

Cycling Unless you are planning a journey almost exclusively on paved roads – when a high-quality touring bike would probably suffice – a mountain bike is recommended. Although touring bike and to a lesser extent mountain bike spares are available in Guatemala City, you'll find that locally manufactured goods are often shoddy and rarely last. Buy everything you can before you leave home.

In the UK the **Cyclists' Touring Club** ① *T0844-736-8450, www.ctc.org.uk*, has information on touring, technical information and discusses the relative merits of different types of bikes.

Motorbikes People are generally very friendly to motorcyclists and you can make many friends by returning friendship to those who show an interest in you. In making your choice go for a comfortable bike. The motorcycle should be off-road capable, without necessarily being an off-road bike. A passport and international driving licence and bike registration document are required. Try not to leave a fully laden bike on its own. A D-lock or chain will keep the bike secure. An alarm gives you peace of mind if you leave the bike outside a hotel at night. Look for hotels that have a courtyard or more secure parking and never leave luggage on the bike overnight or whilst unattended. Also take a cover for the bike.

Hitchhiking

Hitchhiking in Guatemala is reasonably safe and straightforward for males and couples, provided you speak some Spanish. It is a most enjoyable mode of transport: a good way to meet the local people, to improve one's languages and to learn about the country. If trying to hitchhike away from main roads and in sparsely populated areas, however, allow plenty of time, and ask first about the volume of traffic on the road. On long journeys, set out at the crack of dawn, which is when trucks usually leave. They tend to go longer distances than cars. However, it should be said that hitchhiking involves inherent risks and should be approached sensibly and with caution.

Maps

Maps from the **Instituto Geográfico Militar** in Guatemala City are the only good maps available. It is therefore wise to get as many as possible in your home country before leaving, especially if travelling overland. An excellent series of maps covering the whole region and each country is published by **International Travel Maps (ITM)** ① *www.itmb.com*, most with historical notes by the late Kevin Healey.

An excellent source of maps is **Stanfords** ① *12-14 Long Acre, Covent Garden, London, WC2E 9LP, T+44-020-7836-1321, www.stanfords.co.uk, also in Bristol.*

Essentials A-Z

Children

Travel with children can bring you into closer contact with Latin American families and generally presents no special problems; in fact, the path is often smoother for family groups. Officials tend to be more amenable where children are concerned. Always carry a copy of your child's birth certificate and passport photos. For an overview of travelling with children, visit **www.babygoes2.com**.

Transport All airlines charge a reduced price for children under 12 and less for children under 2. Double check the child's baggage allowance though; some are as low as 7 kg. On long-distance buses children generally pay half or reduced fares. For shorter trips it is cheaper, if less comfortable, to seat small children on your knee. In city and local buses, small children do not generally pay a fare, but are not entitled to a seat when paying customers are standing. On sightseeing tours you should always bargain for a family rate; often children can go free. Note that a child travelling free on a long excursion is not always covered by the operator's travel insurance.

Hotels Try to negotiate family rates. It is quite common for children under 12 to be allowed to stay for no extra charge as long as they are sharing your room.

Customs and duty free

You are allowed to take in, free of duty, personal effects and articles for your own use, 5 litres of alcohol, 2 kg of confectionery, and 500 g of tobacco in any form. Temporary visitors can take in any amount in quetzales or foreign currencies. The local equivalent of US$100 per person may be reconverted into US dollars on departure at the airport, provided a ticket for immediate departure is shown. You may not import or export meat, fish, vegetables or fruit.

Disabled travellers

In Guatemala facilities for disabled travellers are severely lacking. Most airports and hotels and restaurants in major cities have wheelchair ramps and adapted toilets. Pavements are often in such a poor state of repair that walking is precarious.

Some travel companies specialize in exciting holidays, tailor-made for individuals depending on their level of disability. Disabled Travelers, www.disabledtravelers.com, provides travel information for disabled adventurers and includes a number of links, reviews and tips. You might also want to read *Nothing Ventured*, edited by Alison Walsh (Harper Collins), which gives personal accounts of worldwide journeys by disabled travellers, plus advice and listings.

Dress

Casual clothing is adequate for most occasions although men may need a jacket and tie in some restaurants.

Dress conservatively in indigenous communities and small churches. Topless bathing is generally unacceptable.

Drugs

Users of drugs without medical prescription should be particularly careful, as there are heavy penalties – up to 10 years' imprisonment – for even the simple possession of such substances. The planting of drugs on travellers, by traffickers or the police, is not unknown. If offered drugs on the street, make no response at all and keep walking. Note that people who roll their own cigarettes are often suspected of carrying drugs and are subjected to close searches.

If you are taking illegal drugs – even ones that are widely and publically used – be aware that authorities do set traps from time to time. Should you get into trouble, your embassy is unlikely to be very sympathetic.

Electricity

127 volts/60 Hz, US-style 2-pin plug.

Embassies and consulates

For a list of Guatemalan embassies abroad, see http://embassy.goabroad.com.

Gay and lesbian travellers

Guatemala is not particularly liberal in its attitudes to gays and lesbians. Having said that, times are changing and you'll find there is a gay scene with bars and clubs at least in Guatemala City; see http://gayguatemala.com, under 'Guía'. Helpful websites include www.gayscape.com, www.gaypedia.com and www.iglta.org (International Gay and Lesbian Travel Association).

Health

Before you travel

See your GP or travel clinic at least 6 weeks before departure for general advice on travel risks and vaccinations. Try a specialist travel clinic if your own GP is unfamiliar with health conditions in Guatemala. Make sure you have sufficient medical travel insurance, get a dental check, know your own blood group and if you suffer a long-term condition such as diabetes or epilepsy, obtain a Medic Alert bracelet/ necklace (www.medicalert.co.uk). If you wear glasses, take a copy of your prescription.

Tip...

The golden rule is boil it, cook it, peel it or forget it, but if you did that every meal, you'd never eat anywhere ... A more practicable rule is that if large numbers of people are eating in a popular place, it's more than likely going to be OK.

Vaccinations

Vaccinations for tetanus, hepatitis A and typhoid are commonly recommended for Guatemala. In addition, yellow fever vaccination is required if entering from an infected area (ie parts of South America). Vaccinations may also be advised against tuberculosis, hepatitis B, rabies and diptheria and cholera. The final decision, however, should be based on a consultation with your GP or travel clinic. In all cases you should confirm your primary courses and boosters are up to date.

Health risks

The most common cause of travellers' diarrhoea is from eating contaminated food. In Guatemala, drinking water is rarely the culprit, although it's best to be cautious (see below). Swimming in sea or river water that has been contaminated by sewage can also be a cause; ask locally if it is safe. Diarrhoea may be also caused by viruses, bacteria (such as E-coli), protozoal (such as giardia), salmonella and cholera. It may be accompanied by vomiting or by severe abdominal pain. Any kind of diarrhoea responds well to the replacement of water and salts. Sachets of rehydration salts can be bought in most chemists and can be dissolved in boiled water. If symptoms persist, consult a doctor. Most towns have at least one laboratory where you can test for parasites (eg amoebas) and other nasties, but be aware that depending on the hatching cycle, you may require several days of consecutive testing before pathogens show up. Tap water in the major cities may be safe to drink but it is advisable to err on the side of caution and drink only bottled or boiled water. Avoid ice in drinks unless you trust that it is from a reliable source.

Malaria precautions are essential for some parts of Guatemala, particularly some rural areas. Once again, check with your GP or travel clinic well in advance of departure. Avoid being bitten by mosquitoes as much as possible. Sleep off the ground and use a mosquito net and some kind of insecticide. Mosquito coils release insecticide as they burn and are available in many shops, as are tablets of insecticide, which are placed on a heated mat plugged into a wall socket.

If you get sick

Contact your embassy or consulate for a list of doctors and dentists who speak your language, or at least some English. Good-quality healthcare is available in the larger centres but it can be expensive, especially hospitalization. Make sure you have adequate insurance (see below).

Useful websites

www.btha.org British Travel Health Association.
www.cdc.gov US government site that gives excellent advice on travel health and details of disease outbreaks.
www.fco.gov.uk British Foreign and Commonwealth Office travel site has useful information on each country, people, climate and a list of UK embassies/consulates.
www.fitfortravel.scot.nhs.uk A-Z of vaccine/health advice for each country.
www.numberonehealth.co.uk Travel screening services, vaccine and travel health advice, email/SMS text vaccine reminders and screens returned travellers for tropical diseases.

Insurance

Insurance is strongly recommended and policies are very reasonable. If you have financial restraints, the most important aspect of any insurance policy is medical care and repatriation. Ideally you want to make sure you are covered for personal items too. Read the small print **before** heading off so you are aware of what is covered and what is not, what is required to submit a claim and what to do in the event of an emergency. Always buy insurance before setting out as your options will be more limited and generally quite costly once you've departed from your home country.

Internet

Public access to the internet is endemic with cybercafés in both large and small towns. Many hotels and cafés also have Wi-Fi. Speeds and connections are often unreliable, particularly with smart phones and data-hungry applications that place strain on the bandwidth. When using public Wi-Fi, please be considerate of other users.

Language

Spanish is spoken throughout most of Guatemala and, while you will be able to get by without knowledge of Spanish, you will probably become frustrated and feel helpless in many situations. English, or any other language, is useless off the beaten track. A pocket dictionary and phrase book together with some initial study or a beginner's Spanish course before you leave are strongly recommended. If you have the time, book 1-2 weeks of classes at the beginning of your travels. Some areas have developed a reputation for language classes, including Antigua and Quetzaltenango. The better-known centres normally include a wide range of cultural activities and supporting options for homestay. A less well-known centre is likely to have fewer English speakers around. For details, see the Language schools boxes in the What to do sections of individual towns and cities, and the Language tuition section below.

Not all the locals speak Spanish, of course; you will find that some indigenous people in the more remote areas – the highlands of Guatemala, for example – speak only their indigenous languages, although there will usually be some people in a village who can speak Spanish. Regarding pronunciation in Guatemala, 'X' is pronounced 'sh', as in Xela (shay-la).

Language schools can be found in major cities in Guatemala. Alternatively, contact one of the following international providers:

AmeriSpan, www.amerispan.com. One of the most comprehensive options, offering Spanish immersion programmes, educational tours, volunteer and internship positions in Antigua and Flores.

Cactus, www.cactuslanguagetraining. com. Spanish language courses in Antigua from 1 week in duration, with pre-trip classes in the UK. Also has additional options for volunteer work, diving and staying with host families.

Spanish Abroad, www.spanishabroad. com. Intensive Spanish immersion programmes in Antigua and Quetzaltenango.

Media

Latin America has more local and community radio stations than practically anywhere else in the world; a shortwave (world band) radio (or an equivalent phone app) offers a practical means to brush up on the language, sample popular culture and absorb some of the richly varied regional music. International broadcasters also transmit across Guatemala in both English and Spanish, these include the **BBC World Service**, www.bbc.co.uk/worldservice/index.shtml for schedules and frequencies, the **Voice of America**, www.voa.gov, and Boston (Mass)-based **Monitor Radio International**, operated by Christian Science Monitor, www. csmonitor.com. **Putumayo World Music**, www.putumayo.com specialize in the exotic sounds of Mexican music.

Newspapers and magazines

The main newspaper in Guatemala is *Prensa Libre* (www.prensalibre.com). The *Guatemala Post*, www.guatemalapost. com, is published in English online. *Siglo Veintiuno*, www.sigloxxi.com, is a good newspaper. One of the most popular papers is *Nuestro Diario*, a tabloid with more gory pics than copy. The *Revue*, www.revuemag.com, produced monthly in Antigua, carries articles, maps, advertisements, lodgings, tours and excursions, covering Antigua, Panajachel, Quetzaltenango, Río Dulce, Monterrico, Cobán, Flores and Guatemala City.

Money

US$1=Q7.65. €1 = Q8.50. £1 = Q11.90 (Jul 2015).

Currency and exchange

While Guatemala has its own currency, the most useful foreign currency is the US dollar. Banks and *casas de cambio* are increasingly able to change euros but the dollar is still the most readily accepted and changed. The 3 main ways of keeping in funds while travelling are still US dollars cash, plastic (credit cards) and US dollar TCs.

The unit is the **quetzal**, divided into 100 centavos. There are coins of 1 quetzal, 50 centavos, 25 centavos, 10 centavos, 5 centavos and 1 centavo. Paper currency is in denominations of 5, 10, 20, 50, 100 and 200 quetzales.

There is often a shortage of small change; ask for small notes when you first change money to pay hotel bills, transport, etc.

Cash

The chief benefit of taking US dollars is that they are accepted almost everywhere. However, in some places they are only accepted if they are in excellent condition – no small tears, rips, nicks, holes or scribbles. Bear this in mind when ordering money at home. Take a selection of bills including several low-value US dollar bills (US$5 or US$10) which can be carried for changing into local currency if arriving in Guatemala when banks or *casas de cambio* are closed, and for use in out-of-the-way places when you may run out of local currency. They are also very useful for shopping: shopkeepers and *casas de cambio* tend to give better exchange rates than hotels or banks (but see below).

Take plenty of local currency, in small denominations, when making trips away from the major towns and resorts.

Whenever possible change your money at a bank or a *casa de cambio*. Black markets and street changers have largely disappeared; avoid using them. Whenever you leave Guatemala, sell any local currency before leaving; the further you get away from the country, the less the value of its money and in some cases you may not be able to change it at all.

Debit and credit cards

Debit and credit cards are ideal for travelling, providing ready access to funds without carrying large amounts of cash on your person. Ideally taking a couple of cards (one Visa and one MasterCard) will make sure you are covered in most options. It is straightforward to obtain a cash advance against a credit card and even easier to withdraw cash from ATMs. (Remove your credit card from the machine immediately after the transaction to avoid it being retained; getting it back can be difficult.) You may have to experiment with different ATM networks; keep a backup supply of cash until you figure out which ones support your card. The rates of exchange on ATM withdrawals are the best available for currency exchange but your bank or credit card company imposes a handling charge which is a percentage of the transaction, so try to avoid using your card to withdraw small amounts of cash. If your card is lost or stolen, immediately contact the 24-hr helpline of the issuer in your home country (find out the numbers to call before travelling and keep them in a safe place).

Traveller's cheques

Traveller's cheques (TCs) are almost obsolete, shops and restaurants won't change them, but they do provide peace of mind against theft. Several banks charge a high fixed commission for changing TCs because they don't really want the bother. *Casas de cambio* are usually a much better choice for this service. Some establishments may ask to see a passport and the customer's record of purchase before accepting. Keep the original purchase slip in a separate place to the TCs and make a photocopy for security. The better hotels will normally change TCs for their guests (often at a poor rate).

Cost of travelling

Thrifty budget travellers can get by on US$25-40 a day, but that means that you won't be able to afford to take many excursions. A more realistic and sustainable budget is US$40-70. Plenty of travellers manage on smaller budgets but it's probably better to spend a little

longer at home saving up, and then have a good time while you're away, rather than find yourself adding up the small change on a Sat night to see if you can afford a weekly beer.

Opening hours

Banks Mon-Fri 0900-1500, Sat 0900-1300. Some city banks are introducing later hours, up to 2000; in the main tourist towns and shopping malls, some banks are open 7 days a week.
Shops 0900-1300 and 1500-1900, often mornings only on Sat.

Photography

There is a charge of US$3-5 for the use of video cameras at historical sites. For professional camera equipment, including a tripod, the fee is much higher. Never take photos of indigenous people without prior permission.

Police

Probably the best advice with regards the police in Central America is to have as little to do with them as possible. An exception to this rule are the tourist police, who operate in some big cities, and provide assistance. In general, law enforcement in Latin America is achieved by periodic campaigns, not systematically.

You may be asked for identification at any time and should therefore always have ID on you. If you cannot produce it, you may be jailed. If you are jailed, you should contact your embassy or consulate and take advice. In the event of a vehicle accident in which anyone is injured, all drivers involved are automatically detained until blame has been established, and this does not usually take less than 2 weeks. If a visitor is jailed his or her friends should provide food every day.

The giving and receiving of bribes is not recommended. Never offer a bribe unless you are fully conversant with the customs of the country.

Post

Postal prices are quite high and pilfering is frequent. All mail, especially packages, should be registered. Check before leaving home if your embassy will hold mail and if so for how long, in preference to the Poste Restante/ General Delivery (*Lista de Correos*) department. Cardholders can use Amex agencies. If you're expecting mail and there seems to be no mail at the *Lista* under the initial letter of your surname, ask them to look under the initial of your forename or your middle name. If your name begins with 'W', look for letters under 'V' as well, or ask. For the smallest risk of misunderstanding, use title, initial and surname only.

Safety

Robberies and serious assaults on tourists are becoming more common. Sensible precautions can minimize risks. Single women should be especially careful. Tour groups are not immune and some excursion companies take precautions. Do not travel at night if at all possible and take care on roads that are more prone to vehicle hijacks: the road between Flores and the Belizean border, the highway between Antigua and Panajachel and the principal highway between the capital and El Salvadorean border. Assaults and robberies on the public (former US) buses have increased. There have been a high number of attacks on private vehicles leaving the airport.

On the street

Generally speaking, in provincial towns, main places of interest, on daytime buses and in ordinary restaurants the visitor should be quite safe. Nevertheless, in large cities (particularly in crowded places such as markets and bus stations) crime exists. If you are aware of the dangers, act confidently and use your common sense, you will lessen many of the risks. The following tips, endorsed by travellers, are meant to forewarn, not alarm.

Personal belongings

Keep all documents secure; hide your main cash supply in different places or under your clothes. Extra pockets sewn inside shirts and trousers, pockets closed with a zip or safety pin, money belts, neck or leg pouches, and elasticated support bandages for keeping money and cheques above the elbow or below the knee have been repeatedly recommended. Pouches worn outside the clothes are not safe. Keep cameras in bags (preferably with a chain or wire in the strap, so it can't be slashed) and don't wear fancy wristwatches or jewellery. Carry your small day pack in front of you.

Asistur, T1500/2421-2810, is a 24-hr, year-round tourist assistance programme for any problem or question. There is also a national tourist police force, **POLITUR**, T5561-2073, or for emergencies: T120/122/123. Other useful numbers include: **national police** T110; and **tourist police** in Antigua T832-7290.

Safety on public transport

When you have all your luggage with you at a bus station, be especially careful: don't get into arguments with any locals if you can help it and clip, tie or lock all the items together with a chain or cable if you are waiting for some time, or simply sit on top of your backpack. Take a taxi between airport/bus station/railway station and hotel, if you can afford it. Keep your bags with you in the taxi and pay only when you and your luggage are safely out of the vehicle. Avoid night buses unless essential; avoid arriving at night whenever possible; and watch your belongings whether they are stowed inside or outside the cabin (rooftop luggage racks create extra problems, which are sometimes unavoidable – many bus drivers cover rooftop luggage with plastic sheeting, but a waterproof bag or outer sack can be invaluable for protecting your luggage and for stopping someone rummaging through the top of your bag). Major bus lines often issue a luggage ticket when bags are stored in the hold; this is generally a safe system. Finally, be wary of accepting food, drink, sweets or cigarettes from unknown fellow travellers on buses or trains. Do not take shared taxis with strangers you have met on the bus, no matter how polite or well-dressed.

Scams

A number of distraction techniques such as mustard smearers and paint or shampoo sprayers and strangers' remarks like 'what's that on your shoulder?' or 'have you seen that dirt on your shoe?' are designed to distract you for a few critical moments in which time your bag may be grabbed. Furthermore, supposedly friendly assistance asking if you have dropped money or other items in the street work on the same premise. If someone follows you when you're in

the street, let him catch up with you and give him the 'eye'. While you should take local advice about being out at night, do not assume that daytime is any safer. If walking after dark on quiet streets, walk in the road, not on the pavement.

Be wary of 'plain-clothes policemen'; insist on seeing identification and going to the police station by main roads. Do not hand over your identification (or money – which they should not need to see anyway) until you are at the station. On no account take them directly back to your lodgings. Be even more suspicious if they seek confirmation of their status from a passer-by. If someone implies they are asking for a bribe, insist on a receipt. If attacked, remember your assailants may well be armed, and try not to resist.

It is best, if you can trust your hotel, to leave any valuables you don't need in a safe-deposit box. Always keep an inventory of what you have deposited. If you don't trust the hotel, lock everything in your pack and secure that in your room. If you do lose valuables, you will need to report the incident to the police for insurance purposes.

Student and teacher travellers

If you are in full-time education you will be entitled to an **International Student Identity Card** (ISIC), which is distributed by student travel offices and travel agencies in over 100 countries. ISIC gives you special prices on all forms of transport (air, sea, rail, etc), and a variety of other concessions and services. Contact the **International Student Travel Confederation** (ISTC), T+31-20-421 2800, www.isic.org. Student cards must carry a photograph if they are to be of any use for discounts in Latin

America. The ISIC website provides a list of card-issuing offices around the world. Teachers may want to take an **International Teacher Identity Card (ITIC)** distributed by ISTC (above), as discounts are often extended to teachers.

Tax

There is a 17% ticket tax on all international tickets sold in Guatemala. There is also a US$30 or quetzal equivalent international departure tax payable at the airport.

The tourist institute **INGUAT** tax is 10%. Service charge is usually an extra 12%.

Telephone

Country code T+502
Directory enquiries T+154. Many of the telecommunications networks have been privatized and prices have fallen considerably. In some areas, services have even improved. Consequently keeping in touch by phone is no longer prohibitively expensive. International telecom charge cards are useful; obtain details before leaving home. For the US AT&T's USA Direct, **Sprint** and **MCI** are all available for calls to the US. It is much cheaper than operator-assisted calls. Internet calls (eg via Skype, Whatsapp and Viber) are also possible if you have access to Wi-Fi.

Using a mobile in Guatemala is very expensive. In addition to the hassle of having to charge your phone, research whether it is worth your while. Mobile phone calls will be cheaper if you buy a SIM card for the local network; in-country calls are likely to be considerably cheaper than using your home-based account. The initial cost of the SIM is getting more affordable, but check the cost of calls. Also bear in mind that the number you use at home will not work. Some networks, eg O2, provide an app so you can use the time on your contract if you access the app via Wi-Fi.

All phone numbers in the country are on an 8-figure basis. There are 2 main service providers: **Telgua** and **Telefónica**. Telefónica sells cards with access codes, which can be used from any private or public Telefónica phone. Telgua phone booths are ubiquitous and use cards sold in values of 20 and 50 quetzales. From a Telgua phone, dial 147 before making an international call.

Most businesses offering a phone-call service charge a minimum of US$0.13 for a local call, making a phone card a cheaper option.

International calls can be made from phone booths; however, unlike the local calls, it is cheaper to phone from an internet café or shop, which tend to offer better rates.

Mobile phone SIM cards are affordable, with good deals costing around US$10-20 for the card, which includes free calls. Comcel and PCS offer mobile phone services. Rates are around US$0.03 a minute for a national call, US$1.20 for international.

Operator calls are more expensive. For international calls via the operator, dial T147-110. For calling card and credit-card call options, you need a fixed line in a hotel or private house. First you dial 9999 plus the following digits: For **Sprint USA**, dial 136; **AT&T Direct**: 190; **Germany**: 049; **Canada**: 198; **UK (BT)**: 044; **Switzerland**: 041; **Spain**: 034, **Italy**: 039.

Collect calls may be made from public Telgua phones by dialling T147-120.

Time *GMT-6*.

Punctuality is more of a concept than a reality in Latin countries. The *mañana* culture reigns supreme and any arrangement to meet at, say 1900, will normally rendezvous somewhere between 2000 and 2100. However, the one time you are late to catch a bus, boat or plane, it will leave on time – the rule is hurry up and wait.

Tipping

Normally 10-15%; the equivalent of US$0.25 per bag for porters, the equivalent of US$0.20 for bell boys, and nothing for a taxi driver unless for some kind of exceptional service.

Tourist information

Guatemala's official tourist office is the **Instituto Guatemalteco de Turismo** (**INGUAT**), 7 Av, 1-17, Zona 4, Centro Cívico, Guatemala City, T2421-2800, www.visit guatemala.com. Mon-Fri 0800-1600. INGUAT provides bus times, hotel lists and road maps. Staff are helpful. They also have an office at the airport, open daily 0600-2400.

The **Guatemalan Maya Centre**, 94b Wandsworth Bridge Rd, London SW6 2TF, T020-7371-5291, www.maya.org.uk, has information on Guatemala, the Maya, a library, video archive and a textile collection; visits by prior appointment.

Regional websites covering some of the more popular areas include **www.atitlan.com**, **www.mayaparadise.com** (Río Dulce/ Lívingston), **www.cobanav.net** (Cobán) and **www.xelapages.com** (Quetzaltenango). **Posada Belén** in Guatemala City run a very informative site packed with information, www.guatemalaweb.com. Of the several

publications with websites, the *Revue*, **www.revuemag.com**, is probably the most useful to the visitor.

South American Explorers, USA, T607-277-0488, ww.saexplorers.org, is a very useful resource. Despite the name, the whole of Latin America is covered and members receive help with travel planning as well as informed access on books and maps covering the region.

Useful websites
www.latinnews.com Up-to-date site with political comment.
www.planeta.com A phenomenal resource, which is staggering for its detail on everything from ecotourism and language schools to cybercafés.
www.revuemag.com Growing regional guide in print and online, focusing on Guatemala with some coverage of Belize.

Visas and immigration

All international travel requires that you have at least 6 months remaining on a valid passport. Beyond a passport, very little is required for citizens of all Western European countries; USA, Canada, Mexico, all Central American countries, Australia, Israel, Japan and New Zealand. The majority of visitors get 90 days on arrival. If you're staying in Guatemala for several months, it is worthwhile registering at your embassy or consulate. Then, if your passport is stolen, the process of replacing it is faster and easier.

It is your responsibility to ensure that your passport is stamped in and out when you cross borders. The absence of entry and exit stamps can cause serious difficulties; seek out the proper immigration offices if the stamping process is not carried out as you cross.

Also, do not lose your entry card; replacing it can cause you a lot of trouble and possibly expense. If you're planning to study in Guatemala for a long period, make every effort to get a student visa in advance.

Visa renewal must be done in Guatemala City after 90 days, or on expiry. Passport stamp renewal on expiry for those citizens only requiring a valid passport to enter Guatemala must also be done at the immigration office at **Dirección General de Migración**, 6 Avenida, 3-11, Zona 4, Guatemala City, T2411-2411, Mon-Fri 0800-1600 (0800-1230 for payments). This office extends visas and passport stamps only once for a further period of time, depending on the original time awarded (maximum 90 days).

Weights and measures

The metric system is used.

Women travellers

Some women experience problems, whether accompanied or not; others encounter no difficulties at all. Unaccompanied Western women will at times be subject to close scrutiny and exceptional curiosity. Don't be unduly scared. Simply be prepared and try not to over-react. When you set out, err on the side of caution until your instincts have adjusted to the new culture. Women travelling alone could consider taking a wedding ring to prevent being hassled. To help minimize unwanted attention, consider your clothing choices. Do not feel bad about showing offence. When accepting an invitation, make sure that someone else knows the address you are going to and the time you left. Ask if you can

bring a friend (even if you do not intend to do so). A good rule is always to act with confidence, as though you know where you are going, even if you do not. Someone who looks lost is more likely to attract unwanted attention. Do not disclose to strangers where you are staying.

Volunteering

Guatemala has fairly well-developed and organized volunteer programmes. Two main areas provide opportunities for unskilled volunteers: childcare – often at orphanages or schools – and nature projects. Be warned, spontaneous volunteering is becoming more difficult. Organizations that use volunteers have progressed and plan their personnel needs so you may be required to make contact before you visit. Many organizations now charge volunteers for board and lodging and projects are often for a minimum of 4 weeks.

Many developed countries have nationally organized volunteer programmes. The **US Peace Corps**, T1-800-424-8580, www.peacecorps.gov, is the most prominent in the region, working on development projects with 2-year assignments for US citizens.

Variations on the volunteering programme are to enrol on increasingly popular gap-year programmes. These normally incorporate a period of volunteer work with a few months of free time at the end of the programme for travel.

Volunteering organizations
Asociación de Rescate y Conservación de Vida Silvestre (ARCAS), T2478-4096, www.arcasguatemala.com. Runs projects involving working with nature

and wildlife, returning wild animals to their natural habitat.

Casa Alianza, *13 Av, 0-37, Zona 2 de Mixco, Col la Escuadrilla Mixco, Guatemala City, T2250-4964, www.casa-alianza.org.* A project that helps street children.

Casa Guatemala, *14 Calle, 10-63, Zona 1, Guatemala City, T2331-9408, www. casa-guatemala.org.* Runs a project for abandoned and malnourished children at Río Dulce.

Comité Campesino del Altiplano, *on Lake Atitlán, 10 mins from San Lucas, T5804-9451, www.ccda.galeon.com.* This Campesino Cooperative now produces Fair Trade organic coffee buying from small farmers in the region; long-term volunteers are welcome but Spanish is required.

Fundación Mario Dary, *Diagonal 6, 17-19, Zona 10, Guatemala City, T2333-4957, fundary@intelnet.net.gt.* Operates conservation, health and education projects on the Punta de Manabique and welcomes volunteers.

Proyecto Ak' Tenamit, *11 Av 'A', 9-39, Zona 2, Guatemala City, T2254-1560, www. aktenamit.org, based at Clínica Lámpara, 15 mins upriver from Lívingston.* This project was set up to help 7000 civil-war-displaced Q'eqchi' Maya who now live in the region in 30 communities.

Proyecto Mosaico Guatemala, *3 Av Norte 3, Antigua. T7832-0955, www. promosaico.org.* An information centre and clearing house for volunteers, with access to opportunities all over the country.

Quetzaltrekkers, *Casa Argentina, 12 Diagonal, 8-43, Zona 1, Quetzaltenango, T7765-5895, www.quetzaltrekkers.com.* Volunteer opportunities for hiking guides and office workers, minimum 3-month commitment.

UPAVIM, *Calle Principal, Sector D-1, Col La Esperanza, Zona 12, Guatemala City, T2479-9061, www.upavim.org.* This project helps poor families, providing social services and education for the workers using fair-trade principles.

Check out the Xela-based volunteering information organization **www.entremundos.org**. Several language schools in Xela fund community development projects and seek volunteers. Make enquiries in town or via www.xelapages.com.

The London-based **Guatemala Solidarity Network**, *www. guatemalasolidarity.org.uk,* can assist with finding projects that look at human rights issues.

Index

Entries in bold refer to maps

Credits

Footprint credits

Editor: Jo Williams
Production and layout: Patrick Dawson
Maps: Kevin Feeney
Colour section: Angus Dawson

Publisher: Patrick Dawson
Managing Editor: Felicity Laughton
Administration: Elizabeth Taylor
Advertising sales and marketing:
John Sadler, Kirsty Holmes,
Business development: Debbie Wylde

Printed in Spain by GraphyCems

Publishing information
Footprint Guatemala
2nd edition
© Footprint Handbooks Ltd
September 2015

ISBN: 978 1 909268 69 2
CIP DATA: A catalogue record for this
book is available from the British Library

® Footprint Handbooks and the
Footprint mark are a registered
trademark of Footprint Handbooks Ltd

Published by Footprint
6 Riverside Court
Lower Bristol Road
Bath BA2 3DZ, UK
T +44 (0)1225 469141
F +44 (0)1225 469461
footprinttravelguides.com

Distributed in the USA by
National Book Network, Inc.

Every effort has been made to ensure
that the facts in this guidebook are
accurate. However, travellers should still
obtain advice from consulates, airlines,
etc about travel and visa requirements
before travelling. The authors and
publishers cannot accept responsibility
for any loss, injury or inconvenience
however caused.